Rethinking Money

How New Currencies Turn Scarcity into Prosperity

Bernard Lietaer
Jacqui Dunne

16
EasyRead Large

RHYW

Copyright Page from the Original Book

Rethinking Money

Berrett-Koehler Publishers, Inc.
235 Montgomery Street, Suite 650
San Francisco, California 94104-2916
Tel: (415) 288-0260, Fax: (415) 362-2512
www.bkconnection.com

Ordering information for print editions
Quantity sales. Special discounts are available on quantity purchases by corporations, associations, and others. For details, contact the "Special Sales Department" at the Berrett-Koehler address above.
Individual sales. Berrett-Koehler publications are available through most bookstores. They can also be ordered directly from Berrett-Koehler: Tel: (800) 929-2929; Fax: (802) 864-7626; www.bkconnection.com
Orders for college textbook/course adoption use. Please contact Berrett-Koehler: Tel: (800) 929-2929; Fax: (802) 864-7626.
Orders by U.S. trade bookstores and wholesalers. Please contact Ingram Publisher Services, Tel: (800) 509-4887; Fax: (800) 838-1149; E-mail: customer.service@ingrampublisherservices.com; or visit www.ingrampublisherservices.com/Ordering for details about electronic ordering.

First Edition
Hardcover print edition ISBN 978-1-60994-296-0
PDF e-book ISBN 978-1-60994-297-7
IDPF e-book ISBN 978-1-60994-298-4

2013-1

Cover/jacket Designer: Nicole Hayward

Cover art: Composite of images © iStock/perets, iStock/James Lee, and Nicole Hayward

TABLE OF CONTENTS

More praise for Rethinking Money

More praise for Rethinking Money

"You have no idea what money is. Read this book and find out how simply changing our money system will lead to a more sustainable and peaceful society."

—Jurriaan Kamp, Editor-in-Chief, *The Intelligent Optimist*

"Bernard Lietaer and Jacqui Dunne's clear and potent voice tells the story of our distorted and dysfunctional money system and how we can finally free ourselves from it and find our way to the future we yearn for. This stunning book should be required reading for every person who wants a world that works and a sustainable future for all of life."

—Lynne Twist, author of *The Soul of Money*

"*Rethinking Money* does a brilliant job of eradicating the concepts and stories that our economists and other professionals in the field hold dear. The authors write that 'money is our last taboo,' but they don't recommend abolishing the fiat zeitgeist. Rather, they wisely call on the various new currencies and other monetary innovations to complement the existing system."

—Nigel Seale, former worldwide Chairman, Earth Day International, and founder of Earth Day Canada

"*Rethinking Money*is required reading for anyone who is serious about transforming our current unsustainable economic system to one where people and planet can prosper. This is a brilliant analysis of our current monetary system and its pitfalls. More importantly, the authors strategize the way forward with solutions that not only rethink money but revalue human beings, long-term planning, and our planet."

—Georgia Kelly, Executive Director, Praxis Peace Institute

"In the midst of the confusion created by today's crises, there are few people who can provide viable solutions that not only serve our local communities but also address the global economy. Bernard Lietaer and Jacqui Dunne are such a brilliant force for good."

—Mariana Bozesan, PhD, integral investor and author of *The Making of a Consciousness Leader in Business*

"The mission of business—the mission of civilization—is to further the path of development that began in nature. We must develop a human ecosystem where we use less and have more. The monetary ecosystem proposed in Rethinking Money makes it possible and provides long-awaited solutions to the crises we face such as climate change, worldwide violence, and the chasm between rich and poor. This book is a must-read."

—Tachi Kiuchi, Chairman, E-Square Inc. and Future 500

"The portrait of an emerging world where issues of lack, intolerance, degradation, and war are replaced by sustainable abundance and economic justice for all is balm for the soul. This shift is brought about, in large part, by *simply*rethinking money."

—Sherry Ruth Anderson, coauthor of *The Feminine Face of God*

"The authors have expertly revealed new distinctions in the monetary domain but without the usual economic explanations of dry theory and abstraction. This book is for anyone who wonders why the system is failing us and, perhaps more importantly, what to do about it."

—Julio Olalla, founder of Newfield Network and author of *From Knowledge to Wisdom*

"An instant classic! Lietaer and Dunne explain how and why our monetary system fails to put supply and demand together, subsidizes and promotes intolerable and unnecessary disparities of well-being, entrenches unearned privilege, undermines democracy, creates boom- and-bust cycles, and rewards unsustainable, destructive growth ... Without undermining or vilifying all that money presently contributes, they provide a guided tour to an array of actual alternatives like time banking and complementary currencies to create a sustainable, more equitable monetary ecosystem."

—Edgar Cahn, creator of Time Dollars, founder of TimeBanks USA, and cofounder of the National Legal Services Program

"Rather than just blaming somebody—dumb politicians, greedy corporations, and banksters—Lietaer and Dunne show us the real issue: a system and a technology that are just built on agreements. And they show how we can change them to fit our real needs, live well, and save the planet in the process."

—Paul H. Ray, PhD, coauthor of *The Cultural Creatives*

"In a time in which money has become a form of madness, this remarkable book offers profound understanding and guidance to the creation of a monetary ecosystem that can build both a better self and a better world. The rethinking of money is one of the most important things we have to do, and the authors succeed brilliantly."

—Jean Houston, PhD, author of *Jump Time* and *A Passion for the Possible*

"New currency systems will not solve *all* the problems generated by physical growth on a finite planet. But we will have zero chance of creating a more satisfactory global future if we do not create new mechanisms for facilitating commerce. *Rethinking Money*is an incredibly practical and inspiring guide for how we could do that."

—Dennis L. Meadows, *coauthor of The Limits to Growth*

"The new understanding this book offers is critical because economics has become the dominant—and increasingly only—discipline with which important decisions are being made. This is a must-read for anyone who wants to be part of the timely conversation on how to move forward to create the just, sustainable, and equitable world we all desire."

—Thom Hartmann, internationally syndicated talk show host and author of twenty-four books

"Lietaer and Dunne describe the many thousands of innovative currencies in use by communities worldwide and how these currencies are facilitating the needed transition of human societies to more peaceful, sharing, prosperous, and sustainable futures."

—Hazel Henderson, President, Ethical Markets Media (USA and Brazil), and author of *Ethical Markets, Planetary Citizenship,* and *Building a Win-Win-World*

To all the monetary innovators and pioneers who've been dreaming and working for a better world

FOREWORD

John Perkins,
author of Confessions of an Economic Hit Man

We have entered revolutionary times.

People across the globe have lost faith in the ability of government and business leaders to resolve the problems facing humanity. The global economic depression has shattered the lives of Andean peasants, African fishermen, corporate executives, and the average house hold alike. Despite claims that the current economic malaise is ending, the general public remains unconvinced, suspicious, and shaken. The promised "recovery" is uneven and uncertain; monumental issues still remain to be resolved.

In our cash-strapped economy, privatization is proffered as a solution for many of our financial woes. The fire sale is so intense that we cannot be faulted for thinking that there is a *going out of business*sign over the doors of governments on every continent.

Officials at all levels are hocking whatever they can—roads, bridges, national monuments, prisons, and even water—to stave off what seems like inevitable bankruptcy. Furthermore, and perhaps most disconcertingly, the very foundations of our social contract, the institutions we once believed would always be honored such as educational and social services, are gutted and sold to private companies. Today, the U.S. taxpayer supports more privately owned soldiers in Afghanistan than members of our national military. Although the public is told that these solutions are more efficient, the fact is they are usually more costly in the long run. Government ownership of these sectors has served us extremely well. Against this emerging social and economic backdrop, part of the agenda of the *Economic Hit Man*that unfortunately worked so well in other parts of the world, taking advantage of developing countries to enslave them with indebtedness to international financial institutions, has come home to roost in what is referred to as the "developed world," including the United States.

Circumstances like these generate revolutions. The Agricultural Revolution. The Industrial Revolution. The American Revolution. We have entered such a time. Future historians, I believe, will define this as a Revolution in Consciousness. People around the world are waking up to the fact that a very few extremely wealthy individuals are enslaving the rest of us. The shackles take the form of the currencies and debt that are interwoven with global monetary systems.

*Rethinking Money: How New Currencies Turn Scarcity into Prosperity*shines a bright light on the problems. It exposes the fallacies of privatization, austerity, tax reform, banking legislation, stimulus packages, and so many other fancy-sounding strategies, and illuminates a path toward a sane and sustainable future. Writing for the layman, the authors explore a largely unexamined culprit—the monopoly of our centuries-old monetary system. They reveal its primary role in the current crisis. They then proceed to answer the essential question: What can we do about it? They illustrate how new currencies can resolve not only the inadequacies of regular money, but also how they can energize new behaviors and outcomes with incentives that will help create the world we fervently desire—for ourselves and future generations.

The monetary innovations described in these pages remove the creation of money from the hands of the banking system. The power returns to communities operating at different levels of society. This allows for the linkage of resources in a given locality to the unmet needs of that community. The ingenuity of the local population can be galvanized; with their own money they are empowered to create the transformations they desire and need.

Surprisingly straightforward in their clarity and simplicity, Lietaer and Dunne point out that money is a human invention. Our current monetary system was designed some 300 years ago, during an era that knew nothing of natural limits and had a completely different set of objectives and priorities. It's a tool that should be serving us, rather than being our master. And since it is a man-made construct, it can be re-thought, re-imagined, and redesigned.

None of this is mere theory. The transformation of money and thus our culture and society is underway. This inspirational book chronicles stories of ordinary people and their communities solving critical problems by using new money systems in tandem with conventional ones. The stories range from addressing hunger to revitalizing neighborhoods, from the crisis of health care to creating work, from providing education for all to the building of sustainable networks.

This is a book that will strike a chord with readers eager to find meaningful, thought-provoking solutions that can be implemented right now—readers who want to take part in this new Revolution.

Introduction

FROM SCARCITY TO PROSPERITY WITHIN A GENERATION

"On the morning after the Depression a man came to work, building a house, and the foreman said to him, 'Sorry chum, you can't work today. There ain't no inches.' The man said, 'What do you mean there ain't no inches? We got lumber, we got metal, we've even got tape mea sures.' The foreman said, 'The trouble with you is you don't understand business. There are *no* inches. We have been using too many of them and there are not enough to go around."[1]

Like the foreman in this famous allegory about money, everyone is missing the point. Most of us fervently believe that our current financial woes and tribulations are occurring because there simply isn't enough money to go around. From this limited vantage point, the usual solutions for scarcity are trotted out, such as austerity mea sures, cutbacks, and privatizations. The rhetoric on all sides of the political divide is stale and has grown cold, turning glacial and unmovable in its stance. Meanwhile, there is real suffering and anguish among ordinary people, and the rainwater in the streets' gullies turns red with protesters' blood.

It's time to rethink money. And that's what this book is about.

Money is to humans what water is to fish. Humanity exists in an unrelenting flurry of monetary transactions that seem as natural and inscrutable to us as how one might imagine a fish to understand its aqueous environment—it's taken totally for granted. In the case of money, its dynamics and distinctions are obfuscated or forgotten over time, and further complicated by the fact that the professionals in the field, economists, never actually define what money *is;* they just describe what it *does:* how it plays the role of a unit of account, a store of value, a medium of exchange.

At present, our unexamined money system perpetuates scarcity and breeds competition. Are you aware that money is created out of nothing, as bank debt? And how that particular process of creation breeds systematic competition among its users? Did you know that the prevailing money system generates several other harmful consequences, including short-termism, compulsory growth pressure, cyclical recessions, unrelenting concentration of wealth, and erosion of social and physical or natural capital? All these factors together create a wholly unsustainable financial structure that is, indeed, disintegrating.

So, how did we get here?

Modern money, the type we use today, was invented in a very different time with a different worldview and another set of priorities and challenges than we have today. Money is not a product of nature, something that grows on a tree and can be harvested.

Rather, modern money is a human construct that was conceived and fashioned back in the 1700s in Europe and then evolved, first in En gland, to become the engine for the Industrial Revolution. Up until that point, the vast majority of people eked out meager existences, while real wealth was obtained mainly through the spoils of war or colonization, marriage or inheritance.

Through the emergence of modern central banking and its conventions during this time, it was possible to make money out of money. This gave birth to the new merchant and middle classes.

Soon money became the tool empires used in a global dash for assets in a world that didn't seem to lack for earth, water, air, and natural resources. A contrivance of competition, it pitted one against the other in a fabricated Darwinian contest of survival, reflecting and perpetuating the values and the Zeitgeist of that time.

This epoch produced remarkable advances, thrusting society out of the shackles of superstition and stagnant social order that had preceded it. It brought about the rigor of science founded in that which could be proven, rather than divine dogma. It enabled the individual, no matter how lowly his birth, to scale the heights of his unbridled imagination and keen ambition through learning and labor.

The mercantile miracle over time became codified as a success story. Those who succeed are free to take their share of the profits after taxes, and those who suffer losses have to bear consequences such as humiliation, bankruptcy, and possible litigation. This has brought about unmatched attainment of wealth, facilitated through competitive markets and driven by a competitive financial system, which, in turn, has spurred on even greater striving for more innovation, ingenuity, and originality. This is the underpinning of the great American dream, which has been triumphantly exported to the rest of the world after the fall of the Berlin Wall and rise of the Iron Curtain. Today, for instance, China, India, Brazil, and Poland, with their meteoric growth and the rise of their own meritocracies, are prime examples.

That dream, however, has turned into a nightmare. We now have scientific proof that the monoculture of a single type of currency is a root cause of the repeated monetary and financial instabilities that have manifested throughout modern history. According to the International Monetary Fund, in the four decades between 1970 and 2010, there were no fewer than 145 banking crises, 208 monetary crashes, and 72 sovereign debt crises. This adds up to an astounding total of 425 systemic crises—an average of more than 10 countries in crises each and every year![2]

One of the much touted remedies is the Chicago Plan. Essentially this would make bank-debt money illegal and government instead would issue a new currency. While this reform would eliminate the risk of bank crashes and sovereign debt crises, there would still be monetary crises.[3]

These stark statistics don't begin to tell the personal and individual stories of struggle and hardship. The extraordinary chasm that has emerged between the superwealthy and the expanding ranks of the working poor is demonstrated by the fact that the combined assets of the family that owns Wal-Mart equal those of America's bottom 150 million people.[4]

All of this begs the question, "Why do we not examine our money system?" Throughout the history of our world, with all its wars, political upheavals, and periods of civil unrest, and with the emergence of political models including capitalism, socialism, and communism in all their variations and adaptations, still the money system was left unexamined. The portraits on or colors of the paper bills may have changed, but the fundamentals of its core structure have not.

The answer is this: Money is the last great taboo. The topic of sex was opened up in the 1960s and 1970s, and death and dying during the AIDS pandemic and natural disasters of the 1980s and 1990s. But the subject of money is still shrouded in darkness, assumed by many to be untouchable.

An even deeper obstacle to examining our system of money resides in the recesses of our collective psyche: We are motivated both by a fear of scarcity and by greed. Fear of scarcity often carries with it a tendency to avoid facing the reality of our finances, and greed brings an obsessive focus on money. The conflict between these two forces leads to a state of approach-avoidance in relation to money—an inner struggle that further exacerbates the trickiness of the inquiry. Money itself becomes highly emotionally charged.

Ironically, financial markets portray themselves as bastions of cool rationalism. Although economists frequently present their work as neutral, objective, and based on irrefutable science, sometimes crucial underlying epistemological or conceptual orientations and presuppositions remain unstated and are thereby kept shrouded from view.

As we begin to lift the shroud in this book, we will see that it's not the structure of the economy or the hue of the political solution, per se, that are the *real* problems. The real problems are money and the monetary system itself, and not in the way one might first suspect. We will see that since money is a human invention, it can be changed. We'll see that there is not only another way, but a multiplicity of ways, to rethink money. And we'll learn that already a quiet evolution is underway, in which people and their communities are helping themselves through a new understanding of money.

Currently, in thousands of communities globally, there are networks of businesses that span a country or a continent and groups of netizens who are reassessing and reengineering money with astonishing results. Individuals, entrepreneurs, businesses, communities, and governments in many countries around the world have already created new cooperative money systems that link unmet needs with resources that remain unused by the dominant competitive currency of each country. These new strategies do not replace the conventional monetary systems but rather work in tandem, shifting the predominant features of scarcity and hypercompetitiveness to ones that provide new options and additional resources for everyone.

Regular people have discovered not only that it is possible to create money in sufficiency for their needs but also that it is simultaneously possible to build their societies with greater cooperation, care, and collaboration. In other words, they are proving not only that it is possible to redesign money but also that doing so fosters very different and highly desirable outcomes.

In fact, the past 30 years has seen a tremendous growth of cooperative currencies around the world—from fewer than a handful in 1980 to more than 4,000 today. These cooperative currencies are often called *complementary currencies.*Examples include *community or local currencies*such as *time dollars*in the United States, long-established *business-to-business* systems like the *WIR*in Switzerland, and newer currencies like the *regio*and the *terra.*There is also a huge potential for more scalable cooperative currencies. In other words, the emergent cooperative currency movement now has behind it enough proven successes to grow up and start tackling the core challenges of the 21st century.

This book provides the road map for this to happen. You will read real-world stories of ordinary people making an extraordinary difference by pulling themselves up by their own boot straps. There are reports of communities going from high unemployment, despair, and high crime rates to self-sufficiency, mutual support, and sustainable abundance. In these pages, businesses, communities, and governments, as well as individual citizens and entrepreneurs, will find actions that they can take right now to create currencies that connect unused resources to unmet needs, moving their participants from scarcity to sufficiency.

This new approach makes possible a potentially radical transubstantiation, a profound shift from a postindustrial era to an Age of Wisdom. Perhaps even a Diamond Age of unprecedented technological breakthroughs may emerge, where the universe becomes malleable in our hands with unparalleled and exceptional advances.

The book is divided into three sections: Part One, *Scarcity,* comprises the first three chapters. This part unfurls the strands of money's DNA, explaining how each constituent component impacts everyone in some very surprising, sometimes devastating, ways. These chapters also show how it is now possible to tweak and make changes to the money system that result in a completely different set of outcomes. It is written in lay terms to give the reader a better understanding of what's really going on with the financial meltdown.

This will enable greater discourse and debate and, hopefully, grounded action.

*Prosperity,*the second part, Chapters 4 through 9, chronicles the pioneers and implementers of cooperative currencies both in the United States and abroad. It reports on their stories of inspiration and transformation under the categories of banking, entrepreneurship, government and NGOs, and we, the citizens.

The third and final part of the book, titled *Rethinking Money,*projects into an available future and shows how a truly cooperative society would function with both competitive and cooperative currencies working in tandem. It then reaches back into recent history and reveals the lessons learned from modern history and how various missteps can be avoided now. With the vital lessons from the past and a clear vision of a desired future, you and your community, whatever its size or structure, can become empowered and grow prosperous.

This book will take you on a journey into some rather unexpected areas. The value of exploring this uncharted territory, usually not associated with finance and money, is to give you insight, by packing your imaginary knapsack with new monetary tools and additional knowledge. When we get to the end of the journey, like reaching the top of a mountain, you can take in the 360-degree vista and see the financial system though a new understanding. From there, it is possible to realize that there is another way, in fact, thousands of other ways to escape the existing financial morass.

So rather than saying, as in the opening story, that there aren't enough inches to build the world we want for ourselves and our children, we could, equipped with a new understanding, create new currencies that link unused resources with unmet needs. We could build vibrant communities. Not only can we attain sufficiency but also we can reach the inherent human goals of cooperation, community, and even contentment. New cooperative currencies would stimulate learning and entrepreneurship. New ideas for banking would create cooperative housing loans and financial support for emergent technologies and businesses. These are constructs that support local businesses, creating prosperity in local communities.

So, let's buckle our safety belts and hang on for an unusual ride.

PART ONE

SCARCITY

Most of us assume that there is only one type of money possible, even imaginable: dollars for Americans; pounds for the English, Welsh, Scots and Northern Irish; pesos for the Mexicans; yen for the Japanese; and so on. Furthermore, most believe that such currencies are simply a medium of exchange, facilitating transactions that would otherwise take place less efficiently, through barter or other forms of exchange. Thus, money is assumed to be *value neutral,* not affecting the type of exchanges made, the kind of relationships among its users, or the time horizon of investments. In this book, we will explore all of these hidden assumptions and show them to be invalid.

We will see that the process by which money is actually created, through bank debt, is wrapped in a veil that even many economists, the experts in the field, haven't seen through. As a result, we are largely oblivious to the devastating consequences of our limitations regarding money, as well as the vast human potential it has failed.

Our current monetary system generates scarcity and competition. The rivalry and contest are so pervasive that we have become inured to its impact in our daily lives in all levels of society—even for those we imagine would have no problems, given the size of their bank accounts and portfolios.

We all suffer. And before something can be changed, it first needs to be understood.

Chapter One

THE FAILURE OF MONEY

The Competitive Society

What need you, being come to sense,
But fumble in a greasy till
And add the halfpence to the pence
And prayer to shivering prayer, until
You have dried the marrow from the bone?

WILLIAM BUTLER YEATS,
Irish poet and Nobel laureate

It's a cold Tuesday morning, and already the line is forming outside the David Ellis Pawn Shop in the upscale neighborhood of Cherry Creek, Denver, bordering the foothills of the Colorado Rockies. It will be another 10 minutes before the doors open. A woman in a fur coat sits in her parked car with its license tags about to expire. She runs the engine to keep warm while others shuffle around in silence, dodging any direct eye contact.

Denver, the Mile High city, is one of the country's top 10 metropolitan areas where people are saddled with the highest levels of personal debt. This is a result of high housing prices, a steep cost of living, and a culture of spending—a hangover from better days.[1] The David Ellis Pawn Shop has been in business in the same location for over 25 years and during this time has seesawed through multiple financial highs and lows. Trade, however, has never been so brisk or with such a dramatically broadened demographic as it is now.

This scramble for money is playing out globally in towns and rural areas alike. Record unemployment, or underemployment, has triggered a vicious cycle of lack of demand for goods and services that leads to more layoffs in key industries. The mood, to put it mildly, grows dark and defaults into despair, sometimes even abdication, as next steps are unclear.

In the history of the United States, this is the first time when the younger generation of people will be poorer and less educated than their parents.[2] In a country that claims to be one of the richest in the world, some 100 million people—one in three Americans—either lives in poverty or in the distressed zone hovering just above the official poverty threshold.[3] More than one in three Americans lived in households that received Medicaid, food stamps, or other means-based government assistance in mid-2010, according to an analysis of the 2010 census. And when Social Security, Medicare, and unemployment benefits are included, nearly half of the nation lived in a house hold that received a government check.[4]

According to the *New York Times,* "Demographically, they look more like 'The Brady Bunch' than 'The Wire.' Half live in households headed by a married couple; 49 percent live in the suburbs. Nearly half are non-Hispanic white, 18 percent are black, and 26 percent are Latino. Perhaps the most surprising finding is that 28 percent work full-time, year round. These estimates defy the stereotypes of low-income families."[5]

The squeeze for cash has gotten more acute recently. Today, 80 percent of Americans report that they are living paycheck to paycheck. This is nearly double the figure in 2007, just before the banking crisis. One in five individuals earning over $100,000 per year report that they, too, are living from month to month.[6] Savings are at an all-time low.[7] Consequently, the need for credit is on an upswing while banks are not lending.

The money system really isn't serving humanity. The world's population could hit 10 billion by 2050.[8] Money is too scarce for many of Earth's human inhabitants. Even those who have enough of it are obliged to deal with its vicissitudes: crashes, devaluations, inflation, whatever the financial crisis du jour may be.

As the stories of financial stress and uncertainty continue to play out in the United States and around the globe, there's plenty of blame to go around. We can point to rampant cronyism in government on all levels, slack or non ex is tent enforcement of regulations, and good old-fashioned greed, from corporate avarice to the covetousness of innumerate plebs who got in over their heads in the real estate market.

Clearly, however, on the flip side of the coin, we do live in a world of unparalleled achievements, facilitated through competitive markets driven by a competitive financial system. The best and the brightest are rewarded at stratospheric levels, which in turn, has spurred on even greater striving for more innovation, ingenuity, and originality.

Yet, the commonly trotted-out explanations for all that ails the financial systems, or conversely what is working, just don't provide the complete picture. There is a yearning to put into language something that still remains elusive, lingering in the shadows of awareness just out of reach. It's that gnawing feeling in the pit of the stomach that something deeper is going on, something that can't quite be brought to consciousness, let alone expressed in words.

That is what this book offers to illuminate. It is not about how to invest, save, spend, hide, keep, or give away money. Rather, the aim is to unmask the true nature of money and the monetary system that we have inherited. Money is merely a human construct, as will be shown, that was designed in and for another age. By understanding how money really works, we might then create a different system that supports the kind of society we desire for ourselves and for future generations. This is about how to make a sustainably abundant future a reality.

And while money is the culprit, it is not guilty in the way one would suspect.

A much deeper systemic issue is at work. Before anything can be changed, it must be understood. To understand, it has to be taken apart, investigated, and questioned before it can be put back together again in a new configuration that would support a truly functioning system. Although many feel we are fast approaching an apocalypse, we might remember that the word comes from the Greek *apokálypsis,* meaning an "uncovering," a "lifting of the veil," or "the disclosure of something hidden," a "surprise,"[9] if you will.

There are both a general lack of awareness and widely held erroneous assumptions as to how money drives trillions of daily transactions and influences every aspect of daily life.

At the core of these assumptions is the false belief that it is merely the lack of money that is the problem. If there were more to go around, everything could be put to rights. However, what you'll discover in the following pages is this: It is not the *amount*of money in circulation that is the root cause of this current malaise. It's the *type*of money that is being used.

The good news is that the know-how and gumption needed to bring about a transformation are already here. We're not talking about conventional "solutions" such as the redistribution of wealth, increased conventional taxation, bond mea sures, or enlightened self-interest from corporate entities. Rather, we're talking about the stories of ordinary people who are jumping outside the prescribed monetary boundaries, rethinking and reengineering money itself.

Recognizing that transformation is possible, emboldened by new monetary innovations, we can realize a brighter future for everyone. In this future, meaningful work would be available to all; the sick and elderly would be cared for, and children would have adequate shelter, health care, nutrition, and education; threats to our environment would end; unstable urban and rural areas would evolve into viable, sustainable communities; and seemingly insurmountable social chasms would be bridged. In short, life and all living systems would flourish.

This is not an idealistic dream, but rather a pragmatic goal, achievable within one generation.

Currently, we stand at an extraordinary inflection point in human history. Several intergenerational, even millennial cycles are coming to a close, including the end of the Cold War (50 years), of the Industrial Age (250 years), of Modernism (500 years), of hyper-rationalism (2,500 years), and of patriarchy (5,000 years). The universe is now more malleable, given advances in science and technology, yet nothing of true value and longevity will materialize until money is mastered and humanity is no longer its slave. Just as computer operating systems become obsolete, incapable of performing the functions needed, so do our systems of money.

The first step is to take stock of where we are. Currently, as infrastructure crumbles in the United States and in many other nations, and the availability of high-quality education and health care plummets, with massively underfunded liabilities, the stark statistics still don't tell the full story of America's sons and daughters and, indeed, the entire global family as it grapples with an uncertain future. The situation is particularly dire in Europe: Greece, Spain, Ireland, the United Kingdom, and Italy are in a credit crunch not seen in generations. Even in the countries that were up until recently considered booming, nations like the BRICs—Brazil, Russia, India, and China—development was highly uneven, with entire regions experiencing scarcity and need. Now it would appear that their economic bloom is wilting.[10] Practically everywhere one finds many tales of how the highly competitive nature of the conventional money system influences our lives.

REQUIEM FOR A DREAM

It takes a moment to get over the initial shock of seeing Fred bagging groceries in a popular national grocery store outlet. Stooped, with his torso almost parallel to the floor, his hands gnarled and disfigured with arthritis, he dutifully double-bags the heavy items. A former lab technician with a degree in chemistry from UCLA, he's been working this part-time job for the past 18 years since his retirement at age 65. He's a proud man and says that he took the job at his wife's insistence that he do something other than hang around their house. He does agree, reluctantly, that the small salary makes a big difference to the house hold.[11]

Marie was one semester shy of her MA degree when she had to forsake her studies and get full-time work, as she could no longer afford to keep herself in school. Now, four decades later, following a series of low-paying jobs, she lost her unionized custodial job at a local university due to an on-site injury. Until recently, she made ends meet by working for two agencies as a caregiver to homebound, usually bedridden, elderly folks. She cleaned houses to further supplement her income. Her employers did not pay any benefits or cover car expenses as she zigzagged across the greater metropolitan area to work her shifts. She was making $12 an hour for backbreaking work, and the agencies she worked for charged $25 an hour for her services. She worked tenaciously and without complaint, as she knew full well about the stack of résumés in her bosses' inboxes from people eager to take her place. One day she collapsed on the job and was rushed to the hospital, where she spent almost 10 days in intensive care due to complications from asthma and pneumonia. With no health care coverage, she now faces a bill of over $300,000, and she has no idea how it will get paid.

On the day-to-day personal level, the mandate to perform and increase profits percolates through all industry sectors, making life stressful and highly competitive for all concerned. Everything is tied to the financial bottom line.

"Unless I can bring in new business each quarter, I'm toast," says Dave, while juggling his iPhone and a venti café Americano. A seasoned public relations executive, he works for a boutique technology agency in northern California. "My strong suit is strategizing and running campaigns. I do pick up new clients by referral, but the heat is on constantly to get new accounts in the door. It's simply cutthroat these days. The office is mostly run by nonpaid interns getting work experience, while my workload increases. I don't have the bandwidth to explain the basics, let alone the nuances, to these fresh-faced grads. The media executives portrayed in the TV series *Mad Men,* with their long boozy lunches and even longer expense accounts, are as dead these days as Elvis."

Rick, a doctor, had just come off the graveyard shift in a large psychiatric hospital and is operating on just four hours of sleep. In his profession, these questions, although politically incorrect, are often bandied about: "Why are your patients going nuts, and why are their numbers increasing?"

He answers: "From what I can see generally, it's the sense of helplessness that is pushing them over the edge and into an institution or into some sort of therapy at least, for the less chronic cases. These people hold the belief that they won't be able to make it financially and that they're powerless to do anything. The workplace for many has become a complete nightmare. The competition for jobs is like the scramble for lifeboats on the *Titanic.*If you have a job, the atmosphere at work is often toxic. Everyone is scared stiff of being sacked. On the other hand, those that do have resources fear that they will lose it all to some slick sales guy conning them out of their last dime so he can make his sales projections. They feel immobilized and unable to navigate the roller coaster of the financial tsunami. It's not pretty, and it's only getting worse."

The picture isn't pretty for first-time job seekers, either. Americans owe more on student loans than on credit cards. The total of outstanding student loans has exceeded $1 trillion for the first time in history.[12] The average U.S. college student is now more than $25,000 in debt by graduation.[13] With this debt load, a young person with a calling to become a teacher, for example, is forced into finding higher-paying work to take care of the crushing debt. A medical student who dreams of a general practice in a rural area or a poor neighborhood or of volunteering with Doctors without Borders in hopes of giving back to society is coerced into relinquishing these aspirations and becoming a specialist to garner higher fees. A graduate with a passion for science is pressed to vacate the idea of teaching and go for a pharmaceutical sales job instead. This leaves a number of critical vocations not attracting the best or the brightest. The current scuttling of jobs is reaching epidemic proportions. An average of five people vie for each job opening in the United States, and the advice to "follow one's bliss" rings hollow.

It's not much better across the Atlantic. Graduates in the United Kingdom, for example, can anticipate 70 applications for one job opening and have been told to flip burgers rather than counting on attaining positions commensurate with their educations, leaving them with no means of addressing their liabilities.[14] Nobel laureate Paul Krugman writes: "In particular, these days, workers with a college degree, but no further degrees, are less likely to get workplace health coverage than workers with only a high school degree were in 1979."[15]

These days, job satisfaction means having any gainful employment.

Money is the most powerful secular force. Financial issues affect all economic classes, from the rich to the poor. Empathy for the plight of those who suffer from scarcity comes easier. The damage created by poverty and want is pervasive, devastating, and easy to understand. Yet the levels of competition and struggle indelibly linked to money propagate through all levels of society. Less recognized and definitely not generally understood or empathized with are the formidable issues of those who are affluent. Rich people don't elicit much sympathy: From a distance, many less well-heeled people would welcome their money issues, or so they believe.

"Money has been such a royal pain for our family. I rarely, if ever, speak to my two brothers," confides Anna, as she takes another sip of her overpriced Upper East Side martini. "Our interactions have always been strained, given the craziness of being shunted off to different boarding schools and, following our parents' divorce, being raised by different branches of the family. However, it was a seven-figure cash inheritance from my grandfather that just ripped us apart. As the girl, I got the largest share of the estate. That didn't go down very well with my siblings. The family has been in litigation for years. The only ones getting rich are the lawyers."

Jungian psychologist Bernice Hill has categorized four levels of what she calls "sacred wounds of money."[16]

Level one is *the burden of* e *xpectations.*Those who are seen as wealthy are often the objects of the fears, needs, and expectations of those who lack money. Society expects those with money to "do the right thing," which most often translates into "give money." The affluent are left to ask themselves, when invited to attend an affair or participate in an event, "Is it me or my checkbook that's being invited?"

Level two is *isolation.* The prosperous must question if their personal relationships are based on money or status, rather than genuine caring and true feelings for the friendship. As a consequence, people of means tend to socialize only with others of similar financial and social backgrounds and ultimately come to experience a deep sense of isolation. The painful question lingers, "Would my friend still be my friend if I didn't have any money?" Love, popularity, and camaraderie can be as paper-thin as money. This lack of trust is reflected in the measures taken to ensure their security—the higher walls built around their homes, possessions, and lives, literally and psychologically. In the end, the well-heeled tend to seek refuge in "golden ghettos."

Third, being well-to-do can lead to *unhealthy family dynamics,*as exemplified by Anna's story. The tabloid press and reality TV are filled with family feuds and the nagging fears and general angst regarding inheritances, wills, and pressures brought to bear regarding proper behavior. Even the most intimate relationships—choosing the *right*partner in marriage—are subject to all-important prenuptial agreements, yet another financially secured contract.

And finally, and perhaps most important, is the *crisis of identity,* particularly for those who have inherited wealth. The questions of self-worth and one's uniqueness, which arise for everyone, become much more painful when one is seen by others as having money. Philosopher Jacob Needleman observes, "The only thing that money will not buy is meaning."[17] Often, wealthy people suffer from guilt, anxiety, and a sense of meaninglessness.

In an environment and culture where so much is shaped by financial worth, the scarcest commodity seems to be trust. Indeed, each of these four conditions shares a common thread—the loss of trust in society, in friends, in family, and finally, in oneself. An all-too-common response to the issues faced by the wealthy is "I wish I had that problem." This denies, however, the depth of the anguish experienced by some and the reality that money has become an equal-opportunity problem maker.

Feelings of futility permeate all strata of society. This sense of worthlessness often manifests as rampant consumerism. An extreme case in point is the recent report of a Chinese high school boy who sold his kidney for $3,500 to raise the funds to buy an iPad and an iPhone. Young girls across the globe trade sexual favors with wealthier men to procure luxury items such as designer handbags and couture. The practice is euphemistically called *compensated dating.*[18,19]

All this leads to the ironic conclusion that the current money system provides genuine individual satisfaction neither for those who suffer from its scarcity nor for those who are wealthy. The drama of money plays out in all segments of society.

THE DASH FOR CASH

Beyond the daily monetary mêlée that is playing out on the personal level, some 44 states in the Union are considering bankruptcy,[20] and dozens of cities across the nation are faced with inevitable bud get shortfalls.[21] The river port city of Stockton, California, is the largest U.S. city to lately declare bankruptcy.[22] In the meantime, at various levels of officialdom globally, it's believed that the only way out of the current credit crunch, on the present trajectory, is the forfeiture of assets in the blaze of fire sales.

Some 28 states have passed private public partnerships (PPPs) enabling statutes.[23] Despite the benign-sounding label, these statutes mean that governments—at whatever level—are selling off existing infrastructure that has already been built and paid for with taxpayers' money to reduce existing debt, if they are unable to meet current governmental expenses. Once something is privatized, the new owners will certainly charge fees for the use of any once-free public utility or will increase existing tolls. Consequently, taxpayers will end up paying twice for the same infrastructure, and the second time could be more expensive than the first, given that many infrastructure assets are monopolies.

The total value of U.S. government fixed assets (at federal, state, and local levels combined) was an estimated $9.3 trillion in 2008. Of this, $1.9 trillion is owned by the federal government, and $7.4 trillion is held at state and local levels. The value of all the highways and roads owned by states and municipalities is $2.4 trillion. There are sewerage assets worth $550 billion at state and local levels, along with a further $400 billion of water assets. And in the real estate sector, the federal, state, and local governments own assets worth $1.09 trillion.

The evidence reveals that PPPs, rather than being entrepreneurial ventures to create work and unleash massive opportunities for the general population, actually favor buying up existing assets instead of building new ones because the time required and risks involved are much higher with new projects.

The competition to acquire real assets, whether through PPP programs or the wealthy simply buying up whatever they can before currency gets devalued, leads to an even greater concentration of wealth as the deepening of privatization plays out. Ordinary people are less and less able to afford access to a local library, for instance, since what was once a public service now requires a subscription, like a membership fee to a private club. Additionally, pressure on authorities to sell their own offices will oblige them to pay rent for the offices that they once owned. And this will be another bill that taxpayers will have to cover.

With this new concentration of monetary and financial power, François Morin, a financial advisor to the highest ranks of European government and the European Central Bank (ECB), asks, "Is this not a cause, probably the main one, of the powerlessness for the public sector to manage the growing economic and social imbalances that manifest in our societies? Is this new global financial paradigm not having a dissolving effect on our democratic societies?"[24]

Americans have always been encouraged to aspire to bold dreams and to believe that diligence, coupled with the benefits of capitalism and democracy, would ensure a bright future. As this reverie dissipates, another reality needs to arise.

There is a way out of this insanity: by rethinking money. In the words of famed computer scientist Alan Kay, the best way to predict the future is to invent it. To invent, one has to first understand why money *really* matters. Only then is it possible to rethink the monetary model.

Chapter Two

THE MYTH OF MONEY

What It Really Is

So you think that money is the root of all evil. Have you ever asked what is the root of all money?

AYN RAND, Russian-born American writer

It is a slow day in the small Saskatchewan town of Pumphandle, and streets are deserted. Times are tough, everybody is in debt, and everybody is living on credit. A tourist visiting the area drives through town, stops at the motel, and lays a $100 bill on the desk saying he wants to inspect the rooms upstairs to pick one for the night. As soon as he walks upstairs, the motel owner grabs the bill and runs next door to pay his debt to the butcher.

The butcher takes the $100 and runs down the street to retire his debt to the pig farmer. The pig farmer takes the $100 and heads off to pay his bill to his supplier, the Co-op. The guy at the Co-op takes the $100 and runs to pay his debt to the local prostitute, who has also been facing hard times and has had to offer her "services" on credit.

The hooker rushes to the hotel and pays off her room bill with the hotel owner. The hotel proprietor then places the $100 back on the counter so the traveler will not suspect anything. At that moment, the traveler comes down the stairs, states that the rooms are not satisfactory, picks up the $100 bill, and leaves.

No one produced anything. No one earned anything. However, the whole town is now out of debt and looking to the future with a lot more optimism.

This amusing anecdote, circulated around the Internet, illustrates the effects of a stimulus package. Apparently, the first iteration appeared during the Great Depression, when local stamp scrip currencies were created to address the crisis. In the earlier version, the kicker is when the salesman who deposited the $100 note on the desk picks it up and lights his cigar with it.

"Counterfeit," he said. "A fake gift from a crazy friend."

So, what is money? What makes it *real?* Or perhaps more important, what makes it *legal?*

Despite its paramount role in our lives, ordinary people and experts alike seldom question or think about what money really is, which suggests that a deep collective blindness is at work.

OUT OF THIN AIR

The ancient Greek philosopher Aristotle, generally acknowledged as the originator of the science of money, claimed that money exists not by nature, but by law.[1] Issuance of money historically has been tightly guarded as the divine right of kings, making it illegal to counterfeit or to establish a rival system, a crime that was punishable by death in bygone days and certain incarceration today.

Some of the earliest records in monetary history date back to ancient Sumer, located where modern-day Iran and Iraq lie. The Sumerians are credited with the development of writing. Their impetus was primarily to keep records of accounts rather than any romantic notions of writing poetry or memorializing victories in battle. Gold coinage started in Lydia (part of Turkey today) during the 7th century BC. More than 1,000 years later, in the same geographical area, the bezant was created, a gold coin that was issued with the same weight (4.55 grams) and same purity (98 percent) for a record 700 years.[2]

The beginning of one form of paper money in the Western world emerged in Venice during the 13th century. It was a prudent practice to store one's money with goldsmiths for safekeeping, who in turn would issue a receipt for the coins and charge a small fee for the service. When money was needed, owners could cash in the receipt, and the goldsmith would pay out the coins. It soon became more convenient to make payments by simply exchanging the promises to pay. Whenever someone accepted such a receipt as payment, they were implicitly entering into an agreement with the goldsmith. This was the origin of modern-day paper money and banking.

In time, a few astute goldsmiths observed that the bulk of the coins stayed with them on deposit, because their clients never retrieved all their coins at the same time. The goldsmiths realized that they could thereby issue receipts in excess of the gold coins they stocked and increase their income by lending out money without having to increase their actual reserves. In other words, they began to issue more money than they actually held in coins.

This process, now called the *fractional reserve* system, and the remaining elements of what constitutes modern banking and monetary standards were largely put in place and became standard practice in Europe by the mid-1600s.

These banking practices are explored in some depth in the next chapter, including how the banking system creates and lends money, which is all debt based, and how one is obliged in the current monetary system to incur debt and compete with others over scarce resources with some devastating consequences.

By the late 17th century, the need to finance wars gave further impetus to the money-creating mechanism. A special relationship began between the emerging private banking systems and governments. The oldest surviving agreement of this type can be traced back to 1668, with the license of the Swedish Bank of the Estates of the Realm (the name was changed in 1867 to *Riksbank,*as the Swedish Central Bank is still known). The agreement gave the power of emission of paper money to a private bank, the Bank of the Estates of the Realm, when the crown urgently needed money to fund a war against Denmark. The same situation took place in Britain a generation later with the founding of the Bank of En gland (1688), to which the monopoly of emission of paper money was assigned by King William of Orange in 1694, when he needed 1.2 million pounds for a war against the French. From En gland, this practice spread around the world. In the United States, this same deal—bank-debt money accepted as legal tender by the government—was part of the Federal Reserve Act of 1913.[3]

This liaison between terrestrial seats of power and the banking system is still with us today.

During the latter days of the gold standard, the actual gold reserves of the Bank of En gland, for example, were treated as a state secret because the amount of gold backing for the British pound was much lower than publicly admitted.[4] The last vestiges of the gold standard in the United States were removed by President Nixon in August 1971, when he officially stopped any convertibility between the U.S. dollar and gold, even for central banks, thereby severing the last link between a physical commodity and the money system. Their values were severed and divorced from each other.

National currencies are now technically defined as "*fiat*" money. *Fiat* takes its origin in the very first word that God spoke in the Latin version of Genesis: *Fiat lux*("let light be"). It implies the godlike ability to create something out of nothing *("ex nihilo")* through the power of the word or, in practice in this case, the stroke of a pen. This means that money isn't something that comes out of a farm, a mine, a mint, or even a printing press. It comes into being by the power of the word or, in these times, a stroke of a computer key.

DEBT AND TAXES

So what makes one form of money more desirable than another? As economics professor L. Randall Wray writes, "In all modern economies the government defines money by choosing what it will accept in the payment of taxes. Once it has required that the citizens must pay taxes in the form of particular money (for example dollars), the citizens must obtain that money to pay taxes. In order to obtain *that which is necessary to pay taxes,*or money, they offer labor services or produced goods to the government (as well as to markets). This means the government could buy anything that is for sale for dollars merely by issuing dollars."[5] Therefore, a sovereign government does not really "need" to raise taxes to pay for its expenses. Once this is understood, it becomes clear that neither taxes nor government bonds "finance" government spending. Instead, taxes are required to give value to money.

In reality, in the money domain, everything starts and ends with government. At the commencement of the process, the government decides what it will accept in payment of taxes. Historically, it has chosen specific commodities, such as wheat or other food products, bronze or copper ingots, beaver pelts, tobacco leaves, or gold or silver bullion. This obligation puts the population to work to find or produce those commodities. Today, with fiat currencies required for the payment of taxes, the population works, trades, and invests in national currencies so they can meet their responsibilities.

It's the same story worldwide. This is true regardless of the country of issuance, the political philosophy (capitalist, communist, socialist, fascist, totalitarian, despotic, or democratic), and the different designations, and despite differences in material composition, shape, or particular motif. The currencies are, each and every one of them, the same type of money that is required by the state for the payment of taxes.

By *type,* what is meant is that all national currencies have the same design features. The design does not mean how the money actually looks—pictures of heads of state looking presidential or regal—but how it is created. This in turn informs how it operates. Like a car, money has an engine that drives certain behaviors, and how that engine is built will influence its performance.

Not only are all conventional national currencies fiat based but also they are hierarchical in that the monopoly of currency creation has been given to the banking system under the supervision of a central bank. Furthermore, conventional currency needs to be kept scarcer than its usefulness to maintain its value, and consequently, there is competition to procure it. The implications of the functional dynamics of national money have some profound repercussions for society at large, which are explored in some depth in the next chapter.

There is yet another layer to the obfuscation of money's true nature. This comes from the science of economics itself.

THE MISSING PIECE

Though each respective school of economics and its thought leaders differ in fundamental ways on a broad range of economic issues, they do share a common oversight—each fails to look at money itself. This blind spot is not a mere coincidence but, rather, endemic to the discipline. Economics textbooks, for example, define *money*by what it does, as discussed earlier—a store of value, a medium of exchange, a unit of account—rather than what it *is.*More important, *never questioned is the assumption that the same monetary tool is needed to play all three roles.*This disregards the fact that some of these roles may operate at cross-purposes. For example, a medium of exchange functions optimally when it is available and circulates, but a store of value can result in a currency's effective removal from circulation. Traditional economics has never decoupled monetary architecture into its constituent parts. To do so would give rise to a very different reality, as will be shown. Yet such considerations are absent in the work of these monetary luminaries.

Suffice it to say here that among the many consequences of this one omission is this: The theoretical postures of several major economics schools are at best compromised. They fail to acknowledge the reality that a monopoly of one type of money, in the form of fiat, scarcity-based, interest-bearing national currencies, imposes a limited set of Industrial Age values and actions on all the economies and cultures of the world. This, in turn, makes a mockery of the very concept of *free*markets, as no one is really free in such a system.

HOW DID WE GET HERE FROM THERE?

No matter whether it's along the corridors of power, in the boardrooms of major corporations, or sitting at the kitchen table working out a family's monthly bud get, government policy relating to all financial matters and monetary procedures is determined by the self-styled *science*of economics.

So, how did economics get to be so complicated and mystifying that it has earned the label of "the dismal science"? And perhaps more important, how devastating are the consequences of government policy following in the misguided footsteps of the economists? And how does that affect the money in our wallets?

The father of economics, Adam Smith, was a moral philosopher. "Smith's true subject was the friction between individual desire and societal norms. What might lead one person to cheat or steal while another didn't? How would one person's seemingly innocuous choice, good or bad, effect a great number of people down the line? In Smith's era, cause and effect had begun to widely accelerate; incentives were magnified tenfold. The gravity and shock of these changes were as overwhelming to the citizens of his time, as the gravity and shock of modern life seem to us today."[6]

Smith's inquiries were set against the background of the development of our modern-day banking system with the formation of central banks in Sweden and En gland, while the earlier discoveries of Newton and his contemporaries ignited the imaginations of the ruling and educated upper class. The Age of Enlightenment's zeitgeist was one of cool-headed rationalism and empiricism, which stood in stark contrast to the era of dark religious superstition that had preceded it. For example, Newtonian physics made it possible to calculate the distance and velocity of a cannonball being shot out of a cannon and to predict the movement of the heavenly bodies in interstellar space, both with precise meticulousness, theoretically down to a fraction of an inch. Consequently, everything had to be measured and codified. If it couldn't be *sensed,* in other words quantified, then it was deemed *nonsense* and duly dismissed.

Subsequently, the burgeoning science of economics was stripped of the moral inquiries and concerns that previously informed it as part of the field of applied philosophy. Economics had to be transformed into a science, meaning that it now required a backbone of mathematical formulae to provide the necessary empiricism.

What is critical to understand is that both the math used and several of the assumptions made to formulate economic theory were fundamentally fl awed. The physics of the time assumed that all systems were closed and static, upholding the Newtonian perfectly ordered view of the cosmos. In his book, *The Origin of Wealth: Evolution, Complexity, and the Radical Remaking of Economics,* Eric Beinhocker details many of the inherent misconceptions in the equilibrium theory used in traditional economics. He concludes that economists' "willingness to make trade-offs in realism for the sake of mathematical predictability would set a pattern followed by economists over the next century."[7]

Newton's neatly ordered view of the universe was shattered some 200 years later by Einstein with his famous equation $E=mc^2$ Energy and matter manifested in an exquisite interchangeable dance. Suddenly the boundaries of reality changed and grew. Matter transforms into energy and energy into matter. But the revolution had only just begun. Newtonian mechanics that had ruled for centuries could only handle two-body astronomical problems, meaning that it could predict with precision, for example, the orbit of the moon around the Earth, assuming no other celestial bodies were involved.

But these equations could not solve for anything beyond two bodies—throw in the sun, the Earth, and the moon, and the equations were hopelessly complex. Realizing this severe limitation, mathematicians and physicists developed statistics that yielded, for instance, a fairly precise way of predicting what happens to billions of molecules in a gas. But the complex, interdependent systems in the *middle,*which is just about everything in our lives and the universe, were well beyond the capabilities of Newtonian physics. This massive blind spot was overlooked by a culture hooked on believing it could understand everything with linear, cause- and-effect thinking. All systems and their inherent complexity were seriously underestimated.

It would be some two centuries later, with the development of computers with massive computational prowess, until equations that would have taken a stadium full of people working for hundreds of years to solve could be solved in a matter of seconds. Relatively precise solutions to the three-body problem were demonstrated. A new field known by various names, including nonlinear dynamics, fractals, chaos, or complexity theory, began to emerge. The concept of the *butterfly effect,* whereby a flutter of a butterfly wing might cause a massive change in the weather countries away, became common knowledge. In short, it was now understood that everything affects everything else in multifaceted, often unpredictable ways. The critical middle, the stuff in between, as it were, is the infinite complexity of systems that are totally interactive, interconnected, and interdependent.

In other words, the fabric of the cosmos is underpinned by a system that is dynamic and open, not fixed and closed, as Newton and his contemporaries believed. Contemporaneously, theoretical physicists, rather than looking into outer space and the movement of large heavenly bodies, focused in the realm of quantum mechanics and observed a waltz of infinite possibilities in the inner space of subatomic particles in atoms and molecules. Danish physicist Niels Bohr presented a counterintuitive newfound reality that views life as a game of chance, a roll of the dice as it were, with infinite probabilities that all coexist in parallel dimensions.

As Eric Liu and Nick Hanauer write, "Science—which we mean broadly to include physical discoveries, insights into behavior, awareness of patterns of experience—tells us today that the world is a *complex adaptive system,* not a linear equilibrium system; that the elements within are *networked,* not atomized, that humans operate in that system as *emotional, reciprocal approximators,*not rational self-regarding calculators."[8]

Clearly, then, the economy does not exist suspended in a vacuum. In reality, the economy has little in common with Newtonian mechanical models, which imply images of perfectly functioning free markets, impeccably efficient corporations, and skillful players who know everything taking place in the markets. Nor does Einstein's more evolved view go far enough. The financial system instead exhibits many traits and emergent properties common to the complex, adaptive, open systems found in nature and the biological sciences, systems governed more by randomness and chance.

Perhaps anthropologist Gregory Bateson summed up the current debacle best: "The source of all our problems today comes from the gap between how we think and how nature works."[9]

THE CONSEQUENCES

While much of the groundwork of conventional economics remains frozen in an outdated Newtonian paradigm, several bright but marginalized economists looked to the natural ecosystems for answers. Biologists and complexity experts have determined that the long-term sustainability of any complex flow network depends on an appropriate balance between two opposing requirements: efficiency and resilience. *Efficiency*is the ability of a complex flow network to process volume of whatever flows through it per unit of time, in an organized, streamlined manner. *Resilience* is its ability to cope with change while preserving its integrity. Both efficiency and resilience of a network depend in turn on two key *structural*variables of the network: its diversity and its interconnectivity. However, this dependency operates in opposite directions: efficiency tends to be increased by streamlining, i.e. by *reducing* diversity and interconnectivity. In contrast, resilience *increases*with diversity and interconnectivity.

For instance, an ecosystem's resilience increases with its diversity and interconnectivity, because they provide options and additional choices to fall back on in tough times, such as a drought, an attack, or a disease. So if an animal in the higher levels of a food chain has only one source of food that becomes unavailable due to blight or illness, most likely that animal will also die. For example, the problem of the panda is that it eats only one type of bamboo, i.e. it lacks interconnectivity. Similarly, if a store or factory has only one source for critical merchandise or parts and that supplier goes bankrupt, that business may also get into trouble.

What is important is that optimal functionality in nature—and by extension in all complex flow networks, such as the electrical grid, the human body, and the money system—requires resilience. And to be resilient, there must be more choices and options to fall back on if attacked, struck by disease, or experiencing business failure. In short, there has to be a minimum of diversity.

In the current systems in business, finance, and economics, the focus is almost exclusively on efficiency, and therefore tends to disregard resilience. With efficiency, the focus is on the volume of throughput within a given time period. Bigger is better. More is best. This has been the yardstick used to mea sure the relative success of a system, whether in nature or in economics. Many economists urge endless growth in the size of the gross national product (GNP), since they assume that growth in volume is a sufficient mea sure of health. Total system throughput (TST) is the equivalent mea sure for ecosystems. But GNP and TST both are poor mea sures of sustainable viability because *they ignore network structure.*Subsequently, the experts cannot, for example, distinguish between a resilient economy and a bubble that is doomed to burst; or between healthy "development," as former World Bank economist Herman Daly describes it, and explosive growth in monetary exchanges simply due to runaway speculation.

The impetus for setting up GNP was indeed noble. Following the crash of 1929 and the Great Depression in 1932, the United States developed a set of mea sures on which to base a new national accounting scheme. With better accounting and better data, it was believed that the horror experienced by so many could be averted.

This set of mea sures, the GNP, computed the value of goods and services produced by American businesses and nationals, both at home and abroad. But though more sophisticated than anything that preceded it, and more comprehensive regarding who was included in its accounting data, its theory regarding price and value still reflected earlier classical economic assumptions. As a result, what the GNP measured was still limited exclusively to adding up the flow of bank-debt money through the economy.

According to the rationale of the GNP, monetary transactions are considered a gain, and anything that does not involve the direct exchange of money is disregarded. Barter exchanges, for example, are not tracked. Domestic care, such as someone taking care of an aged parent or a young child, and volunteer work are likewise not taken into account. Yet the same work performed by someone paid in conventional money, like a nurse or a firefighter, *is*measurable in bank-debt money and, therefore, *does*count.

The consequences of not taking into account such activities are both unfortunate and deeply significant. The decline of a nonmarket economy, such as the social breakdown of a family or community, has a negative impact on society. But from a strictly monetized economic perspective, services rendered without payment are considered to have no value. Worse, if individual decline gets to the point where paid intervention is needed, the costs of social decay then register as an improvement.

Costs associated with psychological counseling, social work, and addiction treatment, which arise from the neglect of the nonmarket realm, are tallied as economic gains. Crime adds billions to the GNP due to the need for legal services, prisons, increased police and private security protection, and repair of property damage. Similarly, the depletion of our natural resources, the cleanup and medical treatments associated with industry's toxic by-products, the costs of ecological disasters such as the oil spills in the Gulf of Mexico and Alaska's Prudhoe Bay, relief efforts following the Haitian and Japanese earthquakes and subsequent nuclear meltdown, the devastation caused by wars, and the hundreds of billions of dollars allocated in emergency stimulus packages all register as improvements to a nation's economy by the curious standards of the GNP.

As economists Clifford Cobb, Ted Halstead, and Jonathan Rowe point out, "The GDP not only masks the breakdown of the social structure and the natural habitat upon which the economy—and life itself—ultimately depend; worse, it actually portrays such breakdown as economic gain."[10] Herman Daly put it this way: "The current national accounting system treats the earth as a business in liquidation."[11]

Gross domestic product (GDP) replaced gross national product (GNP) as the primary mea sure of U.S. production in 1991, without correcting the flaws just described. Yet, despite its obvious limitation, it endures today, warping and distorting the collective worldview. It persists precisely because of the myopic focus on monetary exchanges regardless of the broader-term consequences for society at large.

The devastation of the Great Depression and the dramatic economic ramifications of the 1930s forced economists and nations to reexamine their assumptions regarding the economy, particularly the then-dominant view that a free market, unfettered by government interference, would naturally bring about full employment equilibrium.

This debate still rages, almost a century later. Without needing to parse the theories, ideas from three iconic schools of thought shape current economic and political debates: John Maynard Keynes, Friedrich Hayek, and Milton Friedman and their respective Keynesian, Austrian, and Chicago schools of economics. Their viewpoints, together with those of another once-prominent economist, Irving Fisher, not only show how the views of prominent economists diverge but also highlight what is almost entirely lacking from traditional economic thought.

WHAT'S NOT CONSIDERED

Challenging a paradigm in any field and moving thought and action forward beyond it is always a risky business. In particular, challenging the monetary paradigm can be interpreted as violating an academic taboo. It somehow gets in the way of being invited to the "important" conferences or getting published in prestigious peer-reviewed journals. For example, consider the most prestigious award of all, the Nobel Prize in Economics. Many people overlook the fact that there is a significant difference between the economics prize and the other five awards that were established in 1901: the awards in physics, chemistry, physiology or medicine, literature, and peace. The economics prize is the only one that wasn't created by the will of Alfred Nobel, nor is it funded by the Nobel Foundation. Its technical name is the "Sveriges Riksbank Prize in Economic Sciences in Memory of Alfred Nobel," and it was first awarded in 1969. It is funded by the Swedish central bank. Is it any wonder that none of the 69 Nobel laureates in economics, so far, have dared to challenge the monetary paradigm?[12]

*New York Times*columnist Paul Krugman told one of the authors in Seoul, South Korea, a decade ago that he has always followed one piece of advice that his MIT professors had given him: "Never touch the money system." Krugman was awarded the Nobel Prize for Economics in 2008.

Perhaps Keynes said it best: "The ideas of economists and political philosophers, both when they are right and when they are wrong, are more powerful than is commonly understood. Indeed, the world is ruled by little else. Practical men, who believe themselves to be quite exempt from any intellectual influences, are usually the slaves of some defunct economist. Madmen in authority, who hear voices in the air, are distilling their frenzy from some academic scribbler of a few years back ... sooner or later, it is ideas, not vested interests, which are dangerous for good or evil."[13]

Chapter Three

A FATE WORSE THAN DEBT

Interest's Hidden Consequences

It may sometimes be expedient for a man to heat the stove with his furniture. But he should not delude himself by believing that he has discovered a wonderful new method of heating his premises.

LUDWIG VON MISES, Austrian economist

The small village was bustling with locals proudly displaying their wares, chickens, eggs, cheeses, and bread as they entered into the time-honored ritual of negotiations and trade for what they needed. At harvests, or whenever someone's barn needed repair after a storm, the village-dwellers simply exercised another age-old tradition of helping one another, knowing that if they themselves had a problem one day, others would come to their aid in turn. No coins ever exchanged hands.

One market day, a stranger with shiny black shoes and an elegant white hat came by and observed with a knowing smile. When one farmer who wanted a big ham ran around to corral the six chickens needed in exchange, the stranger could not refrain from laughing. "Poor people," he said, "so primitive."

Overhearing this, a farmer's wife challenged him: "Do you think you can do a better job handling chickens?"

The stranger responded: "Chickens, no. But, I do know a way to eliminate the hassles. Bring me one large cowhide and gather the families. There's a better way."

As requested, the families gathered, and the stranger took the cowhide, cut perfect leather rounds and put an elaborate stamp on each. He then gave ten rounds to every family, stating that each one represented the value of a chicken. "Now you can trade and bargain with the rounds instead of those unwieldy chickens."

It seemed to make sense, and everybody was quite impressed.

"One more thing," the stranger added. "In one year's time, I'll return and I want all the families to bring me back an extra round—an eleventh round. That eleventh round is a token of appreciation for the improvements I made possible in your lives."

"But where will that round come from?" asked another woman.

"You'll see," replied the stranger, with a knowing look.

A year passes and on another market day the stranger with the stylish hat returns, and from his vantage point he observes the village below. While sitting under the broad-limbed oak tree, he reaches into his knapsack and pulls out a silver canteen filled with a single-malt whiskey, takes a swig, savoring its peaty warmth at the back of his throat, and waits for the village folk to file past him with each family's repayment of the eleventh round.

Below on the village outskirts, a family begs for alms, having lost everything in a fire. Focused on their obligations, the villagers pass by without as much as a glance.

The elusive eleventh round like interest itself was not created, but payment for the development of the upgrade in efficiency does seem reasonable to his mind and is exacted nonetheless. The stranger sits and watches the scene below, completely oblivious and unaware of the impact his innovation has caused.

The eleventh round is a very simplified illustration of an important principle regarding money. The point of the anecdote is that, with all other things being equal, the competition to obtain the money necessary to pay the interest is structurally embedded in the current money system. Somebody will have to be without the eleventh round for payment for somebody else to have it and make the interest payment.

So how does a loan, whose interest is not created, get repaid?

Essentially, to pay back interest on a loan requires using someone else's principal. In other words, not creating the money to pay interest is the device used to generate the scarcity necessary for a bank-debt monetary system to function. It forces people to compete with each other for money that was never created, and it penalizes them with bankruptcy, should they not succeed. When a bank checks a customer's creditworthiness, it is really verifying his or her ability to compete successfully against the other players—that is to say, assessing the customer's ability to extract from others the money that is required to reimburse the interest payment. One is obliged in the current monetary system to incur debt and compete with others in order to perform exchanges and pay the resulting interest to the banks or lenders.

HOW IT REALLY WORKS

For each deposit that any bank receives, it is entitled to create new money, specifically in the form of a loan to a customer of up to 90 percent (a *fraction)* of the value of the deposit (held in *reserve),* hence the name *fractional reserve*system.[1] Indeed, a bank is supposed to lend out only the money it has on deposit while keeping 10 percent of it in reserves with the central bank. In practice, however, banks do not wait for excess reserves before making loans. Rather, if faced with a creditworthy customer and a request for a loan, a bank makes the loan. It then operates to obtain reserves as necessary to meet legal requirements. If banks in the aggregate are short of required reserves, the central bank *must*supply them. Indeed, if a bank is short on reserves, this *shortage* is, in fact, accounted as an overdraft on its reserve account with the central bank. This overdraft is an automatic loan from the central bank. So there is no way that a central bank could deny credit to a bank.

Furthermore, when a new loan is made—for instance, a mortgage to buy a house, financing for a car, or a student loan—this usually results in someone making a new deposit somewhere else in the banking system, for example, by the seller of the house. In turn, the bank receiving that deposit is entitled to create another loan for 90 percent of that new deposit. Then that loan is deposited in another account, that bank is permitted to make yet another loan, and the cascade continues from deposit to loan down through the banking system. Although new loans are being created, the interest on the principal is not. Nowhere in the system is this additional money created. This gives rise to scarcity, which, in turn, creates competition to acquire the extra money to cover the loans' interest. This magic, where one person's loan becomes another's deposit, and whereby when you pay interest you are using someone else's principal, is really monetary alchemy. This monetary alchemy is one of the esoteric secrets of the monetary system.

This *fractional reserve multiplier,* as it is technically known, starts with the injection, for example, of 10 million units of *high-powered money from the central bank*directly into the reserve account of a bank. This 10 million makes it possible for that bank to make loans for 100 million. These 100 million end up being deposited somewhere in the banking system by the recipients of these funds, which enables the banks that receive these new deposits to provide a new loan for 90 million to someone else (the other 10 million becoming "sterile reserves," meaning they remain in deposit in the reserve accounts with the central bank). The new loan for 90 million will, in turn, lead to another deposit for that amount somewhere else, enabling the next bank to provide another loan for 81 million (i.e., 90 percent of 90 million), and so on. This is how what started off as 10 million units of *high-powered money*can create up to 200 million units in *credit money*as it trickles down the banking system.

A key point to keep in mind is that this entire money-creation process hinges on loans. If all debts were repaid, money would simply disappear, because the entire process of money creation would reverse itself. Reimbursing all loans would automatically use up all the deposits. Even the central bank's high-powered money would evaporate if the banks were able to repay their debts. There would even be a remaining financial hole, a negative balance reflecting the unpaid interest on all those loans.

In the conventional currency paradigm, one important reason that so much weight is given to decisions made by central banks is that increased interest rates automatically imply a larger proportion of bankruptcies in the future.

Also remember the eleventh round story: When a banker checks a customer's credit score, it is to assess how successful or aggressive that individual or business will be in contending with others to obtain funds that are not created in sufficiency to pay back the interest on the loan.

In a manner of speaking, it's like a game of musical chairs in that there are never enough seats for everyone. Someone will end up getting squeezed out. There isn't enough money to pay the interest on all the loans, just like the missing chair. Both are highly competitive games. In the money game, however, the stakes are elevated, as it means grappling with certain poverty or, worse still, having to declare bankruptcy.

The dynamics of today's conventional money system have led to a number of problems in addition to systematized bankruptcy. These negative consequences not only are misunderstood but also were unintended and, for the most part, have their roots in the application of interest.

INTEREST

Undoubtedly, there are solid reasons for applying interest to a loan. It protects against default and works as a fair precaution by the lender to ensure that he receives back at least the amount he lent out. For instance, if a lender expects 10 percent of his borrowers to default on their loans, then 10 percent interest is charged to ensure that the entire principal is paid back. Furthermore, by providing a borrower with money, the lender forgoes the opportunity to make a profit by investing the money. A lender charges interest as compensation for the missed opportunity to make additional earnings.

Interest, however, has hidden dynamics that result in detrimental costs not only to personal relationships, commerce, and society at large, but also to the sustainability of our fragile planetary home, Earth. The effects are so well concealed, in addition to being so deeply embedded in the money system, that they go, for the most part, utterly unnoticed.

COMPULSORY GROWTH PRESSURE

Debt-based money requires endless growth because borrowers must find additional money to pay back the interest on their debt. For the better-rated debtors (e.g., in normal times, government debt), the interest is simply covered through additional debt, resulting in *compound interest:* paying interest on interest. Compound interest implies exponential growth in the long run, something mathematically impossible in a *finite*world.

There's a famous metaphorical tale about the Persian emperor who was so pleased with a new game called chess that he offered its inventor a reward for his idea. The nameless inventor knew something about mathematics, so he asked for a grain of rice for the first square, twice as much for the second square, and doubling again for each square until all 64 squares on the board had been accounted for.

It seemed innocuous enough to the emperor, and he quickly agreed. On the eighth square, the inventor collected 128 grains of rice. On the 16th, he brought home 32,768 grains of rice. By the time half of the chessboard was accounted for, the emperor was in debtors' prison because he defaulted on his debt to the game's creator because he owed more rice than was produced.

Here's another way to visualize this concept of exponential growth. Let us assume that every week water lilies double the surface they cover in a lake. Initially, their growth may seem quite reasonable. For example, after a year, a quarter of the pond is covered with lilies. How much time will it take for the lilies to cover the entire pond? If the growth were linear, it would take another four years. If the growth is exponential, as is the case in compound interest, however, it will take merely one week to cover a second quarter of the pool of water, and by the second week, the entire pond will be covered!

Stories aside, the exponential growth of money through interest rates has shattering real-life consequences in which entire nations of people are marginalized and stuck in debt forever. For instance, after a G8 summit former President Obasanjo of Nigeria stated: "All that we had borrowed up to 1985 or 1986 was around $5 billion and we have paid back so far about $16 billion. Yet, we are being told that we still owe about $28 billion. That $28 billion came about because of the foreign creditors' interest rates. If you ask me, 'What is the worst thing in the world,' I will say, 'It is compound interest.'"

The Nigerian government by 2006 had paid almost $20 billion to settle its foreign debts to two international bank syndicates, the Paris Club and the London Club of Creditors, and became the first African nation to settle with its official lenders. This was one of the largest transfers of wealth by a third world nation to first world nations.[2]

It is alarming to note that back in the 1990s the developing world was spending $13 on debt repayment for every dollar it received in foreign aid and grants. By 2004, that number had grown to $20 on debt repayment for each dollar of foreign aid. Today the ratio is 25:1.[3]

Sadly, Nigeria's cycle of debt was not absolved with its massive settlement less than a decade ago. With an outstanding debt profile of about $5 billion after the debt pardon was secured by then President Olusegun Obasanjo, the progression of arrears and liabilities has now risen to a staggering $37 billion.[4]

Clearly, it's almost impossible to break from the shackles of debt obligation, given the effect of compound interest on a loan.

Growth by itself, even exponential growth, it should be emphasized, is not necessarily problematic. For instance, there is no reason to worry if one's knowledge base increases exponentially. Healthy growth is facilitated by the influences of innovations and inventions, the expansion of markets into new geographic areas or through internal growth in the labor force, and by rising standards of education and training. The growth induced by compound interest money, however, does not discern. Rather, compounded interest unchecked by countervailing forces blindly pushes the real economy to grow, regardless of the form of growth or its consequences. This mandatory growth obligates everyone to be on an economic treadmill, no matter what the long-term impact may be.

SHORT-TERMISM

"The time horizon for the financial planning for my family is easily 20 to 25 years into the future. There are provisions made for my children's well-being, their education, and once they're out of the house and on their own two feet, I suppose I will be looking at my wife's and my retirement," answered the CEO of a major German corporation spontaneously. He didn't have to think about it or carefully evaluate his reply, it was so spontaneous.

"And what is the time horizon for decisions in your company?" The second question hung in the air for a moment.

"Well, usually there's a three-to five-year horizon in a business plan. But what is really critical is the next quarter and possibly the one after that," came the reply rather matter-of-factly. "If I don't deliver profits each quarter, I'll be quickly replaced by someone else who will."

His response would be typical for most businesspersons who are being candid, particularly in publicly owned companies. In the business and financial world, the importance of the immediate future totally outweighs the long-term future. The upshot is that financial rewards are strongly skewed toward immediacy. Subsequently, there is not enough long-term planning. This has serious consequences. For one, to conserve and protect Earth's finite resources requires long time horizons, even intergenerational thinking. Therefore, whenever decisions are made on a short-term basis, sustainability—whether financial or ecological from local to planetary—tends to be overlooked. For instance, British Petroleum's or Ford's decisions and choices in energy and transport strategies would clearly be different if they were based on a 100-year time line, instead of on a few quarterly results.

Part of this short-termism is in de pen dent of the monetary system: The further in the future that events are located, the more difficult it is to make accurate predictions about them, meaning there is increased risk. Hence the old saying, "a bird in the hand is worth two in the bush."

There is, however, a second key impetus toward short-termism that is entrenched firmly in the conventional money system. Today's money is created through bank debt, as explained in the last chapter, and it requires the payment of interest. In other words, every dollar, peso, or euro that exists today is someone's debt, whether incurred by a state, corporation, or individual. This means that interest is a built-in feature of the monetary system. Furthermore, as known to anyone familiar with the discounted cash flow (DCF) technique used in financial decision making, the readiness to make long-term investments depends, to a significant extent, on the current and anticipated interest rates.

Discounted cash flow analysts know that interest is one of the three factors in discounting any future cash flow. (The other two factors are the intrinsic risk of the investment project and the cost of equity capital.) With the issue of interest, however, an entrepreneur, for example, can put her capital in a bank instead of investing it. If she deposits $61 in the bank at an interest rate of 5 percent, she will have $100 after 10 years.[5] Thus, any investment of $61 today that will have a value of $100 in 10 years is only worthwhile if the money market interest rate is lower than 5 percent. Otherwise, she can make the same amount of money with less risk by leaving it in the bank.

To put it another way, say the same entrepreneur has a choice between two different forestry investments: planting a pine or an oak. With the same interest rate, the short-term thinking process becomes clear when one compares the two. To keep the numbers simple, it is assumed that all numbers are inflation adjusted and that the risk of specific investment projects is in de pen dent of the time frame. A pine tree can be felled in 10 years and would then bring a yield of $100. An oak, on the other hand, cannot be harvested until it is 100 years old, and it would then be valued at $1,000 per tree. With these assumptions, and if one doesn't have to take interest into account, the two investments could be seen as equivalent, as one could harvest and replant the pines every 10 years, ending up with the same $1,000 in 100 years.

Now, the investor asks: "What are these two investments worth as seen from today?" We saw that with an interest rate of 5 percent, the investment in a pine that will produce a yield of $100 in 10 years is equivalent to $61 today. Similarly calculated, with the same interest rate of 5 percent, the value today of the $1,000 oak tree in 100 years is only $7.60! This difference in value of $61 versus $7.60 is due only to the interest feature of the money used. This demonstrates that, while there is a lot of commercial interest in harvesting old-growth forest, there is none in planting trees that will take a long time to mature and be harvested.

More generally, this difference also describes why, in a society using an interest-bearing currency, financial investments are focusing mainly on the short term.

EROSION OF SOCIAL CAPITAL

Social capital is a buzz term related to an individual's goodwill, camaraderie, and favorable social status within his or her community. Perhaps one mea sure of someone's social capital is the number of people who turn up for someone's funeral and the caliber of their eulogies. This attribute is not trivial. It is the glue that transforms a collection of individuals into a human—or perhaps better still—a humane society.

Essentially, social capital is a proven precondition for rendering a democracy functional[6] and for securing economic prosperity.[7] These are possible only when a society has a sufficient sense of responsibility, mutual trust, solidarity, and cooperation. Responsibility and trust are essential for business and the market system to operate effectively. Increasing crime rates,[8] poverty, and the exclusion[9] of ever-growing numbers of a given population[10] are the first indications of the erosion of societal adhesion. Studies show that, at present, social capital is not only undergoing a change in nature but also dwindling quickly.

An entire field of economics is based on the assumption that something in human nature (and *not*the kind of money used) predetermines certain behavior patterns. Money is deemed value neutral; therefore, it is thought to have no effect on one's conduct. What happened with the !Kung tribe over half a century ago, however, clearly illustrates just the opposite: It *is* the type of money used in a transaction that encourages competition or collaboration, stinginess or generosity.

The !Kung are considered one of the very last societies on Earth whose ways of living have remained fundamentally unchanged since prehistoric times. They live in the high plateau of the Kalahari Desert, an area that occupies most of the country of Botswana and parts of Namibia and South Africa. This Iron Age clan remained largely isolated for over 40,000 years. Whatever outside contact they had did not alter the !Kung way of life. This was proven in archaeological digs,[11] which found a range of stone and bone tools and a specific camp layout, excavated from three ancient !Kung sites.

In the 1960s and 1970s, anthropologist John Yellen studied the !Kung lifestyle. This time period happened to be just before and after these people became acquainted with conventional money, which brought about unprecedented change in the !Kung culture in a remarkably short period of time.[12]

Traditionally, the !Kung adhered to a rich set of social values and rules, which regulated the distribution of food and other goods. The practice of sharing formed the core of the !Kung system of values.

Families were expected to welcome relatives who showed up at their camps. Moreover, etiquette dictated that meat from large kills be shared outside the immediate family. By distributing his bounty, a hunter ensured that the recipients of his largess would be obliged to return the favor sometime in the future. In the traditional !Kung view of the world, security was obtained by giving rather than hoarding, that is, by accumulating obligations that could be called upon in times of need.

The layout of a traditional !Kung camp reflected their norms of sharing and reciprocity. Huts were arranged in a circle, with the doorways facing inward, allowing members to directly look into each other's huts. The hearths were placed outside the huts, and each person could see what food everyone else was preparing and, therefore, whether there was any food to share. Individuals also established formal relationships with nonrelatives in which two people gave each other gifts, such as knives or iron spears, at irregular intervals. Reciprocity was delayed, so that one person would always be in debt to the other.

During the 1970s, the Botswana government started to stimulate trade with the !Kung people. This development, as well as more contact with

South Africa, introduced conventional money into the !Kung tribe. With this newfound cash, the !Kung people purchased such goods as glass beads, clothing, and extra blankets, which they hoarded in metal trunks, locked for the first time, inside their huts.

Many times, the items procured far exceeded the needs of an individual family and could best be viewed as a form of savings. As the !Kung hoarded, they stopped depending on others to give them gifts and retreated from their traditional interdependence. At the same time, perhaps because they were ashamed of not sharing, they sought privacy. The layout of the camps suddenly changed significantly, after having remained unchanged for 40,000 years! Hut openings no longer faced inward, distances between the huts increased, and hearths were moved inside. Privacy played a much greater role than before, and reciprocal exchanges lost their importance.

This example confirms that conventional money doesn't simply facilitate exchanges, as generally assumed, but rather actually creates very specific social behaviors. The!Kung, who had a culture of unusual generosity and consideration for the well-being of the group, a culture that had survived practically unchanged for millennia, was altered dramatically in less than one generation with the introduction of money. The tribe's emotional signature devolved into selfishness and parsimony, characteristics far more prevalent in the modern developed world than in their own traditions.

A national survey of Americans found that some 93 percent said that people are too focused on working and making money, and 87 percent responded that we're living in a materialistic world that makes it difficult to teach children ethics and morals. At the same time, several other studies have shown that the key to building communities and social capital is gift exchanges, such as helping a neighbor or mentoring a student.[13] These findings further attest to the unfortunate reality that, as monetized market mechanisms are introduced into ever-greater areas of society, social capital begins to erode.

International financier George Soros concluded, "International trade and global financial markets are very good at generating wealth, but they cannot take care of other social needs, such as the preservation of peace, alleviation of poverty, protection of the environment, labor conditions, or human rights—what are generally called 'public goods.'"[14]

UNRELENTING CONCENTRATION OF WEALTH

It is generally not understood that an interest-based monetary system is also one of the key underlying mechanisms for concentrating wealth in increasingly fewer hands, fueling the growing disparity between rich and poor. This concentration process has been accelerating in most countries, regardless of whether the nation is categorized as developed or developing.

A recent German study on the transfer of wealth via interest from one economic group to another was conducted by Helmut Creutz, a monetary analyst and author. In his 2007 survey of German families, he grouped the entire sample into 10 income categories of approximately 3.5 million households each.

Because of the upward concentration of wealth caused by interest, there was a transfer of wealth from the bottom 80 percent of the population to the top 20 percent, especially the top 10 percent, due exclusively to the interest feature of the monetary system used. This transfer of wealth occurred independently of the cleverness or industriousness of the participants, attributes often assumed to account for differences in income.

The first eight groups of households are in the negative, which means that they have paid out more in interest than they received. In the ninth group, interest gained and paid roughly cancel each other out. However, in the tenth group, the total gains add up to the total losses of the first eight groups.

The highest transfers of interest were from the middle classes to the top 10 percent of the households. Even the lowest-income households transferred a substantial amount of interest in that year to the wealthiest group.

Nobel Prize–winning economist Joseph E. Stiglitz writes: "Economists long ago tried to justify the vast inequalities that seemed so troubling in the mid-19th century—inequalities that are but a pale shadow of what we are seeing in America today. The justification they came up with was called 'marginal-productivity theory.' In a nutshell, this theory associated higher incomes with higher productivity and a greater contribution to society. It is a theory that has always been cherished by the rich. Evidence for its validity, however, remains thin. The corporate executives who helped bring on the recession of the past three years—whose contribution to our society, and to their own companies, has been massively negative—went on to receive large bonuses. In some cases, companies were so embarrassed about calling such rewards 'performance bonuses' that they felt compelled to change the name to 'retention bonuses' (even if the only thing being retained was bad performance). Those who have contributed great positive innovations to our society, from the pioneers of genetic understanding to the pioneers of the Information Age, have received a pittance compared with those responsible for the financial innovations that brought our global economy to the brink of ruin."[15]

Creutz, reflecting on the current euro crisis, remarks, "Thanks to the blindness of our economical experts there is also the danger that after a collapse, which could be worse than that of 1929, the same systemic errors will be put in place again."[16]

Although no equivalently extensive study isolating the effects of interest payments on the concentration of wealth is available for the United States, data indicate an even more dramatic economic disparity, especially in recent decades.

A comparison of real after-tax house hold incomes between 1979 and 2007 revealed that the income of the richest 1 percent in the United States soared 275 percent, but the bottom 20 percent grew by just 18 percent. The income of the richest 1 percent nearly tripled, while increases were smaller down the economic ladder. After the 1 percent, income for the next highest 20 percent grew by 65 percent, much faster than it did for the remaining 80 percent of the population but still lagging well behind the top group. This study illustrates how the better-off have captured the bulk of income gains over the past three decades. The top fifth has seen its share of income increase, while the other four quintiles have suffered declines in their shares.[17]

The renowned historian Arnold Toynbee[18] concluded that the collapse of 21 different civilizations is explainable using only two reasons: excessive concentration of wealth in the hands of the few and the inability of the elite to introduce significant changes in the face of shifting sociopolitical or socioeconomic circumstances.

Excessive concentration of wealth isn't just an economic issue. Zbigniew Brzezinski, President Carter's national security advisor, sees it also as a geopolitical one: "Not to focus on[this issue] is to ignore a central reality of our times: the massive worldwide political awakening of mankind and its intensifying."[19] Awareness about money and its uses may be the change agent that shifts our society away from collapse and toward renewal.

THE PROCYCLICAL MONEY CREATION PROCESS

The economy grows or contracts in a series of repetitive expansions (booms) and contractions (busts). Referred to as the business cycle, this pattern comprises an interlude of escalation of above-average economic growth, reaching a peak, followed by a contraction to below-average economic growth, potentially all the way to a depression at the low point. Then a new business cycle begins with a new swell of growth, and the pattern repeats itself. While business cycles are recurrent, each is unique in longevity, depth of dip, and height of peak.

The way money is created, by bank debt, tends to amplify both the ups and the downs of the business cycle. Banks tend to have a herd instinct when making credit available or restricting it for particular countries or industries. When business is good, banks tend to be generous in terms of credit availability, thereby amplifying a good period into a potentially inflationary boom period. But as soon as the business horizon darkens even just a bit, banks reduce credit availability, which, if not counteracted, can easily lead to a full-blown recession.

Central banks attempt to offset these fluctuations by giving countercyclical interest rate signals, meaning that in a downturning economy, interest rates are cut. The counteractions, however, usually are not very effective. Furthermore, the capacity of central banks to intervene in monetary markets has been significantly reduced in deregulated financial markets. Consequently, despite their efforts, the collective actions of the banking system tend to exacerbate the business cycle in both boom and bust directions.

WHAT'S THE BOTTOM LINE?

Interest is having a devastating impact on life as we know it. For example, there's the Depression of the late 1930s; Japan since 1990; and the developments in the United States leading to the 2008 financial crisis.[20] They were all generated by asset bubbles, and when those asset priced bubbles popped, huge numbers of businesses and banks failed. The assets in which these bubbles focused varied over time and place. For instance, in the 1930s they were U.S. stocks; in the late 1980s real estate in Japan; in the 1990s high-tech stocks in the United States; and again, real estate in America during the first years of the 21st century. What they all have in common is the pro-cyclical debt creation mechanism that overheats the economic engine. Such bubbles invariably burst with catastrophic consequences for everybody. Furthermore, high capital mobility combined with procyclical money creation amplifies the business cycle into destabilizing booms and busts cycles that tend to spread around the world, destroying financial, human, and natural capital.

Furthermore, conventional money reinforces a particular perception of time, through the existence of interest, which automatically mandates short-term priorities. In contrast, if a different currency were available—one that has a negative interest rate (as will be shown in the next chapter)—this would encourage society and business to value long-term opportunities and costs. Consequently, such a change would automatically re orient the entire investment process and directly promote longer-term financial and ecological sustainability.

The constant requirement for perpetual growth is imbedded in the monetary system. It obliges everyone to be on an economic treadmill with mandatory growth, regardless of the long-term consequences. Such pressures must bear some of the responsibility for the erosion of non-renewable natural resources, or the pollution of the air and water with massive tolls on health, social, and environmental well-being.

As the concentration of wealth becomes more and more acute the conversation becomes about more than simply food and prices of the necessities of life. Justice and democracy are at stake. As U.S. Supreme Court Justice Louis Brandeis claimed: "We can have a democratic society or we can have great concentrated wealth in the hands of a few. We cannot have both." The Dalai Lama put it this way: "A society in which the rich are too rich and the poor too poor generates violence, crime and fighting for them." Clearly, violence and war are the exact opposite of well-being and sustainability as it means a *lose-lose* proposition for all segments of society. As John F. Kennedy remarked, "Those who make peaceful revolution impossible will make violent revolution inevitable."

Finally, but not least, social capital is not a mere by-product of society. It is the cement that changes a collection of individuals into a human society. It is a precondition for rendering a democracy functional[21] and for securing economic prosperity.[22] Indeed, political action and efficient markets are both unthinkable without a minimum of social capital and coherence. Democracy and economic prosperity become possible only when a society has a sufficient sense of responsibility, mutual trust, and cooperation. Increasing crime rates,[23] poverty, and the exclusion[24] of ever larger groups from society are clear indications of the erosion of social capital. A series of studies have shown that, at present, social capital is not only dwindling in most parts of the world, but it is also undergoing a change in its very nature.

The entire current financial paradigm begs these questions to be answered now with alacrity: Is there another way? And, if there is, how would that emergent society function in contrast to our present experience?

PART TWO

PROSPERITY

In a world of almost 8 billion souls and rapidly dwindling natural resources, the notion of prosperity is tricky. A better and more accurate term is *sustainable abundance,*whereby there is sufficiency for all. Sustainable abundance supports the inherent dignity of the human spirit, the creative genius, and the unbounded potential of the ever-evolving human race and its nonhuman cohabitants on this planet we call home.

With new currencies and new monetary designs working in tandem with the conventional system, we can achieve sustainable abundance.

In reality, we already live in a multicurrency world, although many don't recognize that fact. Most of us are familiar with frequent flyer miles issued by airline alliances or other loyalty currencies distributed by supermarkets and commercial groups. These systems prove that the technologies for innovative currencies and payment systems can operate in parallel with conventional money, even on a large scale. This breakthrough has been enabled by increasingly inexpensive computing, along with expanding access to the Internet. Existing monetary innovations have already progressed well beyond simple loyalty and marketing currencies to strategies that help heal social breakdown, deal with the consequences of an aging society, educate people from cradle to grave, create jobs, and address climate change.

In this part, we introduce you to some remarkable stories of people all around the world who are in the process of implementing such cooperative currency systems. We explore what they have achieved so far, from innovations in business for entrepreneurs just getting off the ground to large global multinational corporations. Parallel to the commercial applications are ideas for government at different levels, nonprofits, and nongovernmental organizations (NGOs). Perhaps some of the most spontaneously ingenious and somewhat surprising solutions have been in the domain of banking.

Chapter Four

THE FLYING FISH

A New Perspective on Money

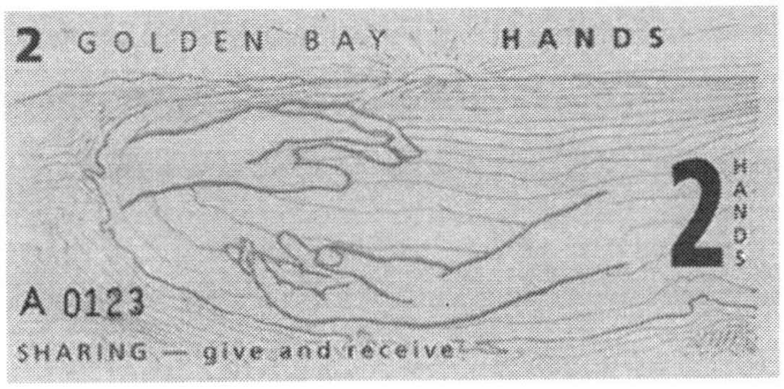

To say that a state cannot pursue its aims, because there is no money, is like saying that an engineer cannot build roads, because there are no kilometers.

EZRA POUND, American poet and economic historian

It's quite common to think of money in terms of its material representations. Although money has taken many forms throughout human history, from shells to zappozats (decorated axes),[1] it is not a material object but, rather, is merely represented as such. For instance, if you are stranded alone on a desert island, a thing, say a knife, is still useful as a knife, but a million dollars in whatever form it takes—cash, coins, or debit and credit cards—ceases to be money. It becomes merely paper, metal, or plastic and no longer functions as currency. For any *thing* to act as money, it requires a community to agree that the particular object is acceptable in an exchange.

That is why our working definition of money is: an *agreement,* within a *community,* to use something standardized as a *medium of exchange.*[2]

These agreements manifest in very different scenarios and levels of society, ranging from tokens used among a small group of friends playing cards or cigarettes traded among prisoners to conventional bank-debt money exchanged among the citizens of a particular nation as "legal tender" (i.e., accepted in payment of taxes). A community can be geographically disparate, such as Internet users; it can exist in virtual realities, such as Second Life; or it can include large segments of the global population, as is the case with the U.S. dollar in its role as the international reference and reserve currency.

Therefore, money really lives in the same space as other social constructs, like marriage, club memberships, and business contracts. These constructs are real, even if they exist only in people's minds. A monetary covenant can be made formally or informally, freely or by coercion, consciously or unconsciously. Most people do not consciously agree to use dollars, euros, or yuan, nor do they consider their nature. These currencies are used automatically, as a means of entering into an assumed and unspoken contract.

There is, however, a broader context of what money is, as money can be found outside the narrow parameters of legal tender. As shown earlier, contemporary national currencies are all interest-bearing fiat currencies, debt based, created through the fractional banking system. They are designed to facilitate transactions (i.e., as a medium of exchange), used both as units of account and as savings (i.e., as temporary stores of value), and are particularly well adapted for business and industrial applications and settings. As already seen, the use of interest, especially compound interest, has very precise outcomes that do not necessarily benefit society at large. However, money can also be architected in other ways.

There are thousands of new monetary pacts operating within communities in the United States and beyond that are not conducted solely with legal tender, leading to some very different outcomes. These pacts are called "common tender," in contrast with "legal tender."

These currencies are also identified under various names, including *complementary currencies*(because they work in parallel with conventional money), *cooperative currencies*(since they are created to encourage cooperation instead of competition among their users), and *local currencies*that are designed to operate within a more limited local community. These currencies can be specialized in ways that conventional money simply cannot. By understanding the constituent parts and their resulting functions, it is possible to remodel money with a specified outcome in mind. This new money can be structured to encourage behaviors that otherwise would not occur without some kind of intervention or deterrent, be they laws and legislation or appeals to moral judgment. For example, a currency can be crafted to encourage people to shop locally, to plant trees and take better care of their environment, to help elderly neighbors, or to provide after-school mentoring.

COOPERATIVE CURRENCIES: LINKING UNUSED RESOURCES WITH UNMET NEEDS

In terms of their creation and operation, cooperative currencies typically are managed by members of a community, a nongovernmental organization (NGO), or a business network, not by banks. Their primary function is to link unused resources with unmet needs within a specific geographical area, business, or segment of society.

Another way to understand these currencies is to compare them with the familiar frequent flyer miles programs introduced by airlines some 30 years ago. The unmet need from the airline perspective was customer loyalty. The unused resource was an empty seat on a flight. The loyalty currency is simply the bridge that links the two.

Creating a cooperative currency is also about building such a bridge, but it aims at inducing behavior changes that are useful to solve some of our more serious challenges of the 21st century. For example, in a small town where the key employer, a factory making cars, closes down and the jobs are shipped overseas, the outcome is massive unemployment in that area. The resulting unused resource is human capital—labor, ingenuity, and expertise—and the unmet need is to get people a way to provide for their families and revitalize the local economy.

Today, we have a plethora of both unmet needs and unused resources. Cooperative currencies tie these together and get the fundamental circuit of giving and receiving, buying and selling, moving again as people get their lives back on track. Completely new circuits of trade are being established by ordinary people as they create new solutions to their area's problems. Accordingly, a community can be anything from a small local neighborhood to a group of multinational companies doing business together. The actual currency can address many issues: for example, the creation of an elderly care currency, an energy conservation currency, or a local food-growing currency. When and wherever there is an unused resource and an unmet need in an economy, they can be linked with a purposefully designed currency. The organization responsible for the issuance of a currency can be a nonprofit, a religious entity, a business federation, a community group, a union, a company, a government agency, or, of course, any body of government from a municipality to the federal echelon. In reality, the only conceptual limitation is imagination. Together with conventional national currencies, they can form what we call a monetary ecosystem.

The creation of these types of money provides to local and state governments a way to resolve problems in ways other than by bond measures or traditional increased taxation, and it eliminates the frustration of trying to secure funding from the dwindling bud gets of government departments and agencies. It empowers groups of people to take control of their collective destiny rather than waiting for some top-down one-size-fits-all solution. It prevents being handicapped in one's efforts—literally cap in hand—while seeking support from overextended nonprofits and philanthropic organizations.

The impressive flowering of these currencies, especially over the last couple of decades, is enabled by communications networks that offer access for greater numbers of people to computers, the Internet, and mobile phones. Recent surveys have indicated that there are approximately 4,000 mature cooperative currencies globally. It was possible to make an inventory of these 4,000 because they have a Web presence. Undoubtedly, many more currencies operate on a more informal and less technological basis.[3] An average smart phone has more computational power than the computers used by NASA to launch the Apollo Space program back in the 1960s, while the cost of computers and mobile phones has dropped by several orders of magnitude. Imagine an airline trying to manage a frequent flyer program by using legions of clerks shuffling paper records. Today, such data are aggregated and parsed in seconds by simply swiping a bar code—a totally paperless and digitized transaction completed in just nanoseconds.

THE GAP BETWEEN HOW WE THINK AND HOW NATURE WORKS

Cooperative currencies have been thought of as curiosities, an interesting trend that might spark and then burn and fizzle like a comet in the night sky. But a solid core of science not only provides the rationale but also proves the necessity for their existence. As touched on earlier, in Chapter 2, nature holds the key not only for provocative insights but also for the solution.

All complex flow networks, like the human immune system, natural ecosystems, and biological systems, consist of complex flows of energy, information, and resources. Though complex, their behavioral patterns are predictable, in de pen dent of what flows through them, be it biomass in an ecosystem, information in a social system, blood in a circulatory system, electrons in an electrical circuit, or money in an economy. What makes their behavior predictable is the universality of their structures.[4]

An example is the illustrious food chain, which is actually a flow circuit: Energy flows into the planet from the sun, plants capture the sun's energy and transform it into biomass, animals eat the plants and each other in a chain all the way to the top predator, which ultimately dies and is broken down and recycled by bacteria and decomposition.

Economic systems are similar: Money flows from one economic agent to another; outputs of one business serve as inputs to other enterprises or to a final consumer in a vast web that processes and circulates energy, information, and resources through the entire planet.

In nature's networks, there is a constant push-pull between two emergent properties: efficiency and resilience. *Efficiency*is defined as a network's capacity to process volume of whatever flows through it in an organized and streamlined manner. *Resilience*is a network's capacity to deal with and adapt to changes, while maintaining the integrity of the network. So for a complex flow network to sustain itself, it must be not only efficiently organized but also able to adjust to changes in its environment, such as droughts, famine, disease, or attacks in a natural ecosystem. What make a network resilient is its options or choices, which can be best expressed as a network having access to *diversity* and *interconnectivity*.

For a real-life economic example, take the case of a factory that has closed down in a small town. If a lunch van has just this one factory as the sole outlet for its fare, the business is going to be in trouble when the plant shuts down. By being mobile, however, the business can seek new customers in other office parks and towns, thus diversifying its clientele. With menus and ordering available online, and with a community of loyal diners, interconnectivity is possible and consequently a viable business with a competitive edge and, ultimately, resiliency.

What is counterintuitive here, yet clearly demonstrated in real-life cases, is that nature does not select for maximum efficiency but, rather, for a balance between efficiency and resilience. Both efficiency and resilience are indispensable for long-term sustainability and health. An excess of either also leads to problems. Too much efficiency leads to brittleness and fragility, and too much resilience leads to stagnation.

Viewing economies as flow systems highlights money's primary function as a medium of exchange. From this perspective, money is to the real economy what biomass is to an ecosystem or what blood is to the human body. Money is an essential vehicle for catalyzing processes, allocating resources, and generally allowing the exchange system to work as a synergetic whole. In economies, currency (with its root interestingly in the word *current* or *flow)* circulates among nations, businesses, and individuals. Money must continue to move in sufficiency throughout the entire system because poor distribution will strangle the supply side of the economy, the demand side, or both.

Seeing the entire global monetary system in terms of a network structure reveals why it is brittle and subject to breakdown: the monopoly of one *type*of money, namely, national currencies, all created through bank debt, that flow within each country or group of countries, as in the case of the euro, and interconnect on a global level. Since there are no other options within the system than this one kind of currency, the entire network is frail. This is clearly borne out by the facts. As mentioned already in the Introduction, according to International Monetary Fund data, in the four decades between 1970 and 2010, there were no fewer than 145 banking crises, 208 monetary crashes, and 72 sovereign debt crises. This adds up to an astounding total of 425 systemic crises—an average of more than 10 countries in crisis each and every year![5]

Nobody questions the efficiency of these huge markets, but their lack of resilience has been demonstrated repeatedly. The justification for enforcing this monopoly of a single currency within each country is that it optimizes the efficiency of price formation and exchanges in national markets. Every nation has tight regulations in place to maintain this goal. Banking institutional regulations further ensure that banks mimic each other in terms of both their structure and their behavior. This was demonstrated among the world's bigger banks, most recently and with a vengeance, with the simultaneous bank crises in 2008 and the continuing economic problems, particularly in the United States and Europe.

DYNAMIC CIRCULATION

The economic importance of cooperative currencies has been underestimated, in part because the impact of their higher velocities of circulation—the number of times they circulate—has been overlooked. Irwin Fisher, a leading U.S. economist during the 1930s, proved that the volume of economic activity depends not only on the *quantity*of money in circulation but just as much on the *number of times it circulates.*

The so-called Fisher equation summarizes this idea thus: $E = Q \times V$, where Eequals the total economic activity in a given time period, Qequals the quantity of money in circulation, and V equals the velocity of circulation measured by the average number of times this money circulates in that time period.

A distinction needs to be made between the two types of money in use within a community: the conventional type, used for both savings and exchange, and cooperative currencies, used only as a pure medium of exchange. Each has its own very different quantity and velocity. Therefore, in this environment, Fisher's equation becomes: $E = (Q_s \times V_s) + (Q_c \times V_c)$ where Q_s equals quantity of money that can be used for savings (i.e., typically conventional money), V_s equals average velocity of circulation of that kind of money, Q_c equals quantity of complementary currency used as pure medium of exchange, and V_c equals average velocity of these complementary currencies.

When a currency is not used as a store of value, it will logically tend to have a higher velocity than a currency that tends to be accumulated. In other words, V_c will be substantially larger than V_s (i.e., mathematically $V_c V_s$). The economic effect of a given quantity of local currencies (Q_c) will therefore be amplified proportionally by the higher velocity of this V_c currency.

There are no current studies on the velocity of circulation of cooperative currencies. In Chapter 10, however, one of the few well-documented recent cases is described, that of a demurrage-charged local currency issued by the city of Wörgl in Austria during the early 1930s. This currency circulated between 12 and 14 times faster than official money.[6]

The positive economic effects of these currencies are, therefore, more substantial than their low intrinsic value and low prestige would lead one to believe.

DUAL CURRENCY SYSTEM

Cooperative currencies are not generally designed to replace conventional money, but rather to work in tandem with the official system. That is why they are often referred to as complementary currencies. They supplement and balance the conventional system by stabilizing the overall competitive structure, dampening its otherwise hyperag-gressive feature.

The practice of dual currency systems is not new. Cooperative currencies have been in wide usage throughout most of history. In Western Europe, for example, they have been used without interruption for hundreds of years, from roughly 800 ad to around 1800AD.[7]

Traditionally, the dual monetary system was comprised of two different types of currencies: One consisted of gold and silver coins, which were acceptable for long-distance trade, and the other was a set of smaller coins of copper, lead, and other metals mainly used for local exchanges.[8] As noted earlier, an example of the former was the *bezant,* a Byzantine gold coin that holds the world record for longevity of a currency.[9] Examples of the latter include the currencies issued by local or regional lords, city administrations, bishops, or monasteries.

Another system, the tally stick, was introduced by King Henry I of En gland. This currency was made of polished wood, with notches cut along one edge to signify the denominations. The stick was then cut in half so each piece still had a record of the notches. The monarch kept one half for proof against counterfeiting, while the other circulated as money. This worked very well for 726 years.

Despite these examples, such local systems are often described as defective, riddled with problems that the establishment of the international gold standard would later claim to remove.[10] The coexistence of different forms of currency is interpreted as a lack of homogeneity and, therefore, as a hindrance to the efficient functioning of exchange and price formation. It is also possible to argue quite the opposite, however, recognizing the differentiation of currencies as an institutional feature expressly designed to keep separate exchange circuits of different natures (local versus long distance) and different monetary functions (store of value versus means of payment).[11,12]

CURRENCY VERSUS BARTER

Given the collective blindness around money, terms are often interchanged in the belief that they are synonymous. Cooperative currencies are typically designed to facilitate transactions, that is, to operate purely as a medium of exchange. But cooperative currencies should not be confused with barter exchanges.

Barter is the direct exchange of goods or services unmediated by any type of money. For example, a boy agreed to cut his neighbor's lawn. The neighbor had two tickets to an upcoming Van Halen reunion concert he couldn't use; he also had an earlier version of an iPod lying around. But the tickets were not of interest to the boy, and the used iPod, the neighbor realized, was far more valuable than the boy's time and effort warranted. Bartering requires matching the needs and resources of both parties involved in the transaction, yet it's not always possible to line up an equitable exchange of goods or services. So the neighbor may decide to pay the boy in cash rather than bartering, and put the items up for auction on eBay.

In most cases, cooperative currencies are not instruments for saving or investment or, in technical terms, to be a store of value. This cuts to the crux of the issue of conventional money. As it is used as a store of value, there is a built-in tendency to save it, while at the same time it functions as a medium of exchange, meaning it's supposed to be spent. This juxtaposition of functionality causes a push-pull conflict. Conversely, cooperative money, by and large, is designed to facilitate transactions by being a medium of exchange exclusively—nothing more, nothing less. Savings and stores of value accrue using other items, such as savings accounts or bonds denominated in conventional money, real estate, gold, or a charcoal etching by Impressionist Edgar Degas.

INTEREST VERSUS DEMURRAGE

In Chapter 3, the singular dynamics of interest were revealed. In contrast to conventional currencies, some cooperative currencies carry a negative interest rate, namely, a time-related charge for holding onto money. This is called a *demurrage*fee. This term comes from the railroad industry, which would levy a charge for a railroad car that was left idle. When applied to money, a demurrage charge means that if money isn't spent within a given time frame, a fee is applied. In the parlance of local currency circles, if the currency isn't spent by a certain date, the money *rusts.*

Applying such a fee generates an incentive to spend the money before that date. This ensures that the cooperative currency is kept in circulation. Remember that most local currencies are designed purely as a way to pay for goods and services and not for savings. The point of these currencies is to get an economy moving again.

There is another important factor to consider, especially in light of efforts to create a sustainable world.

A demurrage charge does not cause the future to be discounted, so long-term projects can be favored and the resources of the Earth can be protected and nurtured. That is why, in a vignette in Chapter 12, a corporation empowered by a money system with a demurrage is rationally deciding to invest in a 100-year reforestation project in sub-Sahara Africa or a multigenerational watershed conservation plan for the Himalayas.

What's more, the boom and bust phases of the business cycle can be addressed effectively when a demurrage-charged currency is designed to be countercyclical. Such a currency would then be issued in greater quantities in a downturned economy, when the banks are not inclined to make loans. This generates a more dependable economic environment, which in turn translates into more employment opportunities, thus averting massive layoffs and business closures. This idea is explored in greater detail in Chapter 7 with the Terra initiative.

Finally, unlike regular interest, demurrage fees do not contribute to colossal concentrations of wealth, so there is greater equality and less income disparity within the system. Consequently, rather than money eroding social capital, demurrage-charged currencies engender a greater sense of community.

CONCENTRATION OF WEALTH

The law of concentration has been sometimes described as the 80-20 rule, and it manifests almost everywhere in nature.[13] It explains, for instance, how big, medium, and small rocks and sand are distributed unevenly in riverbeds. Similarly, it applies to matter and particles (most of it in the universe is concentrated, probably in black holes), waterways (most sweet water ends up in a few big rivers), traffic on the World Wide Web (most goes through a few sensitive hubs), demography (80 percent of the population lives on 20 percent of the land, such as in cities), and even popularity (a few people—politicians, entertainers, corporate leaders—accumulate most of the attention). It also applies to the workforce (80 percent of the work is done by 20 percent of the staff) and commerce (20 percent of customers often generate 80 percent of sales in a given company). Particularly relevant for us is how this applies to the distribution of wealth, where it has also been called the *Pareto distribution.*

In all these cases, *some* concentration is natural, but the concentration doesn't automatically have to be stuck at a *magical* 80:20 ratio. By simply increasing the number of exchange transactions, automatically the concentration effect is reduced.

As stated earlier, in comparison to national money, local currencies have a higher *velocity of circulation*—meaning there are more transactions. There are two principal reasons for this. The first is that for the most part the currencies are designed purely as a medium of exchange: They are intended to be spent, not saved. (The addition of a demurrage charge boosts this function as the money "rusts" by a certain date.) Second, as these currencies are designed for local communities or specific networks, the money remains within the community it is intended to serve. This is in stark contrast to national money. If someone spends a dollar in Harlem on a Monday, that same dollar could be part of a transaction in Anchorage, Alaska, or Dubai in the United Arab Emirates by the end of the week. But a local currency such as a BerkShare or a Brixton Pound will remain within a short radius around Great Barrington, Massachusetts, or within the district in the Borough of Lambeth in south London, respectively, the localities of their issuance.

SUBSIDIARITY: POWER TO THE APPROPRIATE LOWEST LEVEL

Solutions can be generated at any level: neighborhood, borough, village, city, county, region, or state. But who is better equipped to devise an appropriate solution to a problem: the people who are actually involved or a remote, centralized authority?

The principles of subsidiarity[14] state that a central authority should perform only those tasks that cannot be performed effectively at a more local level. This is also one of the tenets of federalism, which asserts the rights of the parts over the whole, as would be exemplified, for instance, by the rights held by states in the U.S. Constitution.

SOLUTIONS INSIDE THE BOX

The fragility of the conventional system has been a concern for quite a while now. Following the 1929 crash, two banking reforms were proposed in the United States to ensure that such a disaster would never happen again. One was the Banking Act of 1933, also known as the Glass-Steagall Act. It strictly separated banking activities between Wall Street investment banks and commercial banks. However, the most prominent academics of the time favored another proposal known as the Chicago Plan.[15]

The quickest way to explain the Chicago Plan is that bank-debt money would be made illegal. The government would itself issue a currency to be used in payment of all debts, public and private.[16] Banks thereby would become simple intermediaries. They would be forbidden to lend out *more*than the deposits they collected. Said another way, banks would have to apply a 100 percent compulsory reserves rule, and since no bank-debt money could be created at all, banks would de facto be limited to the role of money brokers.[17]

The Glass-Steagall Act was repealed with the Gramm-Leach-Bliley Act, signed by President Clinton. Since then, this repeal has been blamed for triggering the subprime crisis and the collapse of Lehman Brothers in September 2008, which in turn precipitated the global banking scramble, leaving so many governments overindebted.

The 1930s debate—whether to reinstate some form of the Glass-Steagall Act or implement some version of the Chicago Plan—is now starting all over again. Although unofficial reports have surfaced that several nations are discussing the latter strategy, there are clear reasons that the Chicago Plan isn't the best solution available, given the current understanding of systems.

First, implementing the Chicago Plan would be replacing one monoculture with another. But for the economic system to be robust, there needs to be diversity in exchange media. Simply replacing a private monopoly with a public one wouldn't resolve the resulting problem of structural fragility.

Second, although it is true that a Chicago Plan reform would eliminate the risk of widespread banking crashes and sovereign debt crises, there would still be monetary crises. In other words, the 145 banking crises and 76 sovereign-debt crises that have hit the world since 1970 would not have happened if such a reform had been in place. The 208 monetary crashes would not necessarily have been avoided.

Third, the Chicago Plan gives the power of creation of money only to the federal government. This could disproportionately empower central governments compared to state, regional, and local ones. Central governments have often tended to concentrate power, thereby reducing the capacity for governing entities at the lower level to take creative initiatives to deal with their problems. In the near future, flexibility will become more critically important than ever. For example, appropriate strategies to adapt to the impact of climate change may be very different in Texas as compared to Vermont or California. Or in the case of bio-regions, the Rocky Mountain caldera might address this issue in contrast with the island of Manhattan. Generally, as will be explained in depth in the next chapter, genuine regional development requires a regional currency. If the funding for such strategies is made available only from the federal level, there will be less flexibility and creativity than if both state and federal levels create their own currencies.

Furthermore, a fourth and a crucial distinction will be made between competitive versus cooperative currencies, and it will be show that *both*are necessary. One can argue that government-issued currency is less competitive than bank-debt – issued currency because it is created without interest. Being less competitive however, still doesn't make it a cooperative currency.

Moreover, although Hayek and the Austrian School of Economics are questionable in several domains, Hayek's condemnation of currency monopolies is compelling: "It has the defects of all monopolies: one must use their product even if it is unsatisfactory, and, above all, it prevents the discovery of better methods of satisfying a need for which a monopolist has no incentive ... But the people have never been given the opportunity to discover the advantage[of using another currency]."[18]

The final argument is about risk. Nationalizing the money creation process cannot be done on a small pilot scale. It must be implemented on a massive national scale or, in the case of the euro, a multinational scale. Any change always involves the risk of unintended consequences. Logically, large-scale change involves greater risk. With these distinctions between the conventional competitive system and the emergent cooperative money system, how would a new divergent monetary ecology work in practical terms?

Chapter Five

THE FUTURE HAS ARRIVED BUT ISN'T DISTRIBUTED EVENLY ... YET!

There is not the slightest indication that we will ever be able to harness atomic energy.

ALBERT EINSTEIN, 1932
(13 years before the atomic bomb was dropped on Hiroshima)

A quiet revolution is happening that has, for the most part, gone underreported. The number of contemporary cooperative currencies operating in the Western world has grown exponentially from two in 1984 to more than 4,000 mature systems today. They are more prominently in use in Latin America, Australia, Japan, and continental Europe than in the

United States, although the current economic downturn is resulting in a significant increase in the United States and globally. The oldest written record of an operational cooperative system still in use today is found in Bali, Indonesia. The island-wide system was first documented in 826 ad, when writing was first introduced in that area, and it's believed the system was thriving for centuries prior to that date.

A diverse monetary ecology is what is needed to stabilize the global economy, but the flowering of cooperative systems and other monetary innovations has tended to be in small pockets, driven by struggling local economies. As futurist John Naisbitt noted, "Change occurs when there is a confluence of both changing values and economic necessity, not before."[1] The cooperative currency movement is a major boon to the million-plus nongovernmental organizations and local communities around the world that Paul Hawken identifies as the most powerful instruments for change in his book *Blessed Unrest.*He observes, "After spending years researching this phenomenon.... No one knows its scope, and how it functions is more mysterious than meets the eye. What *does*meet the eye is compelling: coherent, organic, self-organized congregations involving tens of millions of people dedicated to change."[2]

Interestingly enough, the cooperative currency that most people are familiar with is frequent flyer miles, as mentioned in the previous chapter. Such commercial *loyalty currencies*are the largest complementary currency system in existence today, the most widespread of which are airline reward programs. American Airlines introduced the first of these programs more than 30 years ago as a simple marketing promotion. There are currently about 92 airlines issuing miles. Increasingly, frequent flyer miles are redeemable for a variety of services besides airline tickets, such as long-distance and mobile phone calls, hotels, cruises, and catalog merchandise. They have developed into a *corporate scrip*— a private currency issued, in this case, by airlines. In fact, about 54 percent of miles are not earned from flying. Instead, credit cards that offer bonus miles with purchases have become the most popular way to earn frequent flyer credits.

Just as frequent flyer programs are highly successful and used quite seamlessly by the general public, other currencies have been created and are working to enhance the business and/or social aspects of their communities, from local neighborhoods to states. For example, *Torekes* are operational in a mostly recent immigrant neighborhood in Ghent, Belgium, and the *Chiemgauer* in the prosperous region of Bavaria in southern Germany. There is a time currency that revitalized the Welsh former mining town of Blaengarw, an international currency called the *C3* in Brazil and several other Latin American countries, and last but not least, the grandfather of modern business-to-business systems, the *WIR* in Switzerland.

Most often, cooperative currencies are either mutual credit systems, such as LETS or TimeBanks, both of which are explored later in this chapter. But the possibilities are unlimited: A garbage-backed currency is thriving in Curitiba, Brazil, while other models link their currency to a national currency such as the *regio*in the Germanic parts of Europe, the *BerkShares*in New En gland, and the *Totnes*or *Brixton pounds*in the United Kingdom.

The purpose of these cooperative currencies usually falls into one of two distinct categories. One is for social purposes, where the intention is predominantly to motivate people's behavior and to meet societal objectives, such as creating a more close-knit community and addressing social isolation. A second purpose is to support local businesses, in which the currency is designed principally to circulate and to meet objectives such as stimulating employment or fostering a campaign to buy local products and services.

LETS—MUTUAL CREDIT

The most frequent cooperative currency system in the world today is LETS, an acronym for "Local Exchange Trading System." It was invented in the formerly economically stable middle-class town of Courtney in the Comotz Valley near Vancouver, Canada, in the early 1980s when it was enduring a 40 percent local unemployment rate.

"We are a town of about 50,000 people, and the major industry was a defense base, plus the town was a dormitory for timber, mining, fishing, and a bit of tourism at that stage. In 1982, everything stopped. The defense base moved, and the Bank of Canada was running at 14 percent prime, and mortgages were approximately 18 to 20 percent in some cases. I was a sole proprietor business teaching the Alexander technique with a clientele of mostly schoolteachers. And obviously, it's a very selective market. When the sand ran out of the economy, my business dried up in a matter of months, as it did for many others in our area," remembers Michael Linton.[3]

He observed that there were plenty of things to be done and a large, skilled labor force willing and needing to work. Needs went unaddressed, however, as unemployment persisted. The missing link was money. Without money, the requisite transactions simply could not take place. Linton continues: "The greatest deficiency of conventional money is that for too many, it is simply not available. By its very design, there is only a limited amount of it created. And as conventional money must come from somewhere outside the local community, it inherently doesn't understand or concern itself with the needs of a particular community."[4]

Consequently, LETS was created to facilitate much-needed trade within circuits in local neighborhoods, villages, and towns.

The LETS system can be used for any number of needs and transactions. For instance, Anne cuts hair, John fixes cars, and Lisa is an organic farmer. Anne and John negotiate the price of a haircut and decide on L15 (15 LETS units) and $5. Anne's account is credited L15, while John's is debited L15. With her earned LETS credits, hairdresser Anne negotiates with farmer Lisa to get some organic vegetables for L10. Thus, Lisa's LETS account is credited L10, and Anne's is now debited L10. Meanwhile, Lisa's car now needs a tune-up, and she agrees with the mechanic John on a price of L30 for labor and $15 for parts. At the end of these three interactions, Anne has a net positive balance of L5 (L15 earned giving John a haircut minus L10 spent buying organic produce from Lisa). John has a positive balance of L15 (L30 earned working on Lisa's car minus L15 spent on the haircut by Anne), and Lisa has a negative balance of L20 (L10 earned by Anne's purchase minus L30 for the tune-up by John). With a LETS system in place, Anne, John, and Lisa were each able to use their skill sets to offset costs and the scarcity of national currencies to afford certain goods and services.

In contrast to conventional money, a negative balance in LETS is not a problem. Rather, it is an indication of community activity, showing that people have been acquiring goods and services from others in their neighborhood. Members with a negative balance can be called on to offer goods or services in return, further increasing the community's wealth.

Some programs set debt limits to avoid abuses, but generally there is a common understanding that debts will be repaid. For instance, citing the example given here, farmer Lisa will pay back her L20, whether through organic produce sales or by some other means she has to offer.

The LETS system is an example of a mutual credit system, whereby currency is created by a simultaneous credit and debit in a transaction. As a mutual credit system, the LETS' money supply is self-regulating, since members issue their own currency within the framework of their community. It overcomes the limitations imposed by a scarcity of national currency and, instead, promotes sufficiency by enabling participants to use what is already available within their trading community. It is also customarily transparent, with an open record kept of both credits and debits. This self-regulation and transparency promotes greater trust, and people are held more accountable.

Other advantages of LETS include prompting people to use skills they might not have considered valuable, for example, cooking, driving, Web designing, teaching English, or gardening. It also gives access to services that members may not otherwise be able to afford.

The LETS system is now operating in many different parts of the world. Given the highly decentralized nature of the transactions, nobody has been able to tally an accurate number of exchanges, but its spread around the globe testifies to its success. A partial list of nations in which LETS currently operates includes

Argentina, Austria, Belgium, Brazil, Canada, Chile, Colombia, El Salvador, Finland, France, Germany, Hungary, India, Indonesia, Ireland, Israel, Japan, New Zealand, Nigeria, Norway, Poland, South Africa, Switzerland, Thailand, and the United States.

Australia has many communities actively trading in LETS. One interesting application is QuipShare. The currency, called the *quip,* is the medium of exchange that enables people to pay for the use of a piece of equipment without having to buy it. Think about how often one uses a snake for a blocked sink, a jumper cable, or a blow torch. Usually, house hold, gardening, and do-it-yourself tools just sit in the shed or a drawer unused.

Through QuipShare, one can locate and borrow items, and on the other side of the transaction, lend out various items. By sharing equipment, more use is made of tools and machinery that might otherwise sit idle. All protocols and agreements between the parties are available on their Web site for downloading. This bright idea started at the weekly Tilba Growers Market in Central Tilba, located in the southeast of New South Wales province, and has now spread to other regions.

TIME DOLLARS—TIME-BACKED CURRENCY

The time dollars system was created by attorney Edgar Cahn. As a Fulbright scholar, cofounder of the

National Legal Services, a speechwriter and counsel to former Attorney General Robert F. Kennedy, and a close associate of Sargent Shriver on the War on Poverty and the Peace Corps, Cahn has dedicated much of his life to those less fortunate than himself. He had the idea for the time dollar program while recuperating from an illness.

"There were two separate forces coming together at the time. It was less a matter of coping with my convalescence, but more of my reaction to feeling useless and helpless. I was getting the care I needed, but the notion that I would spend my life as a recipient of services, even affection, was to me not really being alive. I am about making a difference in other people's lives," reflected Cahn.

"Secondly, it was 1980. We had a recession. We had all kinds of people being laid off. I understood that they didn't like feeling useless any more than I did. My opinion was backed by a larger perception that all the advocacy work that my law school had been doing was winning some battles, but basically we were losing the war on the fundamental issues of equity of society, and redress of injustices. We would be championing people who were simply viewed as victims. And as victims they would be fighting over crumbs. But those people would never be perceived as stakeholders or shareholders in a larger society, unless there was some way to value what they could contribute. And in turn, receive in another way than what the market could provide. To the extent that we continued to allow money and the market to define value and contribution, they would always be viewed as redundant, throwaway people."[5]

Cahn devised a cooperative medium of exchange backed by time. The basic unit of account is a time dollar, equivalent to one hour of service, which can be spent for goods and services that are available within a given community. This cooperative currency system allows transactions to occur that would likely not otherwise take place and provides a means by which to acknowledge and honor the contributions and skills of people, matching their offerings with the needs of their community. Everyone's time is valued the same, a reflection of valuing everyone equally.

Dr. Edgar Cahn addressing the Echo Park TimeBank. Photo credit: Zach Lipp.

"While at the London School of Economics, I soon came to realize that we were involved with an ongoing dialogue about the function of interest rates and how that distorted money. Money's primary value is its external trading value. Furthermore, the price—the amount of money one is willing to pay—is defined by its value and that value is determined by supply and demand. In order words, if a thing is scarce, it is valuable; if it is abundant, it is cheap. If it is truly abundant, it is dirt cheap or worthless. And that means that every capacity that defined you as a human being and enabled the species to survive and evolve is worthless. We have created a monetary and pricing system that has devalued many fundamental human capacities."[6]

In comparison, a cooperative currency operates very differently. It is created in sufficiency, and by its very design, it is spent into existence while connecting unused resources with unmet needs. This affords the opportunity to honor people in entirely new ways.

Lisa Conlan is CEO of Time Banks USA, which has a nationwide count of some 286 systems. "The first thing that drew me to time dollars was that I was overseeing a family-run advocacy organization in Rhode Island. So part of the support network is unique in that the families with children with behavioral health issues were helping one another. This type of help touched on child welfare, juvenile justice with kids with high levels of behavioral issues, and mental health needs. Two things struck me, however. One, what would happen if we couldn't find the funding we needed? And how do we really tap into the families' energy and creativity to truly support one another? In my search, I stumbled on time dollars in 2007."[7]

Using time as a unit of account, the families are able to arrange a variety of services and all-important social events. Conlan continues: "Many of our families were isolated, especially due to concerns about their children's behavior in group settings, but they felt more relaxed with a bunch of people who have the same situation and outlook. Transportation is another big issue—being able to get rides when people needed them. Also respite, a short break for a caregiver when someone covers for them, is also critical to the families. So we have been actually expanding and supporting families beyond children's behavioral health across the life span, from children with special needs to adults with developmental disabilities to our elders, in providing their caregivers with respite relief. What's more is that people who are exchanging that support in the TimeBank, they can also get workforce development skills as a bonus."

Cahn reports that TimeBanking is spreading throughout the United States and globally like wildfire. "On average, five new time banks have started up in the U.S. every week since the beginning of 2012. They are using our model, which is coproduction. This is a partnership between the monetary economy and the economy of community."[8]

TimeBanking in Los Angeles. Everyone earned time credits for working for nonprofits and schools as part of a citywide volunteer day. Here the TimeBank members are helping to fix up people's properties for the Watts House Project. Photo credit: Autumn Rooney.

Meltem Şendağ and her associate Ayşegül Güzel met at the University of Istanbul in their native Turkey when they were both studying international business. On graduating in 2005, both left their country to gain work experience abroad. Meltem went to Ireland to work for Google, and Ayşegül to Barcelona, Spain, to work as an innovation consultant. While in Barcelona, Ayşegül became acquainted with TimeBanking. In 2010 they returned to Istanbul, and founded, using their own funds, a social TimeBanking network that they named Zumbara. Zumbara uses

Web 2.0 design and also integrates the next generation of social media platforms, such as Twitter and Facebook. It's now a community of 5,000 people offering services to one another.

Going to the heart of the matter, Meltem remarks: "We both want to move from the competitive society, which we both experienced working in the corporate world, to one of cooperation. With our former careers, we would have to live with the values that we do not believe in. Our lives were laid out for us if we were to have stayed on that path. Now, with the TimeBanking community, we are experiencing how it would be if the world was designed for generosity. In this cooperative world now, we are experimenting with the idea that *we have what we need if we use what we have*by trading services and acts of goodwill, thereby emphasizing the values of time, reciprocity and relationships."[9]

Here are some other examples of time dollars operating across the United States:

- In 27 of Chicago's lowest-ranking elementary schools, fifth- and sixth-graders (many in special education and/or labeled ADD) earned time credits as tutors of first- and second-graders. The need for special education and remediation went down; test scores and school attendance went up; fighting and truancy went down. More than one school ceased to be on academic probation. While there is nothing new about older kids tutoring younger kids, it has proven to be a successful strategy to encourage more students to engage in such a practice.

- In Oakland, California, the Alameda County Department of Public Health funded a TimeBank in a neighborhood beset by racial violence. African Americans are now teaching English to Hispanics, who in turn are teaching Spanish to their neighbors. Violence has gone down. "We see similar bridging of ethnic, national origin, age, gender, and class differences in New York City, where the Visiting Nurse Service has created a Community Exchange with nearly 3,000 members in Chinatown, Washington Heights, the Lower East Side, and Battery Park; 70 percent were born outside the U.S., 100 percent report that their physical health, mental health, and wellbeing have improved and their trust for others has increased. In Allentown, Pennsylvania, Latino patients 'pay it forward' by serving as medical translators for their doctors; with training, they get certification and are hired by the hospital," Cahn continues.[10]
- In upstate New York, the Youth Advocate program has incorporated a pay-it-forward element for youth on probation or subject to confinement at detention centers. Enrolled in a Red Cross – supervised restorative justice program, they earn credits teaching homeless people to use computers and prepare résumés, working in soup kitchens, and collecting canned goods and toiletries. In Washington, D.C., for the past 10 years, teenagers have

earned time credits by serving as jurors in the Time Dollar Youth Court, which hears the cases of peers accused of nonviolent crimes. Offenders may be sentenced to community service, life skills classes, an apology, writing an essay—and duty on the jury. Cahn adds: "Recidivism rates are less than 10 percent. The Urban Institute estimates that the district saves $9,000 for every offender who goes to Youth Court instead of the traditional system."[11]

- The National Homecomers Academy enrolls people leaving prison as students on a journey of personal development, learning, and service. Community service includes providing safe passage for youth to get to school through gang territory or helping reduce violence by teenagers in a mixed ownership-tenant housing development. Nationally, recidivism for persons returning from prison is in the 60 to 70 percent range within three years. "To the best of my knowledge no one involved in this TimeBanking program has ever returned to prison," adds Dr. Cahn proudly.[12]
- According to Stephanie Rearick of the Dane Country (Madison), Wisconsin, TimeBanking program: "In exchange for one TimeBank hour, Madison Gas and Electric Company (MGE) shows TimeBank members simple ways to save energy in their homes or apartments. These tips have resulted in significant savings in members' utility bills. To participate in this project, each TimeBank member who's inter-

ested completes an MGE-instructed energy-saving workshop, and the local utility oversees their work to ensure the information being provided is accurate and achievable."[13]

- Mayor Bloomberg has launched TimeBanking for seniors in all five boroughs of New York, as baby boomers turn 65 at the rate of 10,000 per day for the next two decades. Se niors can live longer in their homes in dependently because they can avail themselves of services offered by people within their TimeBank community, such as rides to a doctor's appointment, help with writing letters to their insurance company, or making sure that the handrail in the bathtub hasn't become dangerously loose.
- Bike repair in the San Francisco Bay area is an interesting and very successful application of TimeBanking. "Bike maintenance and repair tend to be expensive. We now have two locations where people can take their bicycles and do the repairs themselves under supervision by experienced repair people," says Mira Luna, one of the principal organizers. "We started the Bay Area Community Exchange network about two and a half years ago, and it is already the third largest TimeBank in the country." Currently, they offer some 20 different categories of services, from health and healing to urban homesteading.[14]
- In Montpelier, Vermont, the Administration on Aging has invested in a form of TimeBank called

Carebanks. Se niors can get an assurance that informal care and support will be available if they or their families pay regular premiums in time dollars earned helping build community or helping other seniors. In effect, the program uses TimeBanking to create a new form of extended family. It is too early to project cost savings. But a recent study reveals that, as home-based care gets cut by state governments, hospital costs are likely to rise as people put off preventive care or end up rehospitalized due to the lack of transitional care.

Sharon Lee Schwartz is regional director of Legal Aid services of Oregon. "Well, first of all, we're not allowed to charge for our services, so we're not looking at it as payment for legal aid, in Time Dollars, but what we are doing is acknowledging that we can't create social justice without our clients' help. We are asking clients to sign a pay-it-forward agreement, in which they agree to match our time, hour for hour, by earning time dollars within their community. For example, if somebody takes our custody class, and then we meet with them individually to follow up, it might take three hours. We in turn ask the client to volunteer through the time bank to help somebody else for three hours. They then get to keep the time dollars to spend for something that they need. It's a pay-it-forward system, but they still keep the benefit."[15]

According to Cahn, there are now over 286 TimeBanks in the United States and approximately 300 in the United Kingdom, and TimeBanking has now spread to an additional 34 countries internationally. In recognition of the social contributions offered by time dollars, three separate IRS rulings make this cooperative currency the only officially tax-exempt currency in the United States.[16]

REGIO

In the early 1980s, Margrit Kennedy, then professor of architecture at the University of Hannover, Germany, was in charge of the design of ecological buildings for Berlin's International Architectural Exhibition. The response to her designs was mixed. "People would say, 'This is great, but it doesn't make economic sense,'" recalls Kennedy.[17]

After some research, she realized that the current monetary system deeply shapes what "makes economic sense," and as long as a monopoly of this system is in place, sustainable architecture and building, and consequently sustainable communities, will never become widespread enough to make a real difference. Short-term planning and destructive business practices are simply more profitable when interest-bearing money is the only option available. In 1987, she outlined the problems with interest-bearing money in her book, *Interest and Inflation-Free Money: Creating an Exchange Medium That Works for Everybody and Protects the Earth.* Soon, however, she recognized that she had to find a way to create sustainable money:

"I knew if I didn't find another monetary way, our societies would never become truly viable."[18]

Regions, according to Kennedy's definition, are geographical areas to which people "feel connected." That is, they are not artificial political units but, rather, based on people's own perceived identity. A region may have several thousand or several million people and be centered around a town, a watershed, or a river basin. In many parts of the world, regions have strong specific identities and a deep connection to the ecosystem in which they are located.

Many observers have pointed to such bioregions as potentially sustainable alternatives to the globalization currently homogenizing our world. While nation-states are better suited to handle large-scale policy issues, regions may be better at dealing with their own specific social and ecological needs—that is, if they are given the right tools. Regional currencies are one tool necessary for such a strategy. In fact, Kennedy shows that sustainable regional development is impossible without such a monetary reform.[19]

Germany and Austria are now spearheading regional currency projects, generically called *regios,* which complement the euro. Regio currencies give regions the autonomy necessary to deal directly with their particular social, ecological, and financial problems. Moreover, they are designed to benefit the region's businesses and services. As we know all too well, the net cash flow spent in big businesses usually flows in the direction of corporate headquarters outside the region, perhaps thousands of miles away.

A case in point: A study designed to evaluate the economic role played by in de pen dent businesses in the busy Chicago North Side found that every $100 spent with a local firm leaves $68 in the Chicago economy, while $100 spent at a chain store leaves only $43 in Chicago. And for every square foot occupied by a local firm, the local economic impact is $179, versus $105 for a chain store.[20]

Regios, by contrast, support regionally based commerce, adding to the uniqueness and strength of each area.

Particular types of regios—each with a different name, structure, and purpose—are being designed to meet the specific needs of a given region. Within the network, 34 systems are now established and operational. There are another 30 projects still in development by the regio network in German-speaking Europe (Germany, Austria, and Switzerland). These projects are typically not initiated through an infusion of start-up capital but rather through the hard work of groups of volunteers who want to see their region flourish.

Kennedy remarks on the volunteers' dedication: "The time outlay is considerable: It takes three to five years until you get into the zone where the whole operation can be self-financing, so it's not a trivial task. Those who run these groups do it because they love it. They really feel they are doing something useful; for some, it actually gives purpose to their lives."[21]

CHIEMGAUER—DEMURRAGE-BEARING CURRENCY

The Chiemgauer inspired by Christian Gelleri.

The Chiemgauer system is based in Bavaria, southern Germany, and is part of the regio network. It encourages locals to shop at their neighborhood businesses rather than at the larger chain stores, thereby supporting local production and enterprise. It was designed by six teenagers at the local Rudolph Steiner School and has caught the attention of dozens of other communities around Europe and beyond.

Inspired by their economics teacher, Christian Gelleri, these six young women created a money system that increases local employment, thanks to the higher demand for local goods and services. It has a built-in mechanism that makes it possible to financially support charities and good causes chosen by the users themselves.

Regional nonprofit organizations that wish to participate purchase 100 Chiemgauers for their members for 97 euros. This currency is then used at par (one Chiemgauer for one euro) to purchase goods and services in participating stores. It can be cashed back into euros for a penalty of 5 percent, providing an incentive to keep it circulating rather than converted back into conventional money. The tally at the end of the process is that 95 percent remains with businesses, 3 percent goes to the nonprofit chosen by the buyer, and 2 percent goes to the Chiemgauer currency administration to cover overhead.

There is an additional feature to this currency that differentiates it from conventional money: The Chiemgauer is a demurrage currency, meaning that it is time-stamped with a quarterly "parking fee." This creates an incentive to circulate the local currency rather than hoard it. The customers can buy nearly everything with the Chiemgauer: food, clothes, medicine, furniture, and a wide variety of local services.

Today, there are 600 participating businesses with 555,000 Chiemgauers in circulation and a turnover equivalent of over 6 million euros in 2011. It is the largest and most successful scheme within the regio network. The *Sternthaler*currency, which operates in the adjacent area of Upper Bavaria, and partnering with the Chiemgauer, provides access to an additional 500 businesses to the system. Seventy-five percent of the cooperative money is now in electronic form. Now every business participating in the program has received readers since the electronic Chiemgauer was launched. Ten local branches of cooperative banks provide banking services in Chiemgauer.

The government has also introduced a *distance tax*to encourage support of local business. Gelleri explains, "The distance fee depends on proximity and is only charged to those using Chiemgauer in cash. If you buy from your own region or an adjacent one, such as around Munich, you pay nothing. If a business in Munich wants to spend Chiemgauer in Frankfurt, it pays, for example, 1 percent. If it imports something from Spain, it pays 4 percent."[22]

All participating members report that, by using their Chiemgauers, they have a stronger feeling of belonging to the local community and of contributing to its socioeconomic well-being.

BERKSHARES—BACKED BY US$

BerkShares are a local currency for the Berkshire region of Massachusetts, heralded as a "great economic experiment" by the *New York Times.* Launched in the fall of 2006, BerkShares are backed by national currency. The 13 branches of five local banks operate as exchange bureaus and have issued 3.3 million BerkShares to date. Currently, more than 400 businesses have signed up to accept the currency.

At a local participating bank, U.S. dollars can be exchanged for BerkShares, and users can then shop or dine out with the local cooperative currency. The exchange rate is $95 for 100 BerkShares. At a local shop or restaurant, 95 BerkShares has the purchasing power of $100 worth of goods and services. Thus, users of the local currency receive a 5 percent discount to encourage support for local businesses. The merchants can use these BerkShares to purchase local products themselves, give change to customers, or partially pay employee wages. They can also deposit this local trading currency at participating banks.

"We estimate that each BerkShare circulates four times before returning to the banks—but that is anecdotal. Some stay out without returning, facilitating multiple local exchanges. Some go directly back to the banks at the end of each day. So, on estimate, of 12 to 15 million in trade in BerkShares in a region of 19,000 year-round residents, about 135,000 stay out in circulation at any one time," remarked Susan Witt, educational officer of the New Economics Institute, which launched the program.[23]

In addition to keeping money circulating locally and encouraging merchants to buy and sell local products, this local currency also stimulates more home-based industries, possibly inspiring the unemployed to use their uncompensated skills in new business ventures.

According to Witt, once the community has had sufficient experience in using and trading BerkShares, there are plans to provide zero-interest loans for the start-up of new businesses. As trust and transparency are essential for community currencies, members will be kept fully informed about what their money is doing. Future plans may involve BerkShares checking accounts, electronic transfer of funds, ATM machines, and even a loan program to facilitate the creation of new, local businesses manufacturing more of the goods that are used locally. Participating banks are also trying to figure out how to start making loans in the local currency, not tied to federal dollars, which would mean backing the BerkShares with something real: not gold, but a basket of commodities—firewood, apples, wind power—the kinds of things you can produce in western Massachusetts.

Susan Witt showing new BerkShares to Professor Philip Beard.
Photo credit: Sergio Lub.

The currency is now spreading out of the southern half of the county, the Tanglewood Berkshires, into the Pittsfield area and even to a few towns just over the New York and Connecticut state lines.

COOPERATIVE CURRENCIES AND INFLATION CONTROL

One of the strongest objections to issuing currency is that it could create uncontrollable inflation. Inflation is commonly defined by its outcome—higher prices—rather than its cause, which is simply too much money in circulation chasing too few goods and services.

Consequently, the introduction of a local cooperative currency could lead some economists and monetary theorists to conclude that a parallel money system would automatically add to inflationary pressures on the economy as a whole.

The objection would be valid if, and only if, this second currency were a fiat currency, as is the case for the dollar, the euro, the yen, or any other national money. Local currencies, however, are intrinsically different from fiat money and can be designed specifically to avoid contributing to inflation. The most generally accepted economic insight is that inflation results whenever there are not enough goods and services produced for the quantity of money in circulation: too much money pursuing too few commodities. Rather than argue from theory, let's look at three practical examples of increasing complexity.

In the case of simple barter exchanges, where no currency is involved at all, the only effect of such an exchange is who owns what. No inflationary pressures arise from barter exchanges, given that the overall quantity of both goods and currency in circulation remains unchanged.

In terms of mutual credit systems (such as LETS and many other local exchange systems), the supply of the product or service is simultaneous with the creation of the currency. In this regard, such exchanges are similar to barter: For every credit generated, there is a simultaneous creation of a debit within the same community. For example, if Jane drives Fred to a doctor's appointment, Fred is debited while Jane gets the corresponding credit. Jane spends her credit at the farmers' market by purchasing some locally grown apples, while Fred addresses his negative balance by teaching a Spanish class or fly fishing to neighborhood children. The net amount of currency in circulation therefore remains unchanged, exactly as with straightforward barter. In fact, from a monetary perspective, mutual credit systems simply facilitate multilateral barter.

Does issuing airline frequent flyer miles increase the number of times a passenger will fly? The answer is, of course, yes. Does it, however, create inflationary pressure on the airline airfares? The surprising answer is no, because any airline manager worth his or her salt will ensure that anybody using the free frequent flyer ticket is sitting in a seat that would otherwise be empty. That is why there are restrictions such as blackout dates or quotas limiting the number of frequent flyer passengers on a given route.

The ability of businesses themselves to better manage their excess capacity—from a theoretical inflation-control viewpoint—is one of the intriguing aspects of using a cooperative currency approach. Within a fiat currency environment, there is no easy way for businesses to differentiate among customers to improve the use of their spare capacity and thus increase productivity.

But cooperative currencies behave differently than conventional money.

Local currencies can be designed specifically to not create inflation. In contrast, the history of conventional national money over the past century has been one where inflation almost seems to be built in. Today, one would need approximately $405 to purchase the same goods that cost $100 back in 1975.[24] Even the world's least inflationary national money, the deutsche mark when it existed, lost 57 percent of its value between 1971 and 1996.[25]

As Edgar Kampers, Director of Qoin—Money That Matters, a Dutch not-for-profit organization that designs, implements, and supports community cooperative currencies, cogently remarks, "It's critical to understand the definition of the word *currency*.So for me currency is information between a buyer and a seller. Two people are involved in a transaction where the money symbolizes the exchange of value. So, I buy a sweater. We agree that it's worth 20 units of whatever. The sweater is the thing with the value; the money is not, of course. Money is not valuable at all, but money allows you to buy things, which are valuable. This distinction should be understood. And it's not generally known or appreciated by most people."[26]

With this general understanding of the various distinctions at work in the domain of money, let's explore applying cooperative monetary solutions in the sectors of banking, business, government, and finally, last but not least, nonprofits or nongovernmental agencies (NGOs).

Chapter Six

STRATEGIES FOR BANKING

Of all the many ways of organizing banking, the worst is the one we have today. Change is, I believe, inevitable. The question is only whether we can think our way through to a better outcome before the next generation is damaged by a future and bigger crisis.[1]

SIR MERVYN KING, Governor of the Bank of England

Ordinary people all over the world have been rethinking money in an effort to resolve their pressing cash problems. Rethinking money leads us to reconsider the entire banking sector as the source of money and loans. This has generated some interesting and provocative innovations, some by clear intent, others by happenstance.

Dissatisfaction with the banking sector is at an all-time high. The Facebook movement *Move Your Mon-*

*ey*materialized when Bank of America announced plans to increase its bank fees. Within 90 days, 5.6 million U.S. adults changed banks. "Of those switchers, 610,000 U.S. adults (or 11 percent of the 5.6 million) cited Bank Transfer Day as their reason and actually moved their accounts from a large to a small institution."[2]

Community Bankers of America said a poll of its 5,000 members found that nearly 60 percent of community banks are gaining customers who "are sick and tired" of the big financial institutions.[3]

As described in Chapter 4, in functioning systems, nature leans more to resilience than efficiency. Ironically, whenever a banking crisis unfolds, governments invariably help the larger banks absorb the smaller ones, believing that the efficiency of the system is thereby increased. Instead, when a bank has proven to be "too big to fail," why not consider the option of breaking it up into smaller units that compete with each other? This has been done in the United States before; for instance, the Bell Telephone monopoly was broken into competing "Baby Bells." But more often, what tends to happen is that banks that are too big to fail are made into still bigger ones, until they become "too big to bail."

In the midst of today's widespread discontent and lack of access to credit, a number of successful solutions using cooperative currencies have popped up in various parts of the world. Perhaps one of the more entertaining and imaginative solutions spontaneously emerged out of dire necessity.

Ireland, during the decade between 1966 and 1976, experienced three separate bank strikes that caused the banks to completely shut down for a total of 12 months, virtually bringing the country to a standstill. It was impossible to cash a check or carry out any banking transaction while the banks' doors were closed. Consequently, the population of Ireland could not access well over 80 percent of its money supply.[4]

What arose from this seeming disaster was the largest spontaneous nationwide mutual credit system—with the local pubs acting as the center of commerce. Michael Linton commented, "The Irish are an imaginative bunch, and they soon realized if the banks were closed then nothing prohibits writing a check and using this check like cash. So they started writing checks that soon circulated, valued at their facevalue, as if they were official money. A check would make the rounds between several people within a circuit facilitating business and people getting on with their daily lives."[5]

When official bank-issued checks were used up, individuals went to their local stationery shop or news agent for supplies and created their own checks. "Usually a guy would write out a set of checks, written in denominations of fives, tens, twenties, and possibly fifties, because these would be easier to negotiate. The idea caught on quickly. Now, a person from Cork wouldn't necessarily take a Dublin check and vice versa. It was important in these transactions to know the people with whom you were dealing," added Linton.

MONEY BACKED BY THE FULL FAITH AND CREDIT OF GUINNESS

Employers soon became keenly aware that their employees needed access to cash to cover the critical needs of their daily lives. Some of the large employers, Guinness among others, issued paychecks in various smaller denominations, rather than one check for the entire salary. That way, they could be used as a medium of exchange, just like cash. Linton added, "Employers, particularly the brewers, started giving paychecks to their employees in denominated checks, and those checks became fully accepted at every drinking establishment in Ireland."

Additionally, full paychecks for the entire amount of one's wages, especially from trusted employers, could be readily used as an instrument of payment for goods and services. This is reminiscent of the story in the opening of Chapter 2, where the tourist comes to the inn and puts a $100 bill on the counter, and while he's investigating the accommodations, several townspeople circulate the $100 to pay off their debts. But in this case, the pub owner or local merchant could validate the creditworthiness of the check.

Economics Professor Antoin E. Murphy of Trinity College Dublin reports, "The nature of the economy greatly facilitated the emergence of this new system. The Republic of Ireland had a population of only three million inhabitants. The small size of the population meant that there was a high degree of personal contact amongst members of the community. Where information was lacking at the personal level, a substitute collective information existed in the form of retail shops numbering around 12,000 and that well-known Irish institution, the public house, 11,000 of which exist in the Republic[which yielded] a pub to population ratio of 1:190."[6]

The close-knit nature of Irish life, even in the cities, meant that shop owners and publicans knew their regular clientele very well. As Murphy put it, "One does not, after all, serve drink to someone for years without discovering something of his liquid resources."

He continued, "The Irish created an unregulated, totally anarchistic community currency matrix. They were operating on the basis of the Irish pound at the time. But there was nobody in charge and people took the checks they liked and didn't take the checks they didn't like. So the whole world just revolved around that simple fact. And, it worked! As soon as the banks opened again, you're back to fear and deprivation and scarcity. But until that point it had been a wonderful time. High velocity, local circulation, and the pubs as the center of commerce."

To sum up, the Irish developed a system that enabled them to get on with their lives during a very challenging time, with great success.

According to Murphy's research, uncleared checks totaled £5 billion when the banks opened again for business. "The direct use of means-of-payment money (bank deposits) was removed from the transaction process. In the absence of this money, exchange activity remained relatively unaffected because the public was prepared to use undated trade credit as the instrument of exchange."[7]

Another variation of the mutual credit system was used to address a different banking crisis in another decade in another country. In this case, the banks threatened to suspend lines of credit, the lifelines of many businesses. The solution that arose is still in existence today. It is actually a major contributor to that country's ongoing monetary stability and robustness. It is perhaps surprising to learn that the country where this happened is Switzerland, one of the world's most eco nomically conservative and stable countries.

THE WIR

Opinions abound as to why Switzerland enjoys such apparent economic stability. Many suppose that it's because the country was neutral in the

Second World War and didn't have to suffer the economic and social consequences. Whimsically, would it have something to do with some unknown magical ingredient in their Alpine drinking water?

The truth is far more compelling. A major contributor to Switzerland's resilience turns out to be a business-to-business currency and an unheralded dual currency banking institution behind it. The story of this success has its initiation during the bleak days of the Great Depression.

Two Swiss businessmen, Werner Zimmermann and Paul Enz, got together with a dozen or more business associates to decide what they could do to address the financial crisis of the 1930s. They had each received a notice from their respective banks that their credit lines were going to be reduced or eliminated; hence bankruptcy was inevitable. They realized, however, that business A needed the bank loan to buy goods from business B, which in turn needed money to buy materials from its own suppliers. So they decided to create a *mutual credit* system among themselves, inviting their clients and suppliers to join.

Here's an example in very simple terms: A baker who needed flour and eggs incurs a debit from a local farmer in exchange for these goods; with that credit, the farmer gets hardware from the local supplier for the barn he is repairing, and the baker supplies the local car repair shop owner with baked goods for his family, bringing the baker's balance back to zero. All these transactions take place without being mediated by conventional money.

The country's banks mounted a massive press campaign to try to squelch this revolutionary idea. Miraculously, the campaign failed, and this ingenious system saved the businesses involved. These people went on to create their own currency, the WIR, whose value was identical to that of the national money but had the distinguishing feature that it didn't bear interest. A cooperative was set up among the users to keep the accounts dealing with that currency. Over time, the system grew to include up to a quarter of all the businesses in Switzerland.

Although the value of the WIR is pegged to the Swiss franc (1 WIR = 1 Swiss franc), all debts in WIR have to be settled in WIR. There is no convertibility into national currency. Participants can also borrow—that is, secure lines of credit from the cooperative—in WIR currency at low interest rates ranging from 1 to 1.5 percent. All such loans need to be backed by inventory or other assets.

The interesting feature of the WIR is that the currency issuance automatically tends to be countercyclical. During a recession, when regular banks reduce lending, businesses use more WIR to meet their needs. When the economy heats up and the commercial banks are lending Swiss francs again, the number of WIR in circulation tends to decrease. This feature is effective at smoothing out the booms and busts in the Swiss economy and has contributed significantly to Switzerland's economic stability.

Jürg Michel, president of the WIR Bank, sums up the core attractions of WIR in the 2010 annual report: "Trust is an invaluable asset, especially for a bank. This trustworthiness is confirmed by both private and business clients in a representative survey. The WIR clearing system as the central anchor in our business model has been based for over 76 years on the trust in this currency. The WIR system, oriented towards small and medium enterprises in Switzerland, enables a unique economic network amongst the participants."[8]

Today, the WIR Bank employs 205 people at its headquarters in Basel and seven regional offices. While individual memberships ceased in the late 1950s, some 60,000 businesses, an estimated 16 percent of all Swiss enterprises, were trading in WIR in 2010. Although depositors are mostly small- and medium-sized businesses, more than a third of all construction companies in Switzerland—a massively capitalintensive sector—use WIR.[9] Currently, the volume of trade in WIR annually is 1.6 billion WIR, which is just under $2 billion. This is a 1.4 percent increase over the previous year.[10]

Business is conducted by check, credit cards, and the Internet. Mobile phone payments will be available soon. Transaction fees are paid on each deal. Interestingly, the WIR is the credit card in Switzerland that operates in two currencies.

The WIR members have access to an internal database to search for goods and services of all descriptions. Next to each business listing is the percentage it is willing to accept in WIR, or whether the rate is open to negotiation.

Professor James Stodder of the Rensselaer Polytechnic Institute has conducted several macroeconometric studies proving that the secret to the country's legendary economic stability is this WIR currency, circulating among businesses in parallel with the national money. His study proved that the WIR contributes significantly to the stability of the Swiss economy and its low unemployment rates by providing "residual spending power that is highly countercyclical."[11] "Growth in the number of WIR participants has tracked Swiss unemployment very closely, consistently maintaining a rate of about one-tenth the increase in the number of unemployed."[12] This means that when the conventional Swiss franc economy slows, job losses are spontaneously reduced as more people join the WIR economy.

Finally, a more recent study[13] based for the first time on more detailed WIR data explains how it is possible that the WIR, whose volume is only a fraction of a percent of Swiss GDP, can have such a significant macroeconomic effect. The answer is that the WIR volume is not only highly countercyclical, but also highly leveraged, meaning, therefore, that many WIR exchanges are pulling a significant volume of activity in Swiss francs with them. For instance, when a hotel is purchased 50-50 in WIR and Swiss francs, the overall economic impact is double from what it appears by counting only the WIR component. This study also reveals that many of the larger Swiss firms are officially "non-members" of WIR, but accept de facto WIR transactions during economic downturns. A third relevant factor is that the velocity of WIR exchanges among the smaller businesses that are members increases significantly when the economy slows down, so that the same volume of WIR currency generates more business activity, again precisely when it is most needed.

Professor Tobias Studer, from the Center of Economic Studies at Basel University, Switzerland, considers the Stodder research a breakthrough: "For the first time, an in de pen dent American researcher has arrived at a surprising conclusion: Far from representing a factor of disturbance for the national monetary policy, the credits created by WIR constitute a support of the National Bank[the Swiss central bank] in pursuit of its monetary policy objectives."[14]

Stodder added, "So when conventional banks are cutting their credit because there's a big lack of financial confidence, and banks are essentially closing their doors to small creditors, there's no question that historically these periods are those in which cooperative currencies spring up. It happened during the Great Depression, and it's happened again during the current world downturn."

THE WIR IN THE UNITED STATES

The WIR's success has inspired some innovators to take action. An application of the WIR model, although on a very small local scale but inspired nonetheless by the Swiss prototype, has taken root in Burlington, Vermont, spearheaded by the Vermont Businesses for Social Responsibility (VBSR) program. "Quite literally, from my studies of biomimicry, I've been applying what I've observed to the monetary system. And a fiat monetary system simply doesn't resonate, but mutual credit does indeed. Mutual credit really looks to excess capacity where things are being wasted or unused and turns them into inputs. As the saying goes, linking unmet needs and unmet resources within a given community,"[15] says Amy Kirschner, marketplace manager for VBSR.

She explains that every business or industry has a cycle. Few businesses are busy all the time, so they take their trade excesses, things like empty seats in classrooms, matinee screenings in cinemas, off-peak times at restaurants, empty meeting spaces, and unsold advertising and sponsorships, and offer them as employee bonuses and benefits and as promotions without having to use conventional money. Business can find new suppliers and customers, using VBSR trade credits.

"More than 1,500 businesses in Vermont already have access to a system through which they can find new customers using their excess capacity to pay for their unmet requirements," she added.

BRAZIL—A NETWORK OF DUAL CURRENCY COMMUNITY BANKS

João Joaquim de Melo Neto Segundo recalls a fateful neighborhood meeting he attended in Conjunto Palmeira in the late 1990s. His hometown is 14 miles from the seaside tourist town of Fortaleza in northeastern Brazil. Originally, nothing was there but palm trees. It became a shantytown with a population of 32,000 during the 1970s as people were relocated from the coastal areas. While basic infrastructure like housing and some roads had been built, there was little in the way of urbanization: Shops and other basic essential services like health offices that offered rudimentary medical treatment were nonex is tent. Life was basic and bleak and therefore rather depressing.

"Someone at the local meeting of folks from the neighborhood raised the key question that turned everything on its head. That provocative question was 'Why are we poor?' And the response would be that we're poor because we have no money! But the answer may appear obvious, though that it can't be true. It has to be something else. So people in the community started doing research and mapped out the consumption patterns of the population of the area. They figured out that approximately 1.3

million Brazilian reals ($662,570) at that time circulated within the community. So it's not a lot of money, but it's definitely some money. The problem was that 80 percent of that currency was quickly leaving the local economy. We're poor because we lose what we have, and additionally we lose what little savings we have. So neighborhoods are not poor; they become poor. And that realization was the beginning spark of Banco Palmas," recalled Segundo, a former seminary student turned banker.[16]

Conjunto Palmeira near Fortaleza, northeastern Brazil in 1974 during the early stages of building. There was nothing but palm trees when construction first started. Photo credit: Banco Palmas.

Segundo also realized that relatively small cash infusions could make a big difference in people's lives. These microloans can be classified into two categories. First, there are loans for personal needs, known as consumption loans, to cover food, clothing, gas, and items for personal hygiene. Second are comparatively larger loans, called production loans, for setting up or in most cases expanding small businesses, such as street stands, shops, and service providers.Se-gundo's inspiration came primarily from Liberation Theology, a Christian movement that developed in the Catholic Church in Latin America in the 1950s and 1960s and explores freedom from economic and social injustice. Another major influence on Segundo came from the Spanish cooperative movement of the late 1950s, called Mondragon. It is a federation of cooperatives that currently provides employment to some 83,000 people in a network of 256 companies in the Basque region in northern Spain. Its annual revenue is 32 billion euros. [17]

The construction of the Asmoconp, Associação de Moradores do Conjunto Palmeira during the mid-to late 1980s. Photo credit: Banco Palmas.

Henk Van Arkel of STRO recalled the early days of the system in the Palmeira settlement: "We put aside the money for building a school in Fortaleza,

João Joaquim de Melo Neto Segundo, founder Banco Palmas, Brazil. Photo credit: Banco Palmas.

Brazil. We asked the donor, the Dutch NGO ICCO, to be patient. The school would get built, but instead we planned to first put local currency, called *fomentos,* in circulation in the form of microcredits backed by the donor money in the bank. At the start, nobody knew what fomentos were, but the Banco Palmas reps asked people, mostly vendors, who were getting these loans to put signs in their windows saying, 'Fomentos accepted here.' Notices were very quickly all over the place. Then Banco Palmas went to builders and asked them to accept payment in fomentos. By then, it seemed that fomentos could be spent everywhere in the neighborhood, so they agreed. When the builders started work on the school, the fomento process basically tripled the effect of the original development aid package."[18]

The first Banco Palmas bank opened in January 1998 and issued two kinds of loans. One was consumption loans, with no interest fees and just a 1 percent flat fee for administration. These loans were given in the local currency, called Palmas, and were not convertible into national currency. In the neighborhood town, Fortaleza, for example, there are 240 businesses that accept the local currency and even offer discounts of between 2 and 15 percent to people using it.

"The process for getting a loan is very simple," added Asier Ansorena, Asesor Nacional de Crédito do Instituto Palmas.[19] "For a business, there is no need for a business plan. There's simply a meeting with a bank officer to discuss the idea for the business, and this is followed up by finding out about the person's reputation for reliability in his or her: neighborhood. Thereby an assessment is made of the individual's trustworthiness to repay the loan. The process is much easier still with consumption loans. Someone in need of some short-term money to put food on the table for their family can make their case and walk out of the bank with the money."

Consumption loans, which used to be called emergency loans, range from 20 to 100 reals, equal to about $50 at most. They ensure that nobody goes hungry. Production loans can also be provided in national currency, in which case they come with an interest fee attached to them. Production loans typically range between $5,000 to $10,000.

Interestingly enough, in 2003, after issuing the first Palmas currency, Joaquim Melo was accused of running a money-laundering operation in an unregistered bank. The Central Bank started proceedings against him, charging the bank with issuing fake money. Following a court case, the judge presiding agreed that the people were constitutionally entitled to have access to funds, as the Central Bank was doing nothing for the poor areas. The Central Bank created a working group on how to help the poor and invited Melo. In 2005, the Brazilian government's Secretary for Solidarity Economy created a partnership with the Instituto Palmas. Support for "community development banks" issuing new currency is now official state policy.

In 2006, Banco Pop u lar do Brazil, the largest public bank in the country, became a partner of the Brazilian Network of Community Development Banks (CDB), a guarantor of credit lines based on the criteria from PMNPO (National Program of Oriented Productive Microcredit). The CDB estimates that this microloan program had an impact on the lives of more than 200,000 people. There are currently 78 community banks.

Banco Palmas has created over 1,800 jobs and sparked the creation of similar dual currency banking already operational now in some 66 communities around Brazil with the full support of the Brazilian government and the nation's Central Bank.

FROM HUMBLE BEGINNINGS

Aurineide Alves Cordeiro, a resident of Conjunto Palmeira, asked for her first loan of less than $100 more than 14 years ago. Today, she is a very successful local businesswoman working her way up from the bottom with help from Banco Palmas.

"Any person of low income that visits a conventional bank to ask for a loan is highly likely to have his or her dreams crashed in an instant, mostly because the barriers of entry developed are highly bureaucratic. There tends to be a lack of interest in serving the poor, or there's a complete disconnect between the priorities of the banking system and the real economy. Banco Palmas has always fought against the barriers that kept people in the poverty trap," explained Aiser Ansorena.

Aurineide's story is full of struggles. She can easily remember the difficulties she and her family experienced during the days before Banco Palmas existed.

"I always worked as a saleswoman. Before the bank opened, I would sell anything I could to stay afloat, mostly clothes. Since the creation of the bank, the neighborhood has grown a lot, and not only economically. Any problem we had, we would run to the bank to try to find a solution. We are privileged to have a Community Bank in our neighborhood."[20]

Aurineide used her first loan to buy clothes, mostly women's underwear from a textile plant, which she then sold door to door. "Every time I finished paying for a loan, I would ask for another one; I continued this process for four years, until I was able to start my own clothing store."

From 2002 until 2009, Aurineide worked in her own store, which she was able to build thanks to the support she received from the bank. Five years ago, she embarked on an even more ambitious enterprise; she opened, together with her husband, a DYI building construction ware house. For two years, they had to manage both businesses until they could successfully transition to the construction business. Her line of credit is now $7,500.

Aurineide gets emotional as she tells her story, especially when she has to explain what Banco Palmas means to her. "We had no access to credit or any other financial service in our town. Thanks to our Community Bank we have managed to have access to these services. Personally, this has been of tremendous importance. Every time I needed help, people at Banco Palmas were always ready to provide it."

"Our plans are to create 1,000 banks in the near future, of which 300 should be in the northeast of Brazil, and to have at least one community bank in each state of Brazil. Furthermore, we'd like to help spread this community banking network across Latin America. There is a pi lot project to use mobile telephones to facilitate transactions, along with a major push to help in financial education," added Segundo.

Interestingly, there are two regions in Brazil where the network's local currency is used to pay part of government employees' salaries. The first is Silva Jardim in the state of Rio de Janeiro. Employees are paid in *Capivari*operated by the Banco Capivari. The second is in the town of São João do Arraial, located in the state of Piauí. The local bank is Banco dos Cocais and people are paid in *Cocais.*

JAK BANK

JAK (*Jord Arbete Kapital)* stands for land, labor, and capital in Swedish and Danish and was founded to provide interest-free banking services. There exists a loose network of several cooperative banks in Europe located primarily in Finland, Denmark, and Sweden, and lately in Germany, Italy, and Spain.

The loans are financed solely by members' savings. No money is made by the bank for providing these loans, nor is money made by the banks' customers on their savings with the bank. In a nutshell, the bank does not partake in the traditional banking practice of money creation. It's a cooperative, so the bank's clientele are shareholders, with each depositor holding just one share. Each member has equal influence in the annual vote for the board of directors.

JAK's ultimate goal is to see the abolition of interest as an economic instrument and replace it with instruments that better serve the interests of people. The bank's mission rests on offering feasible financial instruments sustainable for the environment and serving the local economy.[21]

Unlike regular banks, JAK doesn't rely on external capital. Government regulations ensure that the bank must hold adequate reserves of its own capital. On the face of it, the way to do this would be to build up reserves out of company profits. Defaults on JAK bank loans are rare, approximately 1 percent, and significantly lower than those experienced by mainstream banks. Low losses mean also that costs to the members are kept low.

"Savings points" are the cooperative currency internally used as the key method by which JAK manages member savings and loans, thus increasing its liquidity. Saving points are awarded for one's saving efforts. For example, saving one Swedish crown for one month yields one savings point, and one crown borrowed for one month consumes one savings point. Thus savings points are used to ensure the sustainability of the system. Savings points are earned by the member on savings that accumulate prior to exercising the loan option and on savings accumulated during the loan repayment period.

"The types of loans we make are usually for home improvements such as renovations or to purchase real estate. We usually are able to provide funding for the entire mortgage for properties in rural areas in comparison to providing approximately half the funds needed on a city property. This is because a house, for example, tends to be less expensive in more remote parts of the country in comparison to major cities, such as Stockholm and Malmö," reports Miguel Ganzo, international relations coordinator for JAK. Loans to pay back student loans are also given.

Oscar Kjellberg, who retired in 2010 as head of the bank, remarks, "This system works really well, over the years, for people wanting to buy a house. Some 80 percent of our loans historically have been for that purpose. An individual must save with the bank, with his or her money being used for someone else's loan first. Then we provide a house loan, which typically gets paid back over a 15-year period. But before the bank will hand back the deeds to their house, they have to carry on making the same monthly savings payment for another 12 years after their loan is paid off, to give other people the use of their money. After that, they can withdraw their money if they wish. The benefit to the depositor is that they have good lump sum available for their retirement. With conventional banks, that sum would have been swallowed up by interest payments."

A Bank without Tellers

Some 32 professional staff members are based in three offices, the main one located in Skvöde, Sweden, roughly 180 kilometers outside Stockholm, and the other two branches are located in Malmö and Orsa. All business is transacted by telephone, Internet, or e-mail through a state-of-the-art computer system. The enterprise is supported by 700 specially trained volunteers who sustain JAK's 22 regional communities. These volunteers provide word-of-mouth publicity as to JAK's benefits and array of services, along with using social media, especially among the younger volunteers.

JAK Bank regularly offers classes to their members. Here, three women students who have completed basic training attend an advanced lecture on how loan officers evaluate a potential loan. Photo credit: Amanda Svensson.

The bank currently has plans to install a system that will offer billpaying services to its customers, including the possibility of cash withdrawal, which brings the bank closer to becoming a full-service bank.

Kjellberg continued, "The trust in the system depends not only on the borrowers but also on the management. They have to balance the interest of the savers, the borrowers, and encourage cooperation among all members. It takes time. The other side of the savers in a savings- and-loan system is the borrowers. Their record as borrowers is a factor of major importance for the trust of the savers, who are saving with the explicit purpose of getting a loan themselves. It is not as bad as it sounds, because the borrowers are earlier savers, just as the savers will become borrowers later on," he explained.

JAK reached 36,300 members during 2010, with an overall 12 percent yearly growth rate. During the same year, members' savings amounted to 111 million euros, of which 99 million euros were granted as loans.[22] Their loan default levels are very low on average: 0.03 percent in 2007, and in 2010 there was no default during the whole year.

In the meantime, Kjellberg looks to new horizons. "I have been very interested in the topic of venture capital and looking at new ways of providing access to money, especially for new business ventures. From my experience, risk is mitigated, although never totally removed, by knowing the players involved. So I am looking at new models of funding local enterprise through crowd financing," he added.

There has been a solid push in recent years to reach out to other countries internationally. According to Miguel Ganzo, "There are projects underway to establish the JAK model in Germany, Spain, Italy, and Finland. The JAK bank in Denmark was established in 1931 and is totally in de pen dent from us. It started off strongly, then went through a period of decline, and is now on the rise again. There is also interest from Arab countries because our model respects traditional Shari'a principles."

In terms of the overall good of the Swedish economy, the JAK bank does have a positive effect on unemployment, but in an indirect way. "As JAK liberates more people from interest expenses, that much money is freed up which can be used instead to buy goods and services. This will stimulate businesses so that they can employ more people," according to a report by a Canadian consultancy group.[23]

THE FREE LAKOTA BANK:A COMMODITY-BACKED BANK

The Free Lakota Bank is another interesting case study. Although it works with conventional money, it is very different from conventional banking standards in that it is the only nonreserve, nonfractional bank in the United States and possibly the world that issues, accepts for deposit, and circulates monies that are compliant with the American Open Currency Standard (AOCS) and uses bullion of 0.999 percent fine silver and gold. All of the bank's deposits are liquid, meaning they can be withdrawn at any time in coins.

The AOCS currencies include Boulder Gaians, John Galts, Dixie Dollars, and Coin of the Realm. These privately issued currencies are backed by some precious metal, most commonly silver.

According to Eddie Allen, director of the Free Lakota Bank, "This movement has been envisioned by many for some time. Several years ago, the OPEC nations began to openly speak of moving away from the dollar to a basket of less volatile currencies; China and Russia among others are now engaging in international trade in their own currencies rather than using the dollar. Now it is openly speculated that national leaders of oil-producing countries who have tried requiring payment of their oil in something other than dollars (e.g., euros or gold) are meeting sudden and undesirable ends. As nations scramble to find new paths to protect their interests, it is expected that they, too, may ultimately reach the conclusion that: Promises to pay are not payment. And yes, this path is being taken by numerous entities in other countries—there is even an international commodity banking association in formation as we speak.

"The power and profits gained by those who own and operate the current banking system are significant. Those who create and manipulate paper currencies have quite an impressive global network of support and beneficiaries who rely on the fiat, debt-based system continuing, and thus it has successfully been propped up for quite a long time. Add to that the power of the well-lobbied state reinforcing and exercising considerable influence to the benefit of those who engage in that style of banking."[24]

The Free Lakota Bank is not affiliated with any government agency and does not recognize the authority of any such organization. "Private insurance companies are more than capable of providing sufficient coverage to our holdings without burdening anyone outside of the principles of the contract, such as the American taxpayer," Eddie Allen remarked.

THE BRISTOL POUND: OUR CITY, OUR MONEY, OUR FUTURE

The Bristol Pound (BP) is both a paper and an electronic currency and is emerging as an interesting example of a trifecta of mutual support among the currency, a local bank, and local government. Payments can be made in cash, by text on a mobile phone, or online. The online and mobile accounts are through the Bristol Credit Union, which is a partner in the project. The Bristol City Council has been supportive and is offering to pay any staff members who are interested a proportion of their wages in BPs. The council will also accept BPs from businesses to pay their taxes.

The cost of paying by mobile phone is 2 percent and 1 percent online, which is paid for by the receiver, usually the merchant. Bristol Pounds can be given in change, traded within the network of businesses and suppliers, paid to the council for business rates, or redeemed for sterling pounds with a fee of 3 percent. Several hundred merchants have signed up so far with the launch of the currency slated for the fall of 2012.

TECHNOLOGY

Technology has been used for some pretty mindless applications: gossipy and vacuous blogs with no real substance and silly games. For example, the world has spent a total of 200,000 years playing the game Angry Birds.[25]

Despite this trend, emergent technology solutions now provide banking services beyond the traditional brick- and-mortar offerings. Soon, there will be full-spectrum solutions that make the remittances, payments, and exchanges of value in a multicurrency environment safe, legitimate, and affordable, where both competitive and cooperative transactions take place seamlessly from an individual's e-wallet. Well underway, though, is a new wave of remedies in which Internet and mobile technologies provide innovative options for accessing financial services, thus leapfrogging over the predominant modes of expensive banking modalities.

At present, there are technology silos that hamper the fluid and seamless movement of money within the marketplace. Mark Fischer, founder of Inspire Commerce and a recognized e-commerce expert, comments, "In closed networks, users are captured in a specific channel. This is a proven business model, yet it is increasingly out of touch with the expectations of digital-era consumers who have come to expect choice and ease of use from online and mobile payment services. Closed solutions are beginning to lose favor, and will either consolidate into a universal platform or be left behind."[26]

He explains that while each new closed network solution promises simplicity and convenience, online payments actually are becoming more complicated and cumbersome. "PayPal, Square, Stripe, Google Wallet, and others are simply not solving this problem as they want to maintain the closed system—their own—to protect their business. This is particularly of value to small businesses and consultancies that *feel the pain*of closed systems as they attempt to work with the inconvenient and expensive options that dominate today's market."

His company is in the early stages of the first platform that connects all the existing payment channels and simplifies the process of requesting, receiving, and making payments. This solution, called InspirePay, is a free application.

The continuing advances in technology, such as the increasing ability to handle micropayments, further open the door to designing new currencies based on and targeted to specific goals. The possibilities are limitless. One random example to illustrate the point is that it's now feasible to envision carbon-backed currencies.

A carbon premium exchange (CPX) system could be an Internet-based information exchange system where additional data about the carbon credit producers are made available to potential buyers—for example, their exact location, type of soil used, volume of crops produced, and individual history of carbon sequestration. Since the verifiability of carbon sequestration is a key criterion for registration of projects under the clean development mechanism (CDM) of the Kyoto Protocol, information about the producers and their sequestering process would, in any case, need to be measured.

Data could be collected with sensors built into the biomass processor equipment. Such sensors could include an automatic satellite positioning mechanism that identifies the exact location at which the carbon credits are being generated. Furthermore, the carbon credits could be in dependently verified by satellite, tracer systems, and/or soil sampling. The payment system for CPX exchanges could use highly advanced payment technologies, more secure and cost-effective on a decentralized basis than those currently used in centralized credit or debit card payment systems.

Corporate buyers of the credits in the CPX system would be able to bid for the carbon credits of specific groups of producers and could exchange the seeds, fertilizers, or equipment they produce for farmers' carbon credits. In short, those corporations would be buying not only carbon credits but also market share in these new and emerging technologies. This would motivate these corporations to bid up the value of the CPX carbon credits at higher levels than the regular carbon credit market. The advantage to the farmers is that the bidding among corporations on the CPX would provide them with a higher value—a *premium* —for their carbon credits than the more anonymous conventional carbon credit markets.

In terms of access to banking services, estimates are that 3 billion people globally do not have a bank account. They do not earn enough money to be deemed desirable bank customers. As a consequence, they are relegated to operate solely on a cash basis. These individuals are left vulnerable to theft; they are excluded from all e-commerce transactions and forced to utilize expensive cash-wiring services.

"More than a billion people worldwide lack bank accounts but do have mobile phones, providing a dramatic opportunity to achieve greater financial inclusion," according to a recent Mobile Money Market Sizing study.[27] Furthermore, and perhaps most important, mobile banking will be free to expand, unfettered legislatively, and "since no deposits are accepted or interest paid, the service provider does not need a banking license."[28]

The convergence between ever-cheaper computing and growing access to the Internet and to mobile phones will drastically change the global banking scene. More important, it will trigger the proliferation of further innovations and real prosperity around the globe, in domains that today seem to be the stuff of science fiction.

Chapter Seven

STRATEGIES FOR BUSINESS AND ENTREPRENEURS

Our Age of Anxiety is, in great part, the result of trying to do today's jobs with yesterday's tools.

MARSHALL MCLUHAN,
Canadian philosopher of communication theory

In response to one U.S. governor's braggadocio about massive job creation in his state during the nation's continued employment slump, some wag responded, "Yes, I know all about his job creation; I've got three of those jobs."

"There's been great progress made since the end of World War II to create a broad base of high-paying jobs, although the bulk of those positions were in unionized manufacturing companies, nearly all of which have cut back, shut down or outsourced. High-wage jobs left urban manufacturing districts to be replaced by low-wage service jobs or occupational deserts."[1]

If this prospect isn't tough enough, Silicon Valley entrepreneur Martin Ford writes about how automation eventually will eliminate most jobs.[2] Jeremy Rifkin makes a similar case in his insightful book, *The End of Work.* MIT economist David Autor predicts that automation will eliminate middle-class jobs, and shows that the trend of demand for mainly high- and low-wage extremes will continue for the foreseeable future.

These views are supported by the official statistics, which show that employers tend to be hiring more temporary part-time workers or volunteer workers such as interns, with most job creation trending to lower-paying work. A staggering 21 million jobs need to be created by 2020 to return America to full employment.[3]

Santa Fe Institute economist Brian Arthur cogently describes the ongoing transition from industrial to information age: "With the coming of the Industrial Revolution—roughly from the 1760s, when Watt's steam engine appeared, through around 1850 and beyond—the economy developed a muscular system in the form of machine power. Now it is developing a neural system. This may sound grandiose, but actually the metaphor seems valid. Around 1990, computers started to talk to each other, and all kinds of connections started to happen. The individual machines—servers—are like neurons, and the axons and synapses are the communication pathways and linkages that enable them to be in conversation with each other and to take appropriate action. So, we can say that another economy—a second economy—of all of these digitized business processes conversing, executing, and triggering further actions is silently forming alongside the physical economy."[4]

The upshot of this second economy is that while it's an engine of growth and prosperity, it does not provide jobs. In fact, it erodes entire sectors of traditional jobs. Much of the job creation that has taken place over the past 20 years has been in small enterprises. Businesses with fewer than 100 employees provided the largest percentage of gross job gains, almost 60 percent.[5] Additionally, entirely new job categories have surfaced that didn't exist a decade ago. Technology, cultural shifts, and changing demographics combine to create new career fields all the time.

As this emergent economy meets with the current harsh realities, new money in the form of cooperative currencies is being designed to address the needs of up- and-coming enterprises with some very interesting early results. Innovative blueprints linking unused resources, such as the time, energy, and creativeness of individuals, are making it possible to pay for labor and services in imaginative ways. Furthermore, work that has not been rewarded financially in the past can be honored now with these new currencies. Besides helping enterprises meet their obligations, these currencies foster greater cooperation and potentially more ingenuity because of the trusting relationships they engender within a business, a network, and a community at large.

One of the most pioneering organizations internationally in the field of research, development, and implementation of cooperative money is the Dutch NGO STRO. Organized and run for more than the last two decades by Henk Van Arkel, STRO grew out of the publishing company he and his brother ran with an editorial focus on environmental and social issues. Using money from a Dutch government program, he was able to hire full-time and part-time employees to research currency models following STRO's early adventures into implementing LETS systems in the Low Countries.

Keenly aware that business is the backbone of any community, Van Arkel focused on the successes in South and Central America of microcredit lending and started to look for new designs and models.

Van Arkel remembers, "We started with the relations we had at the time. The manager that we had in Porto Allegre, Brazil, was a former director of the UN small enterprise program. Prior to working with us, he had initiated a program in Uruguay and introduced IT and new technologies and other innovations. It turned out to be a very successful project that led to Uruguay being one of the most advanced countries in that business."[6]

Van Arkel and he together designed a currency that would address the critical issue of cash flow facing small and medium-size enterprises when their suppliers extend credit for 30 days while their larger customers may not pay for 90 days. Often there's a credit crunch, as banks refuse to provide bridge financing or do so subject to very onerous conditions. Furthermore, if the business is a new one, a credit line can be virtually impossible to secure. These problems are endemic in businesses in both developing and developed countries.

The solution that emerged is called the Commercial Credit Circle, or C3 for short. The C3 plan uses insured invoices or other payment claims as backing for a liquid payment instrument within a business-to-business clearing network. Each recipient of such an instrument has the choice to either cash it in national money (at a cost) or directly pay its own suppliers with the proceeds in a cooperative currency backed by the insured invoice (at no cost).

Participating businesses start by securing invoice insurance up to a predetermined amount, based on the specific creditworthiness of the claims they obtain on third parties.

The business (hereafter referred to as business A) that has obtained such insurance on an invoice accepted by one its clients (called business B) opens a checking account in the clearing network. Business A electronically exchanges the insured invoice for clearing funds (called C3 funds), and pays one of its suppliers (business C) immediately and in full with these C3 funds.

To receive its payment, business C only needs to open its own checking account in the network. Business C now has two options: either cash in the C3 funds for conventional national money (incurring a cost computed as the interest for the period until the maturity of the invoice, plus banking fees) or pay its own suppliers with the C3 clearing funds, at no cost. Whatever the timing of the payment is to business A, business C is in a position to use the positive balance in its C3 account in the network, for instance, to pay its supplier, business D.

Business D needs only to open an account in the network, giving it the same two options as business C: either convert the clearing funds into national money or spend it in the network. And so on. At the maturity of the invoice, the network gets paid the amount of the original invoice in national money, either by business B or by the insurance company in case of default by business B. At that point, whoever owns the proceeds of the insured invoice can cash them in for national money without incurring any interest costs.

Thus, businesses increase their working capital and the use of their productive capacity by using the C3. The size of this increase can be built up to a stable level of between a quarter (covering therefore up to an average of 90 days of invoices) and half of annual sales at a cost substantially lower than what is otherwise possible. Suppliers are paid immediately, regardless of the payment schedule of the original buyer, injecting substantial liquidity at very low cost into the entire small and medium-sized enterprise (SME) network. The C3 network grows rapidly, as both clients and suppliers benefit from joining.

Furthermore, the technology is a proven one that doesn't require any new legislation or government approvals, and the necessary software is available in open source. Additionally, the most effective way for governments at all levels to encourage the implementation of the C3 strategy is for them to accept payment of taxes and fees in the C3 currency. This encourages everybody to accept the C3 currency in payment and provides additional income to the government from transactions that otherwise wouldn't take place. Furthermore, that additional income automatically becomes available in conventional national currency at the maturity of the original invoice. At the end of the process, the government has only to deal with conventional national money, thereby not upsetting any existing procurement policies.

Interestingly, where this concept has gotten the most traction while staying truest to its initial design is in northern Europe. The Europe an Union has agreed to fund a feasibility study for the C3, which will be managed by the Dutch NGO Qoin. Its scope will cover Ireland, the United Kingdom, the Netherlands, Belgium, Luxembourg, northern France, and the western provinces of Germany. It plans to use the procurement power of municipalities and large companies that will buy products and services from companies within the C3 network.

Edgar Kampers noted, "C3 allows injecting working capital in a region's private sector, at no cost to the authorities. SMEs, being the most vulnerable during economic downturns, get funding options that are considerably cheaper than existing options and obtain working capital precisely at the point and time when it is most effective, thus creating or preserving jobs. This financial product will be controlled by the users and opens new markets and marketing channels through e-commerce. It is indeed a small step from processing all your invoices and financial flows electronically, to launching an e-business outlet, further improving the capacity of businesses to successfully compete."[7]

He provides the following example: A municipality or larger company wants to purchase LED lights costing 120,000 euros. The C3 network, with some 3,000 members, allows it to pay in six months. The municipality pays a fee for this service.

The LED installer gets the 120,000 euros immediately in C3 clearing funds. After two months, the LED installer spends the C3-euro with other members of the C3 network, such as a marketing company. After one month, the marketing company spends the credits to pay the printer's bill. The printer needs to pay a party outside the network (say, for taxes or hardware) and exchanges the C3 clearing funds directly to euros at a small exchange rate, called a *malus.*

The C3 will need to borrow 120,000 euros from a financial institution for three months to finance the LED installer. The costs of this loan are much lower for the C3 network than for an individual company. The costs are covered by the fee paid by the municipality and the malus fee.

When this program was launched in Uruguay, political problems arose. "We had everything ready to go, including an agreement for the partial payment of taxes. We had all the major ministers convinced—there are five ministers in the economic cluster in the cabinet, such as finance, labor, and economy. At the moment we were ready to take off, there was a change in government," recalls Van Arkel.

Currently, what is operational in Uruguay and El Salvador is a subset version of the full-blown C3 program.

Koen de Beer, project manager for STRO in El Salvador, makes an interesting observation about the business climate in South America in comparison with the United States or Europe. "Something that has fascinated me is there are so many businesses and entrepreneurial activities here. When I was living in Europe, you think about setting up a business, and after 10 minutes you decide not to do it because there are so many rules, regulations, and laws. And you need so much money. Then you come over here, and everybody's thinking of setting up a business. There

Andrés Noubleau, a chef from Spain, got a line of credit in puntos to upgrade his restaurant and have working capital. Photo credit: Koen de Beer.

is this huge amount of ideas and initiative. Many of them don't make it after six months. But that's OK. People aren't afraid of picking themselves up again and trying another commercial idea."[8]

In El Salvador, the C3 concept is known as *Puntotransacciones,* and the currency is called *puntos.*

Esperanto was a small restaurant in San Salvador, the country's capital city, famous for its international cuisine. It was founded in the house of the parents of Andrés Noubleau, a chef from Spain. After two years, the restaurant moved to a more exclusive place in the city. Although the location was great, the investment was steep, and operational costs rose dramatically. Short of cash and without access to more credit from banks, Esperanto became a member of Puntotransacciones. He got a credit line in puntos to complete several upgrades in the restaurant and for some operational overhead, which he easily paid off when customers paid for delicious meals in puntos.

Today, Esperanto has become one of the best and most exclusive restaurants in town and continues offering its fare to members of the network. Noubleau is still proud of his decision to be the first restaurant joining the business network: "Thanks to this currency we've survived a very critical period of the business cycle."

Artyco is a small family business specializing in furniture and accessories crafted from wrought iron and steel. The products are handmade, and their production cost is high. An economic crisis struck; simultaneously, demand for the company's products dropped, and the business had to be restructured, closing down some shops and points of sale. But the owner, Guadalupe de Artiga, was very creative. She joined the network and bought and sold as much as possible from others in the network, both for her business and for her family, everything from food to medicine on a daily basis. "Economic crisis or not, through this network and currency, I have managed to maintain my way of life and that of my family," says de Artigo.

URUGUAY

Maria, like most women in the Casavalle neighborhood, the poorest area of Montevideo, receives subsidized food for herself and her children on a daily basis, directly from a bakery that is located a minute's walk from her house. Thanks to the C3 system, Maria no longer has to pay for bus fares and leave her children alone at home for several hours to obtain subsidized food.

On the business level, small neighborhood shops that are part of the C3 network can employ this system of paying their suppliers even if they do not have cash on hand. These small businesses have access to short-term affordable credit and also can purchase their supplies online or via a mobile phone SMS. This results in significant time savings compared to using the services of the traditional banking system.

Luis is the human resource manager of one of the largest municipalities in the country. It employs several hundred staff members who get reimbursed for taxi fares and fuel for their own cars. Luis and his accounting administration faced two issues that made this procedure cumbersome: A huge volume of papers, mostly vouchers, were submitted by the employees to justify their travel expenses, and the use of these benefits was not transparent.

Guadalupe de Artiga. Through the Puntotransacciones network and currency, she has maintained her standard of living for her family and herself. Photo credit: Koen de Beer.

The STRO arranged a C3 system with taxi companies, suppliers of fuel stations, and the administrators to facilitate payments and avoid the bureaucracy required to administer the previous arrangement. The C3 network allows the secure and safe handling of transactions.

"This system has great potential to be replicated by other municipalities and eventually spread to a large segment of end consumers, who, in this way, via prepayments will have credit on their phones to pay for taxis or to pay for the fuel for their cars," says Luis.

C3 Circuit of Consumer Cooperatives

Patricia is a schoolteacher who lives in a rural area of Salto, some 500 kilometers from the capital of Montevideo. Patricia pays a monthly fee for her membership in the Cooperative of Teachers. This allows her to make purchases by having her shopping guaranteed by her monthly salary, which is the manner in which she has been able to buy all her house hold electronic appliances. Since the cooperative is located far from her house, the transportation costs of the appliances have been expensive.

Then the Teachers' Cooperative Patricia was part of joined the C3 Program. Like all members of this and other cooperatives (civil servants, professionals, police officers, the retired), Patricia now can view, choose, change, pay, and receive the purchased items from the store closest to her residence. A significant number of consumer cooperatives are keen to be a part of this program, which is only viable when they, together with the chain of suppliers, are all part of the C3 network. The decentralization of services and the social inclusion are part of state policy, and obviously this scheme supports these objectives.

Eduardo Tarragó, the C3 project manager for Uruguay, says, "Currently it isn't possible to convert the C3s into national currency. However, this issue is supposed to get resolved by the Ministry of Economy.

The idea is that one will be able to pay taxes and electricity, water, communication services, and fuel expenses via this system, as all these are state-owned monopolies in Uruguay."

FINANCING FOR LOCAL BUSINESSES

The Local Capital Project of the Mile High Business Alliance (MHBA) in Denver, Colorado, is a two-tiered strategy designed to address the most pressing needs of small local enterprises, namely, access to affordable financing and building a sustainable revenue stream. Typically, small businesses operate within very narrow margins, making them vulnerable. The MHBA has rolled out a plan for an 18-month pi lot program that will engage small business members within a core business district of Denver in two cooperative initiatives: the Revolving Loan Fund and the Local Flavors Re-Circulating Gift Certificate Program. The plan is to enable participating businesses to build and sustain healthy revenue streams and, in turn, play a critical role in strengthening the local economy.

Since 2007, MHBA has produced Local Flavor Guides for 15 neighborhoods in Denver and published and distributed over 150,000 copies. Working in conjunction with the guides, the business alliance will issue the local currency in the form of gift certificates. This ensures that the money stays within the community because they can only be spent at the participating businesses. Furthermore, the Revolving Loan Fund will provide anywhere from $1,000 to $10,000 in loans to eligible member businesses, with a payback period of 3 to 12 months. There is no interest on these loans.

Arthur Brock, cofounder and director of the MHBA and a consultant and technology designer for several global currency projects comments, "A critical element that distinguishes Local Flavors from other local currencies is that it is designed to emphasize recirculation of the gift certificates, rather than redemption by a business for U.S. dollars. A business will be able to redeem Local Flavors for cash only after they have repaid their original loan of Local Flavors certificates to MHBA. Any redemption above the original loan amount will be redeemed at 90 percent of face value for the amount of Local Flavors to be redeemed[i.e., 90 cents in cash for every "dollar" in Local Flavors]. Loans may be repaid to MHBA either in Local Flavors certificates (at 100 percent value) or in cash."[9]

However, a business that continues to recirculate Local Flavors never has to repay the loan. "This will serve as an incentive to keep Local Flavors in circulation among local businesses, multiplying their value and further encouraging local business patronage. In either scenario (recirculation or redemption), the Local Flavors and/or cash will then be available for MHBA to recirculate in the form of another Local Flavors loan," adds Brock.

THE HUB NETWORK

The Hub Network is a social enterprise operating in more than 26 countries globally. Their mission is to "inspire and support imaginative and enterprising initiatives for a better world." They provide a space, along with guidance to take an idea from the drawing board to commercial reality. There are Hub offices from Amsterdam to Zurich, from Atlanta to Melbourne, and from Dubai to Berkeley, with an estimated 1,400 offices in United States alone.[10]

The Hub is a place for purpose-driven people to connect and build solutions for a better world. "Members work at the Hub, attend and produce events, run their own boot camps, access funding and mentorship, source clients and coconspirators, find social networks, build campaigns, launch companies, prototype and test products. The members can create what they want, as it is their space and their community to build upon," says Jean Luc Roux, a member of the board of the Brussels chapter.

The Brussels chapter is planning on creating a pi lot cooperative currency with a view to helping entrepreneurs create a more cooperative environment.

Roux describes the situation: "We have two cooperative currencies. One is the *hubbee*—it's like TimeBanking—and the other one is the *honey,* which is a reputation system. And both are combined.

This means that when I'm giving services to my friend William, William will receive hubbees, measured in time, and I will qualify the relation I had with him in the process with honey. For instance, I will give him one or two pots of honey because we see the Hub metaphorically as a hive. That is why we decided to represent the qualitative evaluation with honey pots. And what happened since we established the system? We see increasing relationships between social entrepreneurs, because our challenge as a hub is to create a collaborative spirit around an entrepreneur instead of a competitive spirit. And, it seems that there is a key difference before and after we've established the Hub money.

"Before, people were working more alone, looking at the other not necessarily as a friend, not necessarily as a collaborator, but more as a potential competitor. And now, because they can offer services among themselves, they see that they have more to win by working together.

"So we have one entrepreneur, he's a web designer but he's not allowed to sell web design to another member because that will go against the guidelines, but what he can do is show a member how to make and design his own Web site. And this kind of service really changes the lives and the relationships of the entrepreneurs. So since we've had the currency in place, many people have learned how to do things they weren't able to do before then. And perhaps more important, the collaborative energy at the Hub has improved greatly," Roux added.

Given the early success of this cooperative money experiment the management team is now considering how best to handle the anticipated taxation issues with the Belgian authorities. In the meantime, John David Boswell, a member of the San Francisco Hub in an unofficial capacity, has launched a Hub Time-Bank with an initial commitment of some 120 people in various Hubs around the world.

Boswell says: "I'm working toward launching the Happy Futures Global Challenge. This is in collaboration with the United Nations' civil working group and the UN Happiness Resolution, which I hope will become a stellar international project. It would illustrate how TimeBanking can be used in many ways, including social projects with many others throughout the world and including Hub members. The goal is to be "an exploration of the heart of happiness," which is compassion, community, and deep connections between each other, envisioning ways to move beyond GDP to Gross National Happiness based on other metrics."

FRIENDLY FAVORS

One of the most consistent outcomes reported by participants involved in cooperative currency initiatives is the development of a renewed sense of community and support from that community. Perhaps surprisingly, as a result of using a currency to acknowledge caring, assistance, or even random acts of kindness, the need to use the very currency that cultivated those behaviors and in a way kept score dissipates over time. This is because the awareness of good cooperative activities and deeds within a given circle or kinship has become explicit and flows naturally, and the use of the currency has become secondary or even no longer necessary.

Friendly Favors is a case in point.

An online networking program, Friendly Favors was started in 1999 by entrepreneur and social networker Sergio Lub and Webmaster Victor Grey, author of *Web without a Weaver.* It is a trust-based networking community that rewards users for generosity and goodwill. Members maintain their own pages, including photos and descriptions of services and products offered. They offer discounts to Friendly Favors users, engendering loyalty and gratefulness. Joining is free but requires an invitation from an existing member. This approach ensures that connections are based on trust and relationships. Currently, the Friendly Favors network has over 62,000 participants living in 196 countries.

Use of its own cooperative currency is perhaps the most innovative feature of the Friendly Favors network. The currency is called *thank-yous* or Ts. These Ts are created through transactions and resulting recommendations and are given by members to each other, recognizing the buyer's savings on a service or product received. One T is equivalent to one U.S.

dollar saved by a discount or friendly favor: it is not redeemable in national currency. In fact, Ts cannot do anything except allow participants to acknowledge the generosity of others. They do not mea sure income, but rather goodwill, and operate as a reputation rating system. As a result, participants feel inclined to use the services of, for example, an accountant or computer technician with the most Ts in their FF account. To aid this process, all participants' balances in Ts are openly displayed in their online profiles, along with all the referrals they have accumulated from fellow participants.

Inherent in the program is the idea of reciprocity. "As members receive discounts and favors from others, they will be more likely to offer the same in return. Tangible measurements honor generosity in the past and encourage it in the future. Friendly Favors itself has benefited from this goodwill: Office and server space, technical skill, and supplies have been donated to the organization, with thank-yous given in recognition. The network has no bank account and uses no legal tender, yet *Wired*magazine estimated that the development alone of an interactive application like Friendly Favors' would have cost over $3 million if undertaken by a corporation," enthuses Sergio Lub.[11]

Lub's inspiration comes from the desire to increase the number of people who are willing to help on a regular basis beyond their small social circles: "What we are trying to do is see how we can do more favors for people who are not in our immediate community. You can meet someone who is normally very generous with family and friends but is callous when someone on the street needs a place to stay. If we are all a little more caring, then we will have enough room for everyone to be taken care of."

Lub, originally from Argentina, knows the importance of such expanded circles of generosity. In fleeing his country after a military coup, he learned that relationships and the kindness of others were much more important than money. As Lub said, "I'm here[in the United States] because many people risked their lives to save mine." Using the currency of thank-yous, Friendly Favors supports the development of relationships and goodwill, creating a more balanced economy that acknowledges the diversity of our human needs.

"What we found after using thank-yous, especially among a close-knit group, was that issuing the currency wasn't necessary as an acknowledgment. It became second nature to be generous with one another," adds Lub.

As we see from these real-life examples, cooperative currencies have a powerful benevolent impact not only on the economic health of users but also on their social functioning as well. Now let's look at how this could be applied on a global scale.

A PROPOSAL FOR A GLOBAL TRADE REFERENCE CURRENCY

A new nonnational currency has been designed both to provide a safety net to support the conventional monetary system and to mobilize global corporations toward a sustainable future. Such goals are most effectively accomplished not by regulation and legislative imperatives or moral prodding, but rather by providing a strong financial incentive in the right direction. A supranational cooperative currency would provide such an incentive.

Many precedents demonstrate that whenever attempts at regulation or moral persuasion run up against financial interests, the latter tends to win. The war against drugs is but one example. The Terra provides a solution that doesn't pit financial interests against human concerns—in other words, it is a real-world solution.

The Terra Trade Reference Currency (TRC) as it is known, is a cooperative currency proposal specifically designed to address three systemic economic issues: alleviating the critical problem of monetary instability, curtailing the booms and busts of the business cycle, and making long-term sustainability possible.

Given the financial upheaval we currently face and what all is at stake, this is a timely and exciting proposal.

The Current Context of the Global Monetary System

The Terra Trade Reference Currency initiative is designed to address several key issues that are global in nature and beyond the scope of a single nation's ability to remedy or repair. Although such concerns may seem like boring economic problems of little interest to the average person, they are, in fact, key issues that are impacting all of us daily, such as massive job losses and the disastrous suffering generated by financial and currency crises. Yet, there continues to be a lack of initiatives from key financial institutions, aggravated by a geopolitical stalemate of the past several decades and exacerbated by the present-day economic downturn in the United States.

If these key global issues are to be redressed in an effective, timely, and feasible manner, we need a response that reaches beyond local and national monetary strategies. Such a response must address the requirements and concerns of the most powerful decision makers of our world today—the multinational corporations—and take into consideration the realities of our present-day geopolitical climate and monetary system.

The TRC, with a unit of account called the Terra, is a supranational cooperative currency initiative intended to work in parallel with the current international monetary system to effectively address global issues. It is designed to create more stability and predictability in the financial and business sectors by providing a mechanism for contractual, payment, and planning purposes worldwide. This would be the first time since the gold standard days that a robust international standard of value, which is also inflation-resistant, would become available.

The TRC is specifically designed to counteract the booms and busts of the business cycle and to resolve the conflict between short-term financial interests and long-term sustainability. It would also act as a lifeboat for international trade if and when an international monetary crisis breaks out. The Terra would provide a safety net in support of the conventional money system. Note that the Terra does not require any new legislation or international agreements to become operational.

Practical Operations of the TRC

The following scenario and Figure 7.1 outline the key elements of the Terra mechanism, from the creation of Terras to their final cash-in. The numbers listed in parentheses in the following description correspond to the steps illustrated in the diagram in Figure 7.1.

1. The Terra Creation Process

1a. ***Excess Inventory Sale.*** The process whereby the Terra is created begins with the sale of some excess commodity inventory to the Terra Alliance by one of its backer-members (e.g., 1 million barrels of crude oil by an oil producer).

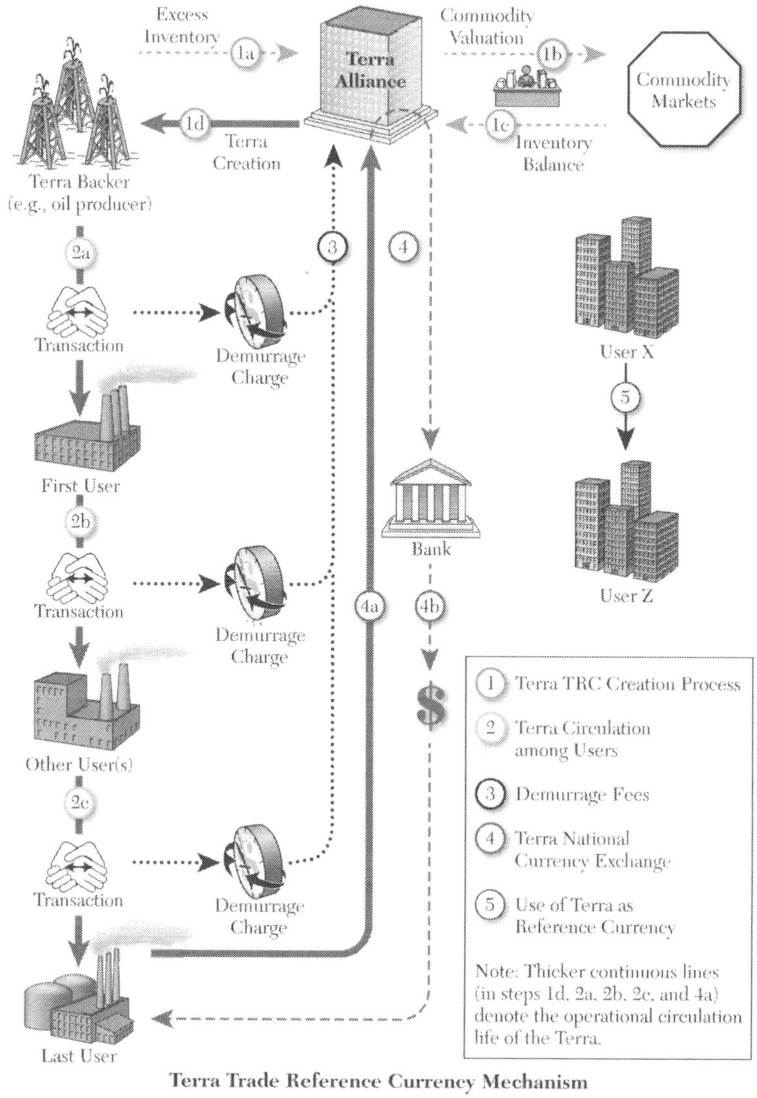

Figure 7.1 Terra Diagram.

1b. ***Commodity Valuation in Terras.*** The value of this sale of oil to the TRC Alliance (i.e., how many Terras the 1 million barrels of oil will be worth) is calculated at market prices. This is accomplished by determining the commodity prices at the time of the sale for both the inventory in question (in this case, oil) and the sum of each of the commodities in the Terra basket.

The formula used to calculate the commodity valuation in Terras is:

$$\frac{\textit{Commodity price per unit} \times \textit{number of units}}{\textit{Terra Unit Value}} = \textit{Terras created}$$

Let us assume in our example that the commodity price for a barrel of oil at the time of the sale is \$100. The Terra Unit Value, or the commodity prices for each of the items in the Terra Basket at the time of the sale (i.e., copper, grains, lead, one carbon credit, and oil), totals \$500. Let us further assume that 1 million barrels of oil are sold. Therefore, 200,000 Terras are created:

$$\frac{\textit{\$100 per barrel of crude oil} \times \textit{1 million barrels}}{\textit{\$500}} = \textit{200,000 Terras}$$

***1c.* Inventory Balance.** The Terra Alliance rebalances its portfolio to take into account the inclusion of the 1 million barrels of oil.

1d. Terra Creation **.**The Terra Alliance credits the oil producers' account with 200,000 Terras. (Note that all Terra currency movements in the diagram are denoted by the thicker continuous arrowed lines.)

2. Terra Circulation among Users

Once the Terra is created, it enters into and may remain in circulation for a period determined entirely by the users. For example:

2a. ***First User (User X).*** The oil producer decides to pay one of its suppliers, a German engineering firm, partially or completely in Terras for the construction of an offshore rig.

2b. ***Other User(s) (User Y).*** The German engineering firm, in turn, decides to purchase specialty steels from a Korean steel mill and to pay partially or completely in Terras. The Korean steel mill, in turn, uses the Terras to pay a mining company in Australia.

2c. ***Last User.*** Each Terra remains in circulation for as long as its users continue to use this currency, from one to an infinite number of transactions and without any particular date of expiration. The process comes to an end only when a particular user determines to cash in the Terra(s), in effect, becoming the last user.

3. Demurrage

Throughout the circulation life of each Terra, from its creation to its final cash-in, a demurrage fee of 3.5 percent to 4 percent per year is in effect. As seen previously, demurrage is a time-related charge on money. This demurrage fee acts like a parking fee, with the charge increasing the longer the parking space is retained. With Terras, this charge is based on how long a user holds the currency.

The demurrage fee serves three key functions: as an incentive to think long-term, as a circulation incentive, and as the way to cover the TRC's operational costs.

- ***Incentive for Long-Term Thinking.*** As explained in Chapter 4, a demurrage fee makes the long-term future more important than short-term. If the Terra is used to make decisions to allocate resources internationally, it would reprogram the users of the Terra toward long-term thinking. This would resolve the prevailing conflict between shareholders' short-term priorities and society's need for long-term planning.
- ***Terra Circulation Incentive.*** The Terra demurrage fee is designed as an incentive to keep the Terras circulating in a timely fashion from one user to another, since the demurrage fee increases the longer the Terra is held onto. The demurrage fee thus ensures the Terras' usage as a mechanism of exchange and not as a mechanism of savings.
- ***Terra Operational Cost Coverage.*** The Terra demurrage fee is calculated to cover the costs of the entire operation of the Terra mechanism (e.g., storage costs of the basket, administrative overhead, transaction costs in future markets). The demurrage fees for a particular Terra transaction can be calculated by the following formula:

(Terra Operation Costs/time unit) × (Terra holding period) × (Terras on account) = Demurrage Fee

Let us assume that the TRC's operation costs are evaluated at 3.65 percent per year, or 0.01 percent per day. Let us further assume that the German engineering firm receives 200,000 Terras from the oil producer and keeps these on account for a period of 10 days, prior to paying the Korean steel mill in transaction 2b in our diagram. Thus, the demurrage fee (represented by the dotted line identified with number 3 in Figure 7.1) in transaction 2b would be calculated as follows:

0.01% per day× 10 days× 200,000 Terras= 200 Terras

4. Terra Cash-In

The circulation and existence of a particular Terra come to an end when the last user decides to cash in its Terras, for example, for national currency to pay its taxes or payroll.

A transaction fee (proposed at 2 percent of the value of Terras cashed in) is charged at that point. This transaction fee serves two purposes:

- ***Terra Circulation.*** The transaction fee is designed as a secondary motivation to keep the Terras in circulation rather than cashing them in too readily, thus continuing the beneficial effects of the circulating Terras. In effect, the 2 percent transaction fee requires those in possession of Terras to consider that cashing in their Terras will cost the same as paying the demurrage fee for more than six months (assuming a demurrage of 3.65 percent per year). It is likely that the holder will be able to pay someone at least partially in Terras over the next six months, as most suppliers would rather be paid earlier than later.

- ***Cash-In Operational Costs.*** When the last user decides to cash in his or her Terras, the Terra Alliance sells the necessary volume of commodities from its basket to the commodity markets to obtain the necessary funds in conventional currency. The cash-in may take place directly with the Terra Alliance itself or, for example, through an intermediary bank, as in any foreign exchange transaction (4b).

5. Reference Currency

Once the Terra mechanism is operational and the advantages of using an inflation-resistant international standard are known, nothing impedes two entities (User X and User Z in the diagram), which may have no direct involvement in the Terra mechanism, from denominating contracts in Terras, even if the final settlement may happen in the corresponding value in conventional currency. The Terra, in this instance, functions purely as a trade reference currency, a reliable standard of value. This is similar to when two parties agreed on contracts denominated in gold during the gold standard days, even if neither party owned gold or had any involvement in gold mining or processing.

Chapter Eight

STRATEGIES FOR GOVERNMENTS

Money is the crowbar of power.

FRIEDRICH NIETZSCHE,
19th-century German philosopher

Trash was a nightmare problem in Curitiba, the capital of the southeastern state of Paraná, Brazil. There was a large slum population dwelling in shanty-towns, makeshift, improvised housing constructed from corrugated steel, cinder blocks, and whatever else was available.

"Back in 1989, the primary problem we faced was garbage in the favelas. We needed to avoid pollution in our streams and, of course, to protect the kids who were playing in what were very contaminated areas. The problem was that we had to have the garbage collected with trucks, but they couldn't get into the favelas because the pathways were too narrow and the terrain was very hilly," recalls Jaime Lerner, who was mayor at the time.

The issue was further compounded because the city simply did not have the funds to deal with the crisis. Raising the necessary money through conventional methods, such as requesting funding from the federal government, was not an option. Something else had to be done.

This dilemma facing governments at whatever level of authority is commonplace some three decades later. Even in better economic times, making the limited conventional currency stretch has always been troublesome. With tax revenues to fund programs and services dwindling today because of the harsher economic climate, everyone is feeling the pinch. National governments have had to slash programs, particularly in Europe, following a series of austerity mea sures to get spending under control.

Lerner, however, took stock of the resources on hand. There was an abundance of food, given the region's rich farmland, proximity to the sea, and subtropical climate. Additionally, there was an underutilized municipal bus system and people with a lot of time on their hands. Lerner, who was trained as an architect and consequently thought in terms of systems and their integration, had an idea!

It was a strategy that developed over time. Large metallic bins were placed on the streets at the edge of the favela neighborhoods. Lerner recalls, "We separated the trash into three unique components: one third, such as paper, glass, and cartons, was commercially recyclable; one third was biowaste (available to produce organic compost); and the other third was trash for the landfill. Those who collected and sorted the trash were given tokens to ride the local bus system."

Thousands of children responded by picking the neighborhoods clean. The children have taught their parents how to do it. Lerner noticed that to earn bus tokens, some slum dwellers even collected and sorted garbage along the highways, making it easier to get the waste picked up by trucks.

People made use of the tokens to travel downtown, often to find work. The bus tokens were soon accepted at local markets in exchange for food. The project expanded from there. In one three-year period, more than 100 schools traded 200 tons of garbage for 1.9 million notebooks. The paper-recycling component alone saved the equivalent of 1,200 trees—each day![1]

Eventually, more than 70 percent of Curitiban households became involved in the various programs. The 62 poorer neighborhoods alone exchanged 11,000 tons of garbage for nearly a million bus tokens and 1,200 tons of food. Other programs were created to finance the restoration of historical buildings, create green areas, and provide housing, all by methods that didn't create any financial burden on the municipality.

Thanks to Lerner and his innovative methods, Curitiba has made major strides in other social sectors, providing the city with some of the best quality-of-life indices in the world. Sixty to 70 percent of Curitiba's trash is recycled in situ, possibly the highest percentage in the world.

The experience gained, along with the lessons learned as mayor of the city of Curitiba, served Lerner well when he later was elected governor of the state of Paraná. The ideas and their implementation served as a blueprint on a larger scale.

Lerner adds, "When I was a governor, from 1994 to 1998 and again from 1998 to 2002, originally we wanted to avoid loans, as in the case of Argentina and the $800 million World Bank loan they took out to clean their bays. We decided that it's not only a question of money but also a question of mentality. It's not only a question of public works but also it's how to successfully stimulate a learning process. So we didn't have the money to clean our bays. So instead we made agreements with our fisherman. When they catch the fish, the fish belong to them. When the days weren't good for fishing, they catch garbage, we pay for the garbage with our tokens. The more garbage they fished, the cleaner the bay became; the cleaner the bay became, the more fish they could catch. It's a win-win solution."

Another major problem is street children. "These children were usually begging for money to feed their families. We tackled that problem by making an agreement with each family: We provided each of them with a monthly basket of food for as long as they kept their children in school."

The idea was to implement this program across all of the 399 municipalities of Paraná, which is home to over 10 million people.

"When we realized the low cost of monthly baskets of food, and how they helped those living in poverty by freeing up their limited resources to pay for other things, everybody got very excited. Instead of having to use all their money to buy food, they could now use the money in different ways and at the same time be sure that their kids were going to school," Lerner recalls.

Garbage that is money. When the fish aren't biting, the fishermen clean the bay instead. Photo credit: Instituto Jaime Lerner.

The many initiatives—environmental cleanup, city restoration, job creation, improved education, disease intervention, and hunger prevention—were each tackled with various cooperative currency systems. This all happened without having to raise taxes, redistribute wealth, issue bonds, rely on charity, or obtain loans from the federal government or organizations such as the World Bank and the International Monetary Fund (IMF). The improvements burdened no one. Everyone benefited.

Curitiba, along with the state of Paraná, discovered a means by which to match unmet needs with unused resources. In 1990, Curitiba was honored with the United Nations Environmental Program's (UNEP) highest environmental award.[2] Curitiba was awarded the Globe Sustainable City Award in 2010.[3] This award recognizes cities and municipalities around the world that excel in sustainable urban development.

None of the exceptional features of what has happened in Curitiba would have been possible without the various cooperative currency systems implemented by Jaime Lerner. Curitiba is the first city to have systematically used a "monetary ecosystem." It is therefore a practical demonstration of what becomes possible within less than one generation when one rethinks money. There have been several PhD studies dedicated to the innovations in city planning and public transport systems of Curitiba. What is surprising is that, not withstanding the availability of 25 years of data, no systemic economic study has been performed on Curitiba.

THE CIVIC: ECONOMIC STIMULUS WITHOUT DEBT

In the case of Curitiba, the results of using a cooperative currency in purely economic terms are worth noting. From 1975 to 1995, the GDP of the city increased by 75 percent more than the rest of the state of Paraná and by 48 percent more than Brazil's as a whole. The average Curitibano earned more than three times the country's minimum wage. If nontraditional monetary gains, such as the exchange of garbage for provisions, are taken into consideration, the real total income for residents was at least 30 percent higher still. The results in human terms—in the renewal of dignity and hope for a better future—are incalculable.[4]

This was accomplished by rethinking money, moving from a model of scarcity that the conventional system inadvertently encourages to one of prosperity with the use of smartly designed cooperative currencies.

Traditional economic stimulus is an effort by government to boost an ailing economy by pumping more money into it, usually by cutting taxes and by borrowing money. With these mea sures, it is hoped that liquidity in the system will increase, which in turn will lead to greater financial resilience, as there is now money for job creation and/or other programs. But this approach has serious negative repercussions: Both increase the national debt. Lately, the net effect has been a tightening of the proverbial belt with drastic austerity mea sures, such as slashing social programs. This has lead to massive civil unrest, particularly in Spain and Greece.

Richard A. Epstein, a senior fellow at the Hoover Institute writes, "Grim is the right word to describe the latest economic news from both the European Union and the United States. Throughout the European Union, austerity programs have failed both politically and economically. In Spain, unemployment rates have soared above 24 percent. The Dutch government is on the edge of collapse because of the popular and political unwillingness to accept the austerity program proposed by its conservative government. Romania is not far behind. Greece, Italy and Portugal remain in perilous condition.... On the American front, the decline of GDP growth to 2.2 percent rightly raises fears that our sputtering domestic recovery is just about over."[5]

There is a solution, as the events in Curitiba illustrate. Government, whether at a local, state, or regional level, can take its economic fate into its own hands and issue a cooperative currency. This cooperative medium of exchange, which can be customized to any given government's needs, is a currency called the *civic.* The key component of such a solution is that it provides a financial Keynesian stimulus with a fundamental and critical difference: It doesn't generate any additional debt.

Indeed, a Keynesian stimulus means that government steps in and launches projects that it funds through deficit spending. The government then borrows from the banking sector, going further and further into debt. This is because the government cannot issue itself the currency. In contrast, if the government launches the same types of projects but issues cooperative currencies to fund them and requires taxpayers to make a contribution payable only in that same currency, no debt is generated.

Furthermore, the process is more bottom-up than the usual top-down central government stimulus plans. It tends to be more successful since the cash injection can be very precisely applied. Residents and local government members clearly have a better insight into a community issue with all its nuances than does a central government bureaucracy. And since the currency's governance needs to be more transparent and easier to manage because of its size, there is less opportunity for fraud and misappropriation. In Chapter 11 the importance of governance issues are addressed.

HOW IT WORKS

A yearly contribution in civics would be requested of all town or city households by their local government authority. Residents would earn civics, which would be issued by the city, by participating in activities that contribute to the city's democratically agreed-upon goals and objectives. Agreement as to the nature of these tasks might be reached by canvassing neighborhoods door-to-door or by online voting. This unit of account could be one hour of time, valued at the same rate for everybody. So, for instance, if a city aspires to be greener and more eco-friendly, the activities could include growing food on terraces, rooftops, or vacant plots of land; taking responsibility for plants and trees in the neighborhood parks; or training people in city-based horticulture.

From a purely economic angle, if an annual tax of $1,000 can be replaced with 10 hours of civic activity per house hold, anyone earning less than $100 per hour should be interested in joining the system. Additionally, the civics system has the added benefit of allowing people to earn an income from civil activities.

Such an approach provides, in fact, a decentralized Keynesian stimulus at the city scale without creating new debt or incurring further costs to the government. Contrast this to what's happening now, as governments try to keep up the social system with the euro, which clearly isn't working.

There is no obligation to personally perform any of the tasks rewarded in civics. To begin, families with children, infirm, or individuals with special needs would be exempt. There would be two other ways of opting out of participation. The first could be by paying an extra amount in dollars as part of one's annual taxes (e.g., $1,000 for the example above). The second option for people not interested or without the time to personally perform any of the tasks would be to purchase civics via an online market, openly and transparently. People who earned more civics than they needed for their annual contribution could sell them in that market. The buyer of the civics could make the purchase in conventional money or as an exchange for any good or service acceptable to both parties.

The government's role should be to ensure that fake civics are not in circulation and that exchanges are transparent and fair. The government should not tie the value of the civic to the national currency. If the government wants the value of civics to rise relative to the national currency, the most effective way would be to require a bigger contribution payable only in civics and, accordingly, if it wanted the value to drop, it could require a smaller contribution to be paid in civics.

Furthermore, the process can be targeted to specific population segments and should be countercyclically tuned to local conditions. For instance, specific programs that pay in civics could be implemented for young people when their unemployment level is abnormally high, as is the case now in parts of Michigan and California, for example, or in Portugal, Ireland, Greece, and Spain in Europe.

The legitimacy of the civic completely depends on the legitimacy of the process by which the choices are made on the activities that can be awarded civics. Bottom-up democratic processes are critical to the genuine success of what is proposed here. This leads to the critical question of appropriate governance for such systems, as will be shown in Chapter 11.

NATIONAL CURRENCY CRISIS SOLUTION?

At the core of our current financial predicament is the issue that the banks aren't lending, and it's not because businesses in general aren't viable. Cooperative currencies, however, can remedy this cash crunch. In terms of a national crisis, a C3 currency, as explored in Chapter 7, could be used to take care of some of the commercial business currently conducted in national currencies. In a case for the eurozone, for example, countries like Spain, Portugal, Greece, or whichever is in trouble could continue using the euro currency for everything having to do with international activities: tourism, shipping, importing, and exporting. Their respective governments could, in addition, create a new version of the peseta, escudo, or drachma to be used for internal social and environmental businesses. This neonational currency essentially could be spent into existence by the government itself, for specific purposes, without incurring debt in the financial system.

Thomas Mayer, former chief economist for Deutsche Bank, made in July 2012 a proposal for Greece that is surprisingly radical for his background. It acknowledges that the great majority of Greeks don't want to leave the euro and that they don't agree with the extreme austerity program imposed in Greece.

Mayer's solution is called the *geuro,*a second currency that would circulate in Greece in parallel with the euro and, Mayer says, "solve all of Greece's problems." For the first time, a mainstream economist, working for a major bank, is endorsing the idea of a complementary currency!

The geuro would be used immediately in most domestic transactions. For the purchase of essential imports, geuros would have to be exchanged for euros, "most likely at a hefty discount of 50 percent or more. Since an increasing number of domestic goods, services, and wages would be paid in devalued geuros, the export sector could reduce its prices in euros and regain competitiveness against foreign suppliers."[6] The main difference between the geuro and the civic is that the geuro would be issued as a central government IOU and the civic would be issued by cities or regions without generating additional debt. But the civic would otherwise provide a mechanism to provide the same benefits as the geuro in terms of gradually rebuilding the competitiveness of Greek labor.

Edgar Kampers, director of the Dutch Qoin ,has been working in the domains of sustainable economic development and cooperative community currencies since 1998. He remarks, "Current legal tender currency systems are very strong in developing high profits and building a globalized society. They have proved less effective, however, in supporting regional economic development, stimulating ecological policy goals and behaviors, and encouraging an active civil society. The current economic and financial crisis faced by many regions in Europe calls for new arrangements for communities to remain or become resilient."[7]

In the province of Limburg in Belgium, for example, there was a waste cooperative between all the municipalities in the province, and this organization calculated the difference in price between new kinds of campaigns. "What they found was if they do a traditional awareness campaign, then they have a response of less than 2 percent. If they do the same thing with the same costs per person in that municipality, and they use a cooperative currency system, then they have a response of almost 40 percent. That's 20 times better! It's the only successful way of changing the behavior of the people on a limited municipal bud get. And coupled with the information society ,which makes computing, smart phones, tablets, and this type of technology so cheap and easy, it is now available everywhere," Kampers added.

Lisa Conlan, CEO of TimeBanking USA, notes, "Given the current credit crunch that states and municipalities are experiencing, there is no reason why a wide variety of services could not be paid for in a local currency, such as time dollars. There's snow removal, garbage collection, even community gardening."[8]

A rich tapestry of initiatives comes to light with the understanding that unused resources can be linked with a whole host of unmet needs. Such exchanges provide solutions for cash-strapped charities and government bodies at different social levels, resulting in huge economic and social benefits.

TOREKES

Ghent, Belgium. Residents pay for their plots of land exclusively in the town's local currency—torekes. Photo credit: Stefanie Overbeck.

Rabot is an immigrant district in Ghent, the fourth-largest city in Belgium. Rabot is the poorest community in the entire region. Most of the population lives in low-income apartment buildings in one of the most densely populated localities in Europe. Well over 20 languages are spoken, with Turkish the most prominent. Rabot suffers from high unemployment and the usual symptoms of urban decay, which have profound effects, both physical and metaphysical.

In 2009, one of the authors was asked what could be done to improve the area. The starting point was a survey to find out what residents wanted for themselves. Many, particularly those living in high-rise apartment buildings, wanted to have access to a few square yards of land for gardening, growing vegetables, and flowers.

The city owned land in the neighborhood, including a site where an old factory had been demolished and the land was left abandoned. Rather than leaving it derelict, the land was divided into plots measuring four square meters each, and these plots became available to rent on an annual basis, at the cost of 150 *torekes,*a newly introduced local cooperative currency. Torekes are available only in paper form for this pi lot project, on the request of the participants themselves. One of the reasons is simplicity.

To earn torekes (Flemish for "little towers," emblematic of the neighborhood), a long list of urban agricultural improvements and beautification activities could be done. Participants were rewarded for activities such as putting flower boxes on the windowsills facing the street, planting and maintaining sidewalk flower containers, placing "no advertising" labels on mailboxes to reduce junk mail, or helping to clean up a neighborhood sports field after a game. In all, 526 different activities were performed.

Wouter Van Thillo, who has been managing the project since 2011, describes the series of events that ensued: "In addition to paying for the rent of the neighborhood gardens, arrangements were also made with the local shops to accept torekes for specific goods that the city wants to encourage, such as low-energy lamps and other green products, or fresh seasonal vegetables. Participating shops can either use the torekes for their own participation in local activities or simply get them reimbursed for euros at the city office. Torekes can also be exchanged for public transport tickets and seats for cultural events or movies. All activities with very low marginal costs for additional participation, such as buses and cinema, are ideal for this scheme.

"We've also found, as this program has gained traction, that well-to-do residents from other parts of Ghent are now participating because it's fun."

This simple paper currency with no demurrage is considered to be a major success. Not a week goes by without visitors from other towns and cities across Europe stopping by to learn from this example. What this experiment has proven is that it produces a much broader social impact with the same euro bud get, providing effective leverage in using conventional currency. Specifically, even at this very early pi lot scale, conservatively three times more activities have been produced with the same amount of euros. If the implementation was fully scaled up, it has been estimated that this multiplier could potentially rise to a factor of 20.

These two colorful models of municipal and state governments finding inventive ways to resolve issues in their respective communities stimulate questions on how these methods can be expanded and improved. For the foreseeable future, government at all levels will continue to grapple with serious bud get shortfalls, thus obliging cuts not only in discretionary programs but also to critical services and benefits. A city-issued currency such as torekes makes it possible to multiply the results achieved with a given bud get in conventional money.

EDUCATION

The cost of education is a burden usually carried at the federal level of government. The seed of a provocative response to bud get concerns was planted over a decade ago in Brazil, when the education fund had grown to more than $1 billion. Conventional solutions—such as the very successful GI Bill approach of the United States that funded education for veterans after World War II—would provide student loans directly to individuals for their own education. Another idea was crafted by one of the authors in cooperation with Gilson Schwartz, an economics professor at the University of São Paolo, Brazil.

The framework of what has since matured into the Creative Currencies Project was to leverage educational funding by using a multiplier that would allow many more students to benefit from the same amount of money with some surprising results.

The first model was the *saber* (meaning "to know" in Spanish and Portuguese), a specialized education paper currency allocated to primary and secondary schools, particularly in economically depressed areas. This currency is first given to the youngest students (7-year-olds), who transfer it to older students (for instance, 10-year-olds) in return for tutoring help with their schoolwork. The 10-year-olds can then do the same thing with 12-year-olds in compensation for the hours spent mentoring, and the latter with 15-year-olds and so on. At the end of this learning chain, the sabers would go to 17-year-olds, who could use them to pay for part or all of their university tuition.

The saber offers a number of advantages. It circulates among students at different grade levels, the last of whom go to college; it promotes better education through learning by teaching; it offers a better chance for students to go to a university; and it allows educational funds to be used for many more students than if they were used for just one scholarship, thereby creating a learning multiplier. For instance, the university would be able to exchange sabers for conventional money through the education fund but at a discount of, say, 50 percent. This makes sense because most of the costs at a university are fixed and, similar to empty seats on an airplane, the marginal expense of an additional student has little impact on those costs.

The total learning multiplier per dollar for the education bud get allocated to this project would, therefore, be a factor of 10 (five times for the exchanges among students of different ages, multiplied by two for the arrangement between the education fund and the university, which discounts the saber by 50 percent). This 10-fold learning multiplier was calculated in terms of the financial effect of $1 billion spent through the saber system, delivering a total of $10 billion worth of education.

Another factor, learning retention rates, further increases this figure. Several decades of research have shown that learning retention depends less on the person or the topics involved than on the delivery system. What is striking is that our traditional educational system commonly uses the two least effective methods available: lecturing and reading, through which, respectively, only 5 and 10 percent of what is taught is retained. At the other end of the spectrum, an impressive 90 percent retention rate applies to whatever one teaches others!

So when the learning retention rates increase from 5 to 10 percent (normal educational methods) to 90 percent (teaching others) is factored in, another 10-fold multiplier effect develops. In other words, spending $1 billion through the saber system could roughly be estimated to generate as much as $100 billion worth of retained learning, in comparison to the conventional scholarship grants approach.

The saber program could also be expanded beyond the conventional classroom: eight-year-olds could teach their newly learned reading and writing skills to grandparents who are illiterate; students could help the elderly or handicapped by reading to them or recording their oral histories. These programs would encourage intergenerational relationships and further learning, not to mention creating extra assistance for the elderly without burdening governmental bud gets.

Demurrage can be used to control the balance each year between the number of students wanting university seats and the availability of seats. A demurrage fee would be applied to encourage students to use sabers for the year that is printed on the saber itself, for example, 2014. If the sabers were not used to pay for tuition before or during that year, they could be exchanged for sabers of the following year—the year 2015—but with a 25 percent penalty. This creates a strong incentive to use sabers on or before their deadline.

"While the project hasn't been adopted on a federal level in Brazil due to the vicissitudes of Brazilian politics, we have created instead two other currencies, *talents* for those involved in the practical application of knowledge, and *alegres*for activities that bring joy or make the world a more beautiful place," adds

Schwartz. Both use the same principles as the saber, in which young people teach other young pupils.

He continues, "We are now working with the Department of Finance and the police. Goods that have been seized because of unpaid taxes or contraband will be available for purchase by our students using any of the three creative currencies."

WISPOS

Back again in the city of Ghent, Belgium, the local educational authority has been challenged by a variety of issues associated with the education of a large immigrant population, many of whom are illegal. Teachers report students having serious deficits in the rudiments of several subjects, the worst being French and mathematics. Falling behind academically undoubtedly contributes to being further marginalized in the future. Something creative to break the cycle had to be found.

Jeffrey Freed, author of *Right-Brained Children in a Left-Brained World,* a best seller and a classic in the field of education, has identified the general learning styles of the Millennials, children born since the turn of this century. "These kids have grown up in a world very different than previous generations. Just think about the impact of technology alone. Many tend to be more right-brained dominant in that they think in pictures. They process information in a nonlinear way. So in doing a math problem, for instance, they can get the right answer, but they can't retrace their steps. They get bored and lethargic easily. The *drill and kill*method of teaching just won't work. What succeeds is if they are taught in short time spurts. They need to understand the context of what is being taught, so learning in field trips and through other rich experiences is the way to go."[9]

With this insight, one of the authors and Igor Byttebier, a resident of Ghent and a consultant to the innovative program, worked with the teachers of the Wispelberg School, one of Ghent's high schools, to design an hour-long program with a class of 12-year-olds that takes place every two weeks. Kids from the senior class participate, too, by assisting the teachers. They designed games around learning so it would be fun and provide novelty. To make it even more interesting, they divided the class into teams that would compete against each other for the entire academic year. *Wispos,* a token currency, was awarded for correct answers and debited for incorrect ones.

Igor Byttebier explains, "French is a difficult language as the pronunciation is so subtle to the ear. So we devised a game called twister. There's a large checkerboard on the floor in bright colors, five squares by five squares, 25 squares in all. The differently conjugated verb endings are placed in different squares. The teacher shouts out a phrase, and the team rep has to jump onto the right square. If correct, two wispos are given; if wrong, one is forfeited."[10]

On average, between 6 and 22 wispo tokens were won by each of the students, who could then purchase fruit and other healthy food items from the school store.

The project has been running for two years now, and, given its success, a second high school, KTA, has adopted the program. "When tested, the students scored 20 percent better than before as a result of the games, and in mathematics, the improvement in test scores was, on average, 10 percent.[11] Just as important is the interaction between students of first and last years, combined with physical and intellectual activity. This is an enormous help to their social integration and self-esteem," adds Byttebier.

Although this project is in its very early stages, it does serve to illustrate that linking an unused resource with an unmet need and introducing a new currency can bring about profound changes.

There are several key takeaways from all these examples. Besides cooperative money's capacity to engender greater collaboration and mutual support while providing cash-strapped governmental agencies with a way to leverage their tight resources, there is an even more powerful motivator at work. Traditionally, efforts to bring about a change in behavior have focused on increasing taxation (for example, increasing taxes on tobacco products to discourage smoking) and regulation, which tries to outlaw certain behaviors (such as Prohibition tried to do to alcohol consumption during the 1920s in the United States). The incentive stimulated by cooperative currencies, however, uses a carrot rather than the proverbial stick.

And perhaps more important, it demonstrates that it is possible to create economic stimulus without the negative effect of increasing debt.

Chapter Nine

STRATEGIES FOR NGOs

Money does not have to be legal tender. It can be what one might call "common tender," i.e. commonly accepted in payment of debt without coercion through legal means.

RICHARD TIMBERLAKE, former Professor Emeritus of Economics at the University of Georgia[1]

Within the space of less than 10 years, the small rural village of Blaengarw, South Wales, with high unemployment and a bleak future, totally transformed itself. David Pugh, a local TimeBanking manager who oversees the currency explains, "On the Welsh index of material deprivation, we were 128th on the scale of 1,800 communities with one being the worst in the country. We've now progressed to 735th in just a decade. So we've climbed more than 600 places. These statistics are based on such things as antisocial behavior, crime, and of course, unemployment—in fact, there is a whole array of indices. We've really come a very long way."[2]

The residents of Blaengarw worked their way out of the all-too-common story of social blight and decay by making an assessment of their unused resources and their unmet needs and, in this case, linking these with a time-banking currency coordinated by a regional and local NGO.

This former mining village of some 1,895 souls was trapped in a postindustrial depression, exacerbated perhaps by its remoteness in the Garw River valley. Although just physically 30 miles from Cardiff, the capital, it might as well be 3,000 miles away, as there is only one road in and out of town and a sporadic public bus service. David Pugh recalls, "The last pit closed in our village in December 1985. We were employing 7,000 men in the four pits in its heyday. Eighty percent of the local population was involved in mining in some fashion. So it was a disaster when all the mines closed down. Deprivation started setting in, as there was no formal employment replacing the mine. People made do with being on the dole[public assistance] or whatever casual work they could find. There wasn't much, though. Furthermore, many people couldn't work because they were disabled through coal dust inhalation and mining accidents. Many were physically incapable of doing any other work. We had to rebuild our village from there—from little or nothing."[3]

Becky Booth is program coordinator and co-founder of Spice, which is part of the Wales Institute for Community Currencies. Spice fosters 40 time currencies in Wales and 12 in En gland. Booth says, "My research has been around postdisaster recovery and looking at the way the agencies that came into disaster situations work through the local community. My prime interest was around empowerment, participation, social management, and really looking at the role of NGOs in that context. I discovered that TimeBanking, along with other designs, is a very simple tool to enable the people to be genuinely involved in a totally different way with NGOs and public services."[4]

Activities are centered around the town's 100-year-old Miners' Welfare Hall. The local activities are run by a community nonprofit or ganization, Creation Development Trust, which employs two workers to oversee the TimeBanking. For each hour of service given to the community, a credit of one hour is exchanged. In the first year, 150 people took part; there are now over 1,000 members and 30 groups; 15 new social enterprises have been established, and new learning opportunities have been created. Participants contribute 60,000 hours of service per year to their community. The hall has an average attendance of 600 visits per week. Entry to events is paid in time money or in conventional money: A two-hour bingo night or movie costs two time credits, and a three-hour cultural performance is valued at three time credits.[5]

The sculpture is a project completed by Blaengarw time credit members. Photo credit: Spice network.

People learn to cook healthy meals in the community food studio and serve it in the café, which prides itself on offering food grown locally in community and individual gardens.

Besides the economic benefits that are cultivated through local currencies, people interact in new ways, creating stronger ties between themselves and their community, transforming crime rates, antisocial behavior, and the general down- and-out demeanor of the place.

CIVICS AND NONPROFITS

Through the lens of cooperative currencies, it becomes evident that there is a new and empowered role for NGOs and nonprofits. These entities traditionally are strapped for resources and often find themselves in vigorous competition with each other for a very limited pot of money and support. Consequently, large swaths of time are spent trying to raise capital, while everybody would really prefer to focus on the organization's core mission. Salaries are usually not competitive in comparison with the commercial sector, which can make hiring and keeping the right people problematic.

Interestingly, in a society with a dual currency system in place, nonprofits not only can play a key role, but also gain access to many more financial resources.

The example of the Civic and its emergent role in government was explored in the last chapter. Such systems provide opportunities for NGOs by playing the same role in the cooperative economy that corporations play in the conventional economy: initiating projects, organiz ing activities, and coordinating and motivating people. Envision also a specially created new type of nonprofit that would be in charge of auditing all the other nonprofits, ensuring transparency and trust in the system. It would take on the role that auditing firms play in the competitive economy, and its reports would be published on the city's Web site. The benefits to nonprofits would be multiple: a powerful new way to reach their objectives, a big increase in their volunteer base, and the opportunity to pay their staff partially in civics.

This generic model can be customized to fit the specific objectives and needs of any given NGO or nonprofit organization.

FREE CLINICS AND ITHACA HOURS

Health care is a critical issue in the United States. Approximately one in four adults do not have health care insurance coverage. Paul Glover, creator of the community currency Ithaca HOURS, offers innovative solutions to a wide variety of issues, including most recently health care. It all started back in 1991, with a local paper currency experiment in his hometown of Ithaca, best known for its Ivy League school Cornell University, in upstate New York. Initially, the primary focus of this cooperative currency system was to address underemployment among the townspeople by connecting them to one another in a skills directory.

Ithaca HOURS is a paper currency that comes in six denominations. Each Ithaca HOUR is worth one hour of basic labor. Thousands of individuals and over 500 businesses have earned and spent HOURS. They have made millions of dollars worth of trades with HOURS, representing hundreds of job equivalents at $20,000 each. Businesses accepting the local currency include the Ithaca Health Alliance, Cayuga Medical Center, Alternatives Federal Credit Union, the public library, many local farmers, movie theaters, restaurants, healers, plumbers, carpenters, electricians, and landlords.

Paul Glover comments, "Ithaca HOURS is local tender rather than legal tender, backed by real people, real labor, skills, time, and tools. Acceptance of the currency is voluntary, and it is interest-free. These are two prime differences between national and local money. Approximately 11 percent of HOURS are issued as grants to community organizations. Over 100 nonprofits have received grants in HOURS. Five percent of HOURS may be issued to the system itself, primarily paying for printing HOURS. Loans of HOURS are made to local businesses, with no interest charged. These loans have ranged from $50 to $30,000 in value."[6]

A half hour denomination of the Ithaca HOURS. Notice the logo "In Ithaca We Trust."

At the height of Ithaca HOURS' popularity, some 80 communities around the United States conducted their affairs partly with local currency. Those that thrived did so by hiring a full-time networker to facilitate circulation.

Against this backdrop and many years of experience, Glover's latest initiative is the Patch Adams Free Clinic in Philadelphia. The American physician Hunter Doherty "Patch" Adams is involved in the project, which uses humor and play to heal people.

His life story was the basis of the popular 1998 movie *Patch Adams,* starring Robin Williams. Since the 1990s, Adams has endorsed the Ithaca Health Alliance (IHA), founded by Glover as the Ithaca Health Fund (IHF). The Philadelphia clinic is the first clinic beyond Adams's Gesundheit Institute in rural West Virginia to bear his name. The clinic will locate in a low-income neighborhood that has 250,000 uninsured residents. Unemployment and crime rates are high. Remarkably, this clinic will be member-owned and operated.

Glover explains, "The clinic will provide community-based health care that is genuinely nonprofit, preventive, humane, and, in the spirit of Patch Adams, fun. It is a refuge for doctors and nurses who want time to heal patients. It is a refuge for patients who want to be treated with dignity. For a small annual fee, members will own this clinic, gaining diagnosis and referral, dentistry, chronic and urgent care, counseling, pediatrics, birthing, hospice care, massage, family planning, chiropractic, acupuncture, and other therapies. "More than a health facility, the clinic is an economic development model that solves several urban problems. Existing medical facilities are overcrowded and underfunded. Suffering is untended, both mental and physical. Infectious disease rates are high."[7]

Glover sees this clinic as a cornerstone of a healthy community and an economic engine to drive the area back to financial viability.

The clinic will be created using the earthship model of constructing passive solar buildings from used materials, in this case, discarded tires filled with earth. Community gardens around the buildings will grow food for the clinic.

"Expenses are kept low by relying least on U.S. dollars. To the maximum possible, we rely on the gift economy, barter, and credit systems such as Time Dollars and HOURS ('MediCash'). Staff members are primarily volunteers: professionals, students, religious congregants, neighbors, and members. Membership may be paid with labor to maintain the facility and its grounds. Both volunteers and staff may be rewarded with Philadelphia MediCash, (HOURS) gift certificates, health care, sweat equity credits, college course credit, and scholarships. Barter agreements will also meet personal needs," he adds.[8]

FIVE BILLION DO NOT HAVE ACCESS TO THE INTERNET

Inspired by the Curitiban example, a young American entrepreneur from Los Angeles, Kosta Grammatis, has conceived of a new currency that links community service in developing countries with donated time on the Internet.

"Our nonprofit, A Human Right,[9] is building a bandwidth bank where unused satellite, cellular, and fixed-wired Internet access that is donated by telecommunications companies will be put to work for social and humanitarian causes. Access to the Internet is a luxury in many countries. Currently, 5 billion people do not have access to the Internet. Although we aim to give everyone the opportunity to get online, there are many ways to go about doing this in a way that honors the access and ensures its sustainability," says Grammatis.[10]

Kosta Grammatis with the Echostar 16 communications satellite at Loral headquarters in Palo Alto, California. Photo credit: A Human Right.

He explains that by getting involved in community projects such as garbage collection and a variety of renovation projects, people can earn a local currency that, in turn, is good for Internet access. As a *Time* magazine feature noted: "One of the surest signs that you're in a developing country is the trash beneath your feet, which has less to do with bad habits than the fact that arranging garbage pickup and disposal is a low and expensive priority for a poor government."

Grammatis adds, "Users and their contribution to their community will be tracked. Solid metrics will gauge the direct impact of community service (one ton of trash gathered for 2,000 hours of Internet) and also the social impact of Internet access (2,000 hours of Internet were used to address the long laundry list of tasks needed to be undertaken in their neighborhood)."[11]

FUREAI KIPPU

At his retirement in 1991, Tsutomu Hotta, a highly respected former judge in Japan's Supreme Court and minister of justice, decided to focus his energies on the growing issue of elderly care in Japan. Japan has the fastest-aging population in the world. For this purpose, he created the Sawayaka Fukushi (Sawayaka Welfare) Center, which later became Sawayaka Fukushi Institute. Hotta's idea was to entice 12 million volunteers with the *fureai kippu* ("caring relationship tickets"), which were officially launched at that point.

The catalyzing event was a powerful earthquake that hit the Kobe area in January 1995. The capacity of the Japanese government to intervene and assist during an event of this scale was clearly overstretched. Consequently, a grassroots volunteer movement sprang up to provide help with the wide range of needs that arose during this crisis. Hotta started two significant initiatives. First, he became one of the key lobbyists for introducing the first legislation for nonprofit organizations in Japan. This lobbying was successful, and new legislation was enacted in 1998.

He also was instrumental in launching a major symposium that took place in September 1995 in Osaka for the promotion of volunteer organizations, focusing on time-based cooperative currencies. The fureai kippu currency and movement came out of this meeting.

Rui Izumi, an associate professor at the Senshu University School of Economics in Tokyo, points to government support as a major contributor to the growth in cooperative currencies: "The central government and many local governments are supporting local currencies in positive ways. For example, they have given financial support to some organizations, and[both] the Minister of Economy, Trade and Industry and the president of the Bank of Japan have made several encouraging remarks publicly about these systems."[12]

A former minister for economy and industrial policies described government support for complementary currencies in surprising terms: "The use of cooperative currencies can bring an end to the long-lasting deflation of the Japanese economy by supplying additional monies of various types at the local level."[13]

Government-sponsored projects were implemented in various communities of very different scales, ranging from small villages to entire prefectures (roughly equivalent to a U.S. county) and involving millions of people. All of them were designed to link unused resources with unmet needs within neighborhoods, districts, and networks. These trials were initially run for a period of three years or so, and the results were carefully observed. The purpose for this massive investment in complementary currency experiments, estimated to be well over $10 million per year, was and still is to fully understand what works best and under what circumstances.

The fureai kippu system provides elderly or handicapped people with any service not covered by the official national health care program. Its units are accounted for in hours of service. Different kinds of services have different valuations—for example, bathing an elderly person is given a higher hourly rate than shopping for an elderly person. In what amounts to a health care time-savings account, caregivers who provide for the elderly in the fureai kippu system accumulate credits and may draw on such credits in a variety of ways. They may use these credits themselves if they are ill, or they may elect to electronically transfer part or all of their fureai kippu credits to parents or relatives who require care and may live in another part of the country. Electronic clearing houses perform these credit transfers. Such options ensure that ever more people are cared for.

The elderly themselves prefer the services offered by these caregivers to those paid in conventional yen currency because the relationship is different—it is more personal on both sides. Caregivers themselves often perceive the elder recipients as surrogates for their own parents.

An estimated 387 fureai kippu systems are now operational throughout Japan.[14] The economic savings are substantial. As in the case of Curitiba, there is no need to raise taxes or divert funds from other programs. The human support network it creates makes it possible for the elderly to stay in their own homes longer or return home sooner after a medical intervention. The human interaction involved, along with the greater sense of community that is engendered, benefits all.

The city of Sankt Gallen, Switzerland, is the first municipality to implement a Japanese-style fureai kippu outside of Japan. During the feasibility study for this project, it turned out that only one significant change needed to be made to the Japanese model. Citizens insisted that the city would have to guarantee that services would be provided in a different configuration if the project failed in its current iteration. The city provided that guarantee and the system is now becoming operational.

EMERGENCY RELIEF CURRENCY

Hurricane Katrina, which destroyed the U.S. Gulf Coast, China's Sichuan Province 7.8 earthquake, the devastating effects of the flooding of the Mississippi River hinterland, and the nuclear meltdown of the reactor in Japan have provided enough opportunities to learn how to better address the plight of displaced people and their communities in extreme circumstances. This usually involves a constellation of NGOs and other government agencies.

Meeting villagers in their new home, an emergency shelter, after the Yogyakarta Earthquake of 2006 (Stephen DeMeulenaere, second from left). The cooperative currency implementation project continued, although many villagers lost their homes in the earthquake. Photo credit: Stephen DeMeulenaere.

The following idea was originated by the Social Trade Or ganization (STRO), to which Stephen DeMeulenaere was one of the contributors,[15] and provides the framework for a local currency that would help manage community resources more effectively during the reconsolidation phase and sustain the community once volunteers and aid organizations have left. Called the BONUS, it is a local voucher, an emergency cooperative currency designed to maximize the efficacy and productivity of relief funds by encouraging money to remain in the local economy, whose revitalization is essential for recovery. Ordinarily, with typical disaster relief programs, funds flow from donors to the local NGOs and eventually into the hands of individuals and businesses. Goods and services, however, are inevitably purchased from nonlocal sources, reversing the flow of money back out of the community. Eventually, almost all of the money leaves the area, abandoning the local NGOs to search for longer-term funding.

The BONUS strategy attempts to counteract this cycle by introducing a local voucher currency that can be used only within the community. In this system, national money is used for resources that absolutely must be purchased from outside suppliers, and everything else is purchased in the local currency. Each voucher credit is backed by a unit of national money, which allows the exchange of local currency back into national currency at any time, thus increasing the acceptance of and confidence in this currency as a valid medium of exchange. Ideally, the money would be used in the form of extremely low or zero percent interest loans payable in local currency, further increasing the ac ceptance of voucher money by individuals and businesses.

The effect of the BONUS program is, in essence, very similar to the effects of the saber, only in this instance instead of a learning multiplier, there is a "reconstruction multiplier," dramatically increasing the positive impact that donors or implementing organizations have in a disaster relief situation.

Besides increasing employment, economic activity, and local access to goods and services, emergency currencies also have the potential to reduce the amount of fraud, which is endemic in cases of crisis and common in many disaster relief situations. For example, the Government Accountability Office (GAO) estimates that 16 percent of FEMA's assistance for housing and emergency provisions in the Katrina aftermath was misspent, leading to a total loss of between $600 million and $1.4 billion to fraud. One man in Texas actually used FEMA money to buy a diamond ring worth over $3,700.[16] By issuing local voucher currency, the likelihood of money being spent fraudulently is significantly reduced, as goods and services can be purchased only from known vendors within the local economy.

Although the BONUS system does not explicitly endorse a demurrage for its currencies, it is suggested that any emergency relief currency carry a small demurrage fee to promote its continuing circulation, as well as to counteract the hoarding mentality that is all too common in the aftermath of large-scale disasters.

Stephen DeMeulenaere comments, "This blueprint was used very successfully by the French agency Triangle, using my design for a simplified revolving microfinance circle in Aceh, Sumatra, in Indonesia following the 2004 tsunami. And emergency currencies were used in the recent Haiti disaster."[17]

Perhaps Edgar Cahn, founder of TimeBanking, puts it best. Reflecting on the power of cooperative currencies to create community, no matter if they're organized by a business, NGO, or government, he commented, "Rebuilding community takes creating organic networks of trust, reciprocity, and engagement. Sustaining that is vital. A way to bring energy and vitality to that effort would be for a gathering to ask, 'What kind of memories would I like my child to have about growing up in this neighborhood? What are the stories we would like them to tell their children and friends about something memorable they did growing up in that particular place?' Suppose they could say, 'We had a TimeBank or cooperative currency that helped veterans' families and made sure that no third-grader went on to fourth grade without being at a third-grade reading level and having a buddy or mentor as they passed to fourth grade.' Suppose it was a tree-planting campaign as a way of reducing the carbon footprint. Why not have a brainstorming session to create place-based memories?

"Set up a TimeBank Rotating Loan Club wherever anyone who has a cause, a dream, a vision of what they would like to change or what they would like to see happen could get a time commitment of 90 days to make that happen. Like Rotating Loan Clubs, everyone would have a chance to do that: I'll help with your cause for 90 days if you will help with mine. Imagine the possibilities."[18]

PART THREE

RETHINKING MONEY

In the process of rethinking money, mistakes and accidents have occurred, some by design, some by happenstance. Whatever the causes, there have been some dire consequences. Individuals who have questioned the orthodoxy of modern-day money have, for the most part, been marginalized and ridiculed. Extraordinary successes that generated unprecedented prosperity, such as the local currencies that sprang up in Europe during the austere years between the two world wars, were dismantled. In more recent history, cooperative currencies have failed due to ignorance of the participants themselves, as they lack awareness of the hidden dynamics of money.

So what can be learned from the past so that we are not obliged to keep repeating our mistakes in the future? And what would a truly cooperative society, which has not existed since the dawning of the Modern Age, look like? In the following chapters, we will explore this available future that stands in such stark contrast to our world today.

Success, in the words of Winston Churchill, "consists of going from failure to failure without loss of enthusiasm." The greatest barriers to success so far have been the fear of failure and the failure to learn from mistakes.

Chapter Ten

TRUTH AND CONSEQUENCES

Lessons Learned

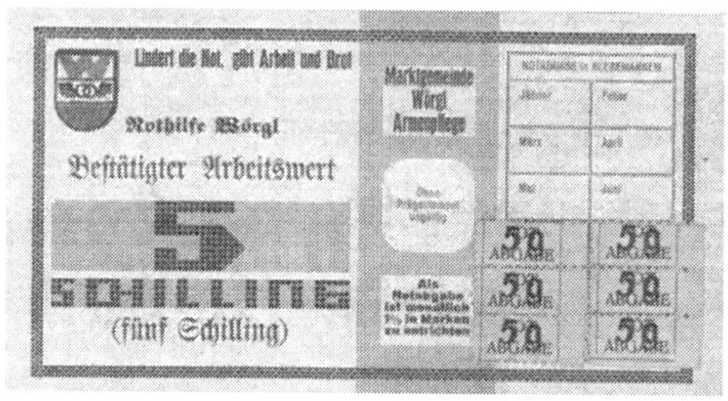

In dreams begin responsibility.[1]

WILLIAM BUTLER YEAT,
20th-century Irish poet and playwright

It was hard to contain the emotions that were surprisingly welling up inside while I was standing on the bridge in the small Tyrolean village of Wörgl. The bridge was so different from how it had been described in various books and articles. It seemed in real life more diminutive, plainer, and definitely shorter, yet its impact was unexpectedly overwhelming. Back in the dreary days of the 1930s Great Depression, this nondescript yet iconic overpass symbolized the dreams of full employment and a decent standard of living for all. Scholars, government officials, and thousands of others traveled to this Austrian community to personally witness and learn from the miracle of Wörgl. Today, the town has little significance, noted mostly for its railway junction connecting the line from Innsbruck to Munich with the inner-Austrian line to Salzburg. A small museum run by volunteers bears homage to Wörgl's short-lived chapter in monetary history.

Here, the black- and-white photos of Wörgl's long-departed citizens going about their daily lives seem strikingly ordinary, given the backdrop of this extraordinary moment in time. To appreciate the full panorama of what happened in German-speaking Europe in the years between the two world wars, besides the earlier example of the WIR, a look at Wörgl and the Wära provide some important insights.

Mostly forgotten today is that the large number of cooperative currencies arose in the aftermath of the German hyperinflation of the 1920s, when the Reichsmark, the German currency at the time, became worthless. Similarly, there was an explosion of local currencies in both Western Europe and North America following the economic crash of 1929 and, more recently, in Argentina, following the collapse of its national currency in 2001. And now, at present, there is a resurgence of cooperative currencies and other innovations as the shadow of recession looms, but the dire consequences and tough lessons from these experiences seem to have lapsed from memory.

Back in the day when Michael Untergugenberger was elected mayor of Wörgl, in 1931, some 30 percent of the workforce was unemployed, leaving 200 families absolutely penniless. The mayor-with-the-long-name, as the renowned U.S. economist Irving Fisher from Yale would call him, was familiar with Silvio Gesell's work. A German economist and merchant, Gesell's conceptual framework for demurrage and for other theories made him, some argue, the grandfather of modern-day cooperative currencies. His monetary designs are often referred to as *freigelt,* or "free money" in English.

The mayor decided to put Gesell's ideas to the test, as there was much to be done around the town and many willing and able-bodied folks looking for work. The rub was, however, that there were only 40,000 Austrian shillings remaining in the bank, just enough to pay the salaries of a couple of dozen people for one month, far short of what was needed.

Instead of spending his entire bud get, which would have been gone in a matter of weeks, the mayor decided to put the money on deposit with a local savings bank and issue *labor certificates.*The deposit served as a backing or guarantee for the town's own cooperative currency, which became known as simply the Wörgl. Untergugenberger's idea was to get the town back to work and the economy moving again. So he designed the Wörgl currency to function solely as a medium of exchange. To that end, a demurrage charge was applied through a stamp affixed each month at 1 percent of face value. Like all other demurrage charges, this *relief tax*acted as an incentive to keep the currency in circulation. Everybody who was paid with the Wörgl made sure he or she spent it quickly before the stamp's date expired.

Interestingly enough, only the railway station and the post office refused to accept the local money, most likely because they were part of the national government. When people ran out of places to spend their local currency, they would pay their taxes early, resulting in a huge increase in the town's revenues. Over the 13-month life span of the Wörgl, the town council not only carried out all the intended works projects but also went on to build new houses, a reservoir, a ski jump, and the famous bridge. The people also used their cooperative currency to replant forests, planning ahead to generate revenues from felling mature trees for timber.

Alex von Muralt, who made an in-depth investigation of the Wörgl at that time, reported the mayor's delighted comments that "taxes were eagerly paid," sometimes even in advance. Von Muralt concluded, "This eagerness to pay taxes may be, in my opinion, simply owing to the fact that the businessman who finds, at the close of the month, that he holds a considerable amount in relief money[Wörgl], can dispose of it with the greatest ease and without loss by meeting his parish[local tax] obligations. A change of attitude has manifestly taken place. If formerly the paying of taxes was deferred to the last, now it occupies first place."[2]

People in line to cash in their Wörgls.

Wörgl soon became the only town in Austria with full employment. As pointed out in Chapter 5, local currencies are exchanged more frequently than conventional money because the latter is used for savings as well as exchanges. It is estimated that the Wörgl stamp scrip circulated in transactions from 12 to 14 times more frequently than the national currency,[3] a major factor in the town's recovery.

According to Irving Fisher, "Free money may turn out to be the best regulator of the velocity of circulation of money, which is the most confusing element in the stabilization of the price level. Applied correctly it could in fact haul us out of the crisis in a few weeks.... I am a humble servant of the merchant Gesell."[4]

Word of the success of this cooperative currency spread like wildfire. French Prime Minister Edouard Dalladier even made a special visit to see for himself the miracle of Wörgl. Soon more than 200 other towns and villages in Austria wanted to use this system as well.

It was at that point that the Austrian Central Bank panicked and decided to assert its monopoly rights by making it a criminal offense to issue Wörgls. The town of Wörgl, almost overnight, returned to 30 percent unemployment.

THE GERMAN WÄRA SYSTEM

By 1923, the monetary situation in neighboring Germany was wretched. Prior to World War I (1913), one U.S. dollar was worth 4.2 German marks.[5] By the time inflation peaked in November 1923, the exchange rate for one dollar was 4.2 trillion marks. A postage stamp cost billions, a loaf of bread required a wheelbarrow full of money, and 92,844,720 trillion German marks were in circulation.[6] Daily wage negotiations preceded work. Salaries were paid twice per day and were spent within the hour.

Based on Gesell's teachings, an organization was formed in Germany in 1929 to "fight stagnation of the market and unemployment."[7] Called the Wära Tauschgesellschaft (the Wära Trading Company),[8] it issued demurrage-charged *wära*bills. The term *wära* is a combination of the German words *ware* ("goods") and *währung* ("currency"). Wära, demurrage-charged scrips, were circulated for a period of one year, at the end of which they could be traded for new ones.

The wära, like the Wörgl, drew international attention when it was used by a local entrepreneur to help save the coal mine in the small town of Schwanenkirchen. Like many other businesses in Germany during this severe economic downturn, the mine had filed for bankruptcy and was shut down. Max Hebecker, the former production engineer, had a chance to purchase the mine for 8,000 Reichsmark, far below its estimated value. As Hebecker had no access to a bank loan, however, he decided to apply the concept of the wära. He gathered the workers and explained that the coal mine could be reopened and they could work again if they were willing to be paid in wära. This currency would be backed by the coal they were extracting, rather than national currency. A predictably lively exchange between the miners, villagers, and local shop keepers followed. In the end, all agreed to accept payment in the new wära currency.

The wära stamp scrip not only saved the coal mine and the town but also began to circulate nationally. Soon, over 2,000 corporations throughout Germany began accepting and paying each other with this local money. A growing number of banks even opened wära accounts.

Here again, the Reichsbank, Germany's central bank, felt threatened by the wära's enormous success and by other local currencies in circulation during the 1920s. With the enlisted help of the government, these cooperative currencies were declared illegal in October 1931 through the "Brüningsche Notverordnungen."[9]

RISE OF THE NAZI PARTY

The repression of cooperative currencies, together with other anti-inflationary decisions by the Reichsbank, led to a sharp decline in the German money supply.[10] As a result, the Schwanenkirchen mine and hundreds of other businesses were forced to shut down, and unemployment soared again. As helping themselves on a local level became increasingly more difficult for people, advocates of centralized solutions gained appeal. In the beer halls of Bavaria, an obscure Austrian immigrant began drawing audiences to his fiery speeches that promised a return to jobs and glory. His name was Adolf Hitler.

What was Hitler's formula for political success? No one knew better than Hjalmar Schacht, chairman of the Reichsbank and considered the leading German central banker of his generation.[11] According to Schacht, the Nazi Party's popularity was primarily fueled by "poverty and unemployment."[12]

The statistics invite conjecture: Between 1924 and 1930, the period when cooperative currencies were in their greatest use in Germany, unemployment hovered around 1 million people. During that same period, the percentage of seats held by the National Socialist (Nazi) Party declined from 6.6 percent to 2.6 percent. In contrast, as the cooperative currencies were outlawed and unemployment shot up by almost 500 percent in just three years,[13] the percentage of seats obtained by the Nazi Party climbed first to 18.3 percent in 1930, then to 43.9 percent by the end of 1933, enough to bring Hitler to power.[14]

THE UNITED STATES

During the Great Depression of the 1930s, the success of the Wörgl experiment caught the attention of U.S. policy makers struggling with unprecedented unemployment in their country. Key conversations ensued between Irving Fisher, the Yale economics professor; Professor Russell Sprague from Harvard; and Dean Acheson, undersecretary of the Treasury. All three became convinced that the Wörgl model offered a way out of the Depression. Economist Fisher stated for the record, "The correct application of stamp scrip would solve the Depression crisis in the United States in three weeks!"[15]

The idea of stamp scrip was, therefore, recommended to President Roosevelt. As reported by Fisher, though Roosevelt was himself impressed, the final decision on whether to officially endorse cooperative currencies was left to advisors, who instead favored a series of new centralized programs for which political credit could be more easily claimed. These new programs included the expansion of the Reconstruction Finance Corporation and large-scale work-creation projects managed by the federal government, all part of what would become popularly known as the New Deal. Roosevelt announced by executive decree that he would prohibit *emergency currencies,*the code name given for cooperative currencies. This decree applied to any and all such currencies then in existence and any that might be proposed.[16] The United States thus chose not to take advantage of such monetary innovations to address the economic crisis of the 1930s.

Contrary to popular belief, the centralized initiatives taken by the Roosevelt administration did not actually pull the United States out of the Great Depression. Certainly, the centralized initiatives and programs enacted did assist in providing valuable employment to many hardworking people. But most economic historians today agree that for the United States, as well as for Germany and Austria, it was the economic shift in preparation for, and eventual participation in, World War II that ended the Great Depression. Roosevelt himself admitted that much when he stated, "It was Dr. Win-the-War, not Dr. New Deal that ended the Depression!"[17]

HISTORY REPEATS ITSELF?

It's impossible to prove that the ghastly years of Nazism wouldn't have taken place if the grassroots currency initiatives had been allowed to thrive.

What is known is that monetary crashes invariably leave people in fear, despair, and anger. This is an explosive social mix that irresponsible demagogues can and do exploit, even today. What started as a monetary problem in the former Yugo slavia, for example—exacerbated by the IMF readjustment program in the late 1980s—was swiftly transformed into intolerance toward "others." Minorities were used as scapegoats by ethnic leaders to redirect anger away from themselves and toward a common enemy, providing the sociopolitical context for extreme nationalist leaders to gain power in the process. Within days of the 1998 monetary crisis in Indonesia, mobs were incited to violence against Chinese and other minorities. Similarly, in Russia, discrimination against minorities was aggravated by the financial collapse of the 1990s. With the fall of the Berlin Wall and the collapse of Soviet communism, it could be argued that the identified archenemy of the United States has now been supplanted with a new foe, immigrants and the poor. Today in the United States, there are some 1,018 identified hate groups compared to *only*602 in 2000.[18]

Another important lesson, and an expensive one in terms of human misery with regard to cooperative currencies, is revealed by the more recent economic crisis in Argentina.

THE ARGENTINE CREDITOS

As a model debtor nation, from 1991 to 2001 the Argentine government adopted all the policies suggested by the IMF, including privatization of government assets and a fixed parity between the Argentine peso and the U.S. dollar. Instead of leading to economic stability, however, these policies created an overvalued peso and a massive economic contraction.

People at the grassroots level responded to the economic tightening with several mutual aid initiatives. In 1995, the first *trueque*("barter") clubs were started to enable groups of friends and neighbors to exchange goods and services. Trueque clubs soon spread throughout the greater Buenos Aires region and into other provinces. Various clubs then began to issue their own *credito*currency notes, and, by early 2001, there were several dozen currencies in circulation. An informal network, the *Red Global de Trueque*("Global Trading Network"), allowed the different systems to interact.

In December 2001, Argentina went into a financial meltdown: Banks closed for months, and people could not access their accounts. The peso suffered a massive devaluation, and chaos reigned. Without the availability of cash, huge numbers of people joined the trueque clubs to make ends meet, and the amount of trading in credito currency exploded. By July 2002, an esti-

Club de Trueque in Buenos Aires, 2001 Zona Oeste. Photo credit: Sergio Lub.

mated 7 million people were using cooperative currencies on a regular basis. By November of that same year, however, the trueque movement had shrunk back to about 70,000 participants, roughly a 99 percent drop.

Sergio Lub is an entrepreneur born in Argentina and the founder of thank-yous, a global reputation currency used by the Friendly Favors network. Lub has traveled back to his native land frequently over the years and is very familiar with this chapter in its history: "The Papelitos system worked very well in the beginning. In 2001, when Tom Greco and I visited their clubs of trueque, they had hundreds of vendors who alternated as customers. They call themselves 'prosumidores,' a combination of 'producer' and 'consumer.' One participant could bring tomatoes from her garden and return home with ravioli for dinner, a voucher for a prepaid dentist visit, furniture, or fishing equipment, and all these goods and services exchanged hands at a dizzying speed using these crudely made papelitos, a substitute for money that people improvised to stay alive when banks closed and there was no more legal tender. They collectively have broken the illusion that people could not issue money on their own."[19]

Heloisa Primavera, a cofounder of over 200 barter clubs recalls, "We started off as part of a group of teachers and researchers in 1996. We were working with socially at-risk groups, such as homeless children, prostitutes, and former convicts, and trying to promote self-esteem and small jobs in the face of growing unemployment due to the structural adjustment plans imposed by the International Monetary Fund (IMF) to debtor countries, especially in Latin America. One of our activities was to train people to form knowledge exchange networks in which every member was supposed to both learn something and teach something else. This strategy came from the French group Réseau d'Échanges Réciproques de Savoirs. We created then the Economic Literacy Program, and the project expanded by leaps and bounds."[20]

Lub and Primavera see the reasons for the failure of the trueque movement as twofold: The value of the creditos became highly inflated because the money was fiat-based and run by a small group of leaders. Furthermore, the system, for the most part, was not transparent to its users; therefore, organizers were able to keep their actions secret.

"Another major problem was that the creditos were primarily created as paper currency, without adequate safeguards against forgery. For example, in 2002, outside one of the big fairs, a couple of men were selling papelitos at a huge discount; you could buy $50 worth of creditos for $1 of official money. They were denounced, and a sympathetic judge ordered their arrest but had to release them the next day because counterfeit laws only protect legal tender. Furthermore, they were both employees of one of the large banks that had color copiers to make papelitos at will. To me it was clear that the bank, after reopening, counterfeited the people's money as a way to destroy their competition and regain their monopoly on issuing money," adds Sergio Lub.

Such an accumulation of flaws provided ample temptation and opportunity for corruption, which led to the collapse of these systems. To aggravate the chaos, professionally counterfeited creditos had begun circulating, sabotaging the system.

According to Primavera, "What we learned from this incredible experience in terms of governance is that money is a key aspect of democracy, that it is possible to distribute wealth instead of concentrating it, if we use social money. But we also learned it is very hard to sustain such a system, if a rigorous management is not available to promote permanent transparency of accounts and decision-making processes. Still, much deeper than the technical issue, we consider the aspects of human behavior that could explain the significant growth of Argentinean networks, which occurred exponentially during almost seven years: How was it possible that a group of 23 people became 2 million in seven years? Where can you find such an example anywhere in the world, without any external support? With only self-management of groups?"

Lub reflects, "Ironically, we had already a transparent accounting system online with our thank-yous that could provide all the safeguards they needed to move their accounting online, where it would remain transparent and cannot be counterfeited (unlike cash transactions, every online transfer has to have a buyer and a seller to be recorded, so crooks cannot be anonymous). I offered our application as a gift to the leadership of one of the largest clubs, but the users were not computer literate and they were in a survival mode, unable to concentrate enough to learn how to access the Internet and make a transfer. So another important lesson for me was to do the preparations and training *before*the crisis starts. Today, I foresee the interface to be easier, thanks to cell phones, so people can access their accounts and make payments through their phones. I saw phones used to buy sodas in 2002 in Japan, and in South Africa in 2005, so eventually we shall have it in the United States as well."[21]

ROTTERDAM

Curiously, even well-designed and successful currencies have hit the rocks. In Rotterdam, the Netherlands' second largest city with the largest port in Europe, over 10,000 people participated in an alternative currency in 2001. The *NU-card*experiment was designed specifically to advance a long list of green activities, from taking public transport to recycling or volunteering. Green products could be purchased using *ooins*in one of the 100 participating shops. The currency was good at the zoo and in cinemas, theaters, museums, and other recreational outlets. It was backed by the European Union and one of the largest banks of the Netherlands.

The program was stopped after 18 months because the political climate in Rotterdam changed dramatically, following the assassination of Pim Fortuyn, an ultra-right-wing politician. Fortuyn's party won half of all the seats in the city council in the elections that followed shortly after his death, and on assuming power, it halted all environmental projects in the city.

"What we learned from this experience was invaluable. It is critical that all key players are stakeholders in the process," Edgar Kampers submits.[22]

It would be wise to heed history's hard lessons. This is even more important today as there are greater possibilities for successful applications, given the convergence of new technologies, more access to information, and the maturity of local and regional currency system designs. Additionally, governments are learning that affording greater opportunities to their citizens bodes well for society and avoids the circumstances that give rise to civil unrest and turmoil.

So what are the design features that bode well for a sustainable currency strategy?

Chapter Eleven

GOVERNANCE AND WE, THE CITIZENS

An Ancient Future?

The economy of the future is based on relationships rather than possessions.

JOHN PERRY BARLOW, former lyricist for the Grateful Dead and founding member of the Electronic Frontier Foundation

Bali is a small island in the Indonesian archipelago that fervently embraces and preserves its Hindu culture, though it is situated in a huge, mostly Islamic nation. What makes Bali compelling is the longevity of its complex cooperative currency system, which is inextricably interwoven with its cultivation of rice, allocation of vital water rights, celebrations of festivals, and hyperdemocratic system of governance.

From this ancient civilization, there are gripping and undeniable guidelines and strategies that may have some useful lessons relevant for our collective future.

The community at large is organized into three main networks:

- *Banjar:* the most important civic organization, which is in charge of the social aspects of the community
- *Pemaksan:* a group responsible for the coordination of religious rituals
- *Subak:* water irrigation cooperatives for rice production

John Stephen Lansing, a professor at the Santa Fe Institute whose research explores the ecology, common property, and social theories of Bali, as well as integrative modeling of environmental changes, explains that an agrarian system of rice cultivation flourished there for almost 1,000 years.[1] Then, in the 1970s, the World Bank insisted, as part of its financial aid package, that the "unsophisticated traditional methods" be replaced with modern techniques and know-how, coupled with the use of chemical fertilizers. The well-documented experiment was a disaster, causing crop failures and massive ecological issues, such as the depletion of large swaths of native coral reefs. It was then decided that the customary agricultural practices could be reintroduced. So the Balinese went back to producing two bountiful crops a year while managing pest control naturally.

Interestingly, what Lansing and his associates demonstrated, using agent modeling,[2] is that the Balinese traditional, socially complex, multitiered, hyperdemocratic methods of sharing precious water, along with the timing of planting and harvesting, mirrored their optimal scenario for the environment at large.

Intertwined with their time-honored agricultural and social practices is the longest-surviving cooperative currency ecosystem in the world. Before Indonesian in dependence in 1945, the conventional currency was the Dutch guilder, followed by the Indonesian rupiah. Working in parallel with this conventional money is a social currency networked through the Banjar system, which has been in use since before written records. Everyone in the Banjar is obliged to contribute to the well-being of the community by helping with jointly decided projects. The Banjar system extends beyond religious or cultural events and may include civic activities, such as support for building local roads, especially when the central government is unable to provide funding. In short, local resources are mobilized regularly to support a full spectrum of undertakings, whatever the community chooses to focus on. It is this system of mutual cooperation and assistance that accounts for the resiliency of Balinese culture.[3]

Additionally ,a physical form of money—an odd-looking Chinese coin with a square hole in its middle called the *uang kepeng* ("coin money")[4]—was also used. This coin money was minted in China and used as trading tokens, much in the same manner that trading beads were used in North America by indigenous peoples.[5] This coinage was outlawed, however, in the 1950s.

"Chinese money, known also as *pis bolong*in Bali, has circulated as a local medium of exchange here for at least the past 1,000 years and only ceased to be used for local purchases in the early 1970s. Up until that time, a Balinese could use uang kepeng in many ways, from buying meat and vegetables in the market or snacks in front of the school, to watching movies with friends at an outdoor theater," says Stephen DeMeulenaere, founder of the Cooperative Currency Resource Center and a long-term resident of Bali.[6]

According to DeMeulenaere, uang kepeng became the official medium of exchange of the Banjar and could be taxed, spent on public works projects, and circulated as a fully functioning currency. Thus its significance to Balinese society was formalized.[7]

It was only when new national banking and currency laws were put into effect, after Indonesia gained its in dependence, that the Balinese were forced to accept the Indonesian rupiah in place of the uang kepeng.

"The decline of uang kepeng as a medium of exchange corresponded with a shift in economic behavior toward earning the Indonesian rupiah. Although many significant elements of traditional life remain vibrant in Bali, mostly thanks to the Banjar-based social currency, the monetary protection blanket they once had with uang kepeng has been stripped away, leaving the Balinese people and society increasingly vulnerable to situations beyond their control and subject to the same financial and consumption pressures faced by all of us living in the modern world," DeMeulenaere adds. The social currency, the nayahan Banjar, continues today as the mainstay of the Banjar system and has served to partially fill the void created by the banning of the uang kepeng.

The Balinese system of governance is of particular interest. A leader of any given Banjar is elected by a majority vote of members and, though this is rare, can be dismissed by another majority vote at any time. He or she receives no remuneration for this role. Anthropologists Clifford and Hildred Geertz describe the leader as "more an agent than a ruler."[8]

Each family has one representative in the *krama,* the Banjar council, in which every member is considered equal and has one vote. No special status is granted to wealthier or higher-caste members. When addressing one another in the krama, they do not use the formal form of language for those of a superior class, which is a prerequisite of daily interaction outside a Banjar meeting. At monthly meetings, new activities are proposed, and ongoing projects are discussed. The contributions of in-kind and conventional money for each project are then decided on, customarily by a majority vote. In short, the Banjar functions as a community-based planning and implementation organization, and it bud gets all its activities in two currencies: the national currency and the nayahan Banjar time currency.

Modern-day pressures on Balinese society, as in any developing country today, are increasing and whittle away relentlessly not only at indigenous culture but also at resources. Stephen DeMeulenaere adds poignantly, "Property values have as much as tripled in the past couple of years, especially following the success of the popular book and movie *Eat, Pray, Love.* The rice fields are being abandoned and sold to the highest bidder, and resorts and hotels are being built in their place."[9]

To romanticize the Balinese experience would be a mistake, but to dismiss its many teachings out of hand would be one, too. The rhetorical question of the relevance of some small island's curious culture could well be proffered. The answer is that they have managed their resources and culture for centuries through a multitiered, highly participatory democracy that has survived countless foreign intrusions. There is a clear distinction to be made, nonetheless, between wisdom and education. One can be a lowly farmer toiling on the lands of the Ngong Hill in Kenya or be pushing a broom in some sweatshop in Shanghai, have little or no formal education, and be truly wise. The corollary to that also stands.

A modern governance system, although very different, reflecting the fractal nature of the Balinese system, is holacracy. Its structure and procedures integrate the collective wisdom of people while aligning a venture, network, or business with its "broader purpose and a more organic way of operating and the result is dramatically increased agility, transparency, innovation, and accountability."[10]

DEMOCRACY, TRANSPARENCY, AND ACCOUNTABILITY

The key aspects of the Balinese cooperative currency system—democratic governance, transparency, and accountability—are clearly necessary conditions for a cooperative currency to succeed over time. These are the same lessons learned from the Argentinean debacle, for instance, that convinced the German regio movement to incorporate the following principles into their eight conditions for a currency to be granted the use of the regio label, according to Margrit Kennedy, the initiator for the regio movement.[11] These conditions state that these criteria need to be satisfied:

1. The system needs to be a win-win model for all participants.
2. Its aim is to support a public good.
3. It needs to be professionally managed.
4. Total transparency of the accounts and the mechanisms for all participants.
5. Democratic control by its users.

6. Sustainable finances or at least a sustainable financial strategy.
7. Guaranteed circulation of the currency.
8. Willingness to collaborate with other regio projects.

Finally, there is a preference that the currency does not bear interest. This is not a formal obligation, but so far all regios have been implementing that ninth principle as well.[12]

As we have seen repeatedly, economic hardship gives birth to a multitude of local currencies. The trend toward cooperative currencies will be stronger now than at any time previously because of the convergence of cheap computing, the Internet, and the technology to launch such systems. The vast majority of the initiatives that arise as a consequence of the current global depression will be started with a lot of good intentions. But good intentions may not always be sufficient. Inevitably, some initiatives will be technically flawed, some may be outright frauds, and some may even be deliberate attempts at sabotage, as appears to have been the case in Argentina.

Dee Hock is the founder and a former CEO of the VISA credit card association. Back in 1968, he convinced Bank of America to give up ownership and control of their BankAmericard credit card licensing program. The new entity was a nonstock membership corporation owned by its member banks. In 1976, its name changed to VISA. This new structure he calls a *chaord,* a word that comprises both the terms *chaos*and *order.*

He writes, "We must conceive of and help implement wholly new forms of ownership, financial systems and measurements, free of the attempt to monetize all values that bind[us] to next quarter's bottom line, gross mal-distribution of wealth and power, degradation of people, and desolation of the ecosphere, or our stories will be increasingly immoral and destructive."[13]

John Boik, a medical doctor who specializes in new cancer treatments, has applied his knowledge of natural systems to governance. He presents intriguing and important ideas on the functioning of an integrated cooperative currency and governance system.[14] He addresses two key mechanisms of contemporary society that make it unsustainable: (1) The financial (banking and investment) system demands continuous economic growth, and (2) financial and political power is centralized within a small subset of the population.[15]

"The Earth has finite resources and a limited capacity to absorb the waste products of human economic activity; unlimited growth is unsustainable due to real ecological constraints. And the country suffers from inherently undemocratic hyper-inequalities of power that cause widespread suffering and will likely lead to greater civil unrest."

Boik contends that the current financial, economic, and governance systems require an overhaul. "Tweaks and reforms, while important," he says, "will ultimately fail to address foundational failures on which they rest." His proposal calls for developing demonstration projects at the local level and on a volunteer basis to test and refine sustainable financial, economic, and governance systems. These projects, called "principled societies," are essentially local membership clubs open to anyone who wishes to participate.

In his blueprint, financial and political power is decentralized, in part through collaborative direct democracy, the governance system a principled society employs when adopting and refining rules. In this form of mass online democracy, members participate in the full creative problem-solving process rather than simply voting yes or no on proposals advanced by a small group. The system relies on built-in design elements that ensure efficiency, transparency, and effectiveness.

Boik adds, "Power is also decentralized through the democratic features built into the proposed financial system, a local currency system called the Token Exchange System." Unique to Boik's proposal is a crowd-funding – like mechanism, which pools small amounts of resources and money from a diverse group of people, usually via the Internet. This generates investment funds for business, as well as a steady stream of donations for funding social services such as schools, nonprofits, clinics, universities, and other groups. Members must use a certain portion of their incoming tokens to make interest-free loans to businesses and make donations to participating nonprofits. Individuals choose the programs they want to support.

Some of the interest-free loans would go to principled businesses, new socially responsible hybrids that contain elements of the nonprofit and for-profit models. This profit-neutral investment system accomplishes three goals: First, every individual participates and becomes a member of the investing class. Second, decisions are based on social concerns rather than profit. Third, in a profit-neutral investment system, funding will tend to flow toward those businesses that provide the greatest community benefits. Principled businesses have a competitive advantage here in that they are designed to deliver social gains.

Boik adds, "Since investment is not motivated by profit, the system does not demand continual economic growth and can remain robust even under steady-state conditions. Profit-neutral investing is compatible with long-term ecologic viability. Thus, collaborative direct democracy is integrated with decentralized investment and social services funding. Each major aspect of a principled society—governance, finance, and economics—serves to distribute financial and political power to all system participants."

Boik asserts that from its core foundations, principled societies and those that follow this plan are inherently democratic.

The first step that cooperative currency networks should urgently consider is to establish international standards of quality and security with an Internet-based rating agency that produces a *Cooperative Currency Consumer Report,* complete with a reputation rating similar to that on e-Bay's auction site. The criteria for such a rating should include not only the technical aspects, such as how the currency is created, its delivery mechanisms, and its security, but also its scale and liquidity, its transparency, its governance, and its underlying social values. Bottom line: It should become possible for anybody to consult the rating of a currency before accepting it.

For any cooperative currency system that is destined to go mainstream, security mea sures should be commensurate with those of the conventional monetary system. There is one advantage that the cooperative currency domain has over the conventional system in this regard: Cooperative currencies should embrace transparency to its users and accountability. This is in stark contrast to the conventional system.

Additionally, the electronic technologies now available make it feasible to trace the use of any currency from its birth to its final retirement, making it a less attractive target for fraud, disruption, or sabotage.

Henk Van Arkel, founder of the Dutch nonprofit STRO, makes an interesting observation: "One of the reasons why systems fail is because there are too many meetings and the initiative gets bogged down. Additionally, a currency needs to be funded so the basic infrastructure and administration costs are covered. Otherwise, there's burnout."[16] Michael Linton adds, "In a mutual credit system such as LETS, your money is as good as your word. If your word is no good, neither is your money. It doesn't have to get overly complicated."[17]

This clearly works well in smaller, more close-knit communities, which form the backbone of most local cooperative movements, but what happens when a program goes truly global?

A CURRENCY THAT MARRIES EFFICIENCY AND EQUITY

The airline business is fiercely competitive, yet airlines need to collaborate when some unexpected disruption occurs. For instance, if a plane is delayed for whatever reason, its arrival and departure gates may have to be changed. This may affect other airlines, competitors of very different sizes and financial power. The old solution was to expand the airport. But that approach is less favored since most of the world's important airports can no longer expand their footprint—it is too expensive, and the land is simply not available.

So, as necessity is the mother of invention, something quite out of the box had to be devised. Geert Jonker, who now works as a software engineer in his native Holland, decided to tackle this dilemma.[18] His starting point took into consideration psychological studies showing that collaboration requires minimum levels of equity, which means that the benefits from the outcomes should be roughly proportional to the input of the different players. Individuals care about the payoff for others besides their own and are even willing to incur personal loss to reach a more equitable outcome.

The methodology Jonker used to unravel this complex issue was agent modeling, whereby a computer simulates all the factors of choices and opportunities between all the players and assesses the impact on the system as a whole. In this case, options and actions are replicated based on specific goals for each airline, as well as their interactions with each other.

"What we found was when conventional money was used in the time-slot exchanges, and all the airlines were fair, the results showed that the free market system actually worked well. As soon as even one airline exploited the situation, however, by leveraging its clout to obtain more than its fair share of benefits or delivering less than promised, all the airlines would also become self-centered, and cooperation broke down," recounts Geert Jonker.[19]

Bottom line: Conventional money can make a market efficient but not equitable, unless all participants keep behaving fairly forever, which is unrealistic. The erosion of community collaboration and its devastating consequences were seen in the !Kung tribe story back in Chapter 3. As soon as conventional money was introduced into their highly cooperative and supportive community, their community disintegrated.

What Jonker proposes is a new system in which the airlines work cooperatively by allocating scarce gate-time slots among themselves via a currency specifically designed for this purpose. He calls this a *spender-signed*currency.

Jonker describes how the currency works: "This is a mutual credit system like LETS where people can issue their own money. Basically, the credits count as an IOU, which has the issuer's name on it, so whoever gives that IOU will do something in repayment. It's called a multi-issuer currency, so there are multiple parties who might issue money, as this IOU can be passed along. In the case of air traffic management, however, I made a variation of that system, creating a *spender-signed*currency. Every user in the scheme has to add an electronic signature to every credit that goes through his or her hands. So, at any moment, every credit will have all the names of all the people who have used that credit in a payment up until that time."

In addition, every user has a reputation on a scale from one to three, with one being low and three representing high regard. The likelihood of a currency being accepted is a reflection of how well one knows the end issuer or the lineage of issuers and the reputation of each of them.

If the issuer or several of its users are known exploiters or swindlers, that currency ends up with a lower exchange value in a free market. For example, if one were offered the choice between 10 units with a pedigree that is aligned to one's values or 10 units for the same transaction but with a history that conflicts with one's principles and ethics, which one would be preferred? One may decide, however, to take a lower-rated currency but at a lower value.

As Jonker points out cogently: "The fact is that spender-signed currency enables a group of agents to *punish*an exploiter in a robust way, that is, in a way that doesn't break down as soon as the first of the group starts to *defect*from common cooperative principles."

He continues, "What happens is that the credits that have my name on them tend to stay close, or around me, and will tend to circle around me from the people I know and then come back to me, when the IOU is redeemed, and it disappears. The upshot is that everyone has his own little economy or exchange sphere around him or her. All these circles, all these local economies, stay interconnected and form a global economy. I think that that very nicely models the social exchange as we do in real life. So I exchange socially with people I know and people I trust, and not with the people I don't know or don't trust. The *spender signed*currency enables lots of local economies around each user's own local economy, together interconnected into one big universal economy while keeping the efficiency of a normal monetary open market—a market with money."[20]

MONEY THAT SMELLS?

The Roman historians Suetonius[21] and Dio Cassius[22] both reported a conversation between Emperor Vespasian (emperor from 69 to 79 ad) and his son, Titus. Titus was complaining to his father about the disgusting nature of a particular tax that his father had recently introduced. It was a urine tax, levied on the disposal of urine in the famous Roman sewer system. In response, Vespasian held up a gold coin and told Titus, "*Pecunia non olet!*" ("Money doesn't smell!").

This phrase is still used today as a way of saying that money is unaffected by its source or its users.[23] What Jonker invented, by contrast, is a system of money that tracks all its users. The currency's originator and its users leave an indelible imprint so that subsequent users can express their opinion. It is now possible to have "smelly money," as a previous user's reputation may stink!

A possible application of this is described in the next chapter, with two Irish lads working out their deal on buying a car. The clincher as to whether a bargain is struck is the origin of the funds over time.

Since available information technologies are now capable of making Vespasian's statement untrue for the first time, imagine the role and effect of a currency such as Jonkers outlined in a monetary ecology. This currency could circulate in parallel with conventional money, using the existing economic framework, but it would change the economic market into one where collaboration and reputation for fairness become as important as profit and competition. The very fact that a participant is willing to use it would be a sign of its reputation rating, and it could even make corporate whitewashing or "greenwashing" counterproductive, because any dishonesty immediately shows. It just wouldn't pay to misbehave.

This type of currency assumes, as in classical economics, that all relevant information is always available to every participant in the market, which clearly is not the truth with conventional money. Mobile Internet access, however, could create a space where a lot more information could be pulled into a decision than was ever the case.

An economy of relationships is trying to emerge: An economy in which interconnectivity empowers the individual, along with his or her various communities, evolving into a more democratic, transparent, and viable economic life, enabled by various consciously created currencies operating at all levels of society, from local neighborhoods to the world at large.

TOWARD A MONETARY ECOSYSTEM

Revising our monetary systems through the inclusion of cooperative currencies fosters the possibility of building a better world, one to enjoy now and one worthy of bequeathing to future generations.

What could be some of the components of what we have described a monetary ecosystem?

That it provides *balance* between competition and cooperation, as measured, respectively, by the system's efficiency and resilience, is crucial to the long-term health of any given complex flow system. As already discussed in Chapter 4, in all sustainable systems, the optimum point between resilience and efficiency invariably lies much closer to resilience. And these two factors for resilience are diversity and connectivity.

What could elements of a mature monetary ecosystem look like one generation into the future? For example, a multitiered monetary system could consist of:

- a global reference currency
- three main multinational currencies
- some private international scrip
- scores of national currencies
- dozens of regional currencies
- a multitude of local cooperative currencies
- a wide variety of functional currencies

Of course any one individual or business would participate in only a few of these systems. Just like today, nobody uses all of the conventional national currencies in existence. This list just describes what is available as choice of media of exchange.

Let's now explore what each of the items in the currency menu could look like.

A Global Reference Currency

The need for a global currency that is nobody's national currency has finally been recognized. It has taken the form of the Terra described earlier, or some variation of it, and arose from a systematization of corporate barter.

Three Multinational Currencies

It has indeed become obvious that regional economic integration can reach maturity only when a single currency levels the playing field for all economic participants. A single currency is the only way to structurally guarantee a unified information field. After some serious start-up problems in Europe, various multinational alliances have evolved from the original euro. There are also multinational currency zones in Asia (triggered by a deal between Japan and China) and in the North and South Americas (around a new Amero, or federal dollar, after a reform of the U.S. dollar).

Some Private International Scrip

The airline loyalty currencies were the first large-scale application of an international corporate scrip. Today, Facebook is trying to dabble in the same direction. Google may be tempted to do the same. The net result will be that several corporate scrips will be competing on the Internet, issued by the likes of Amex, Microsoft, or an alliance of European and Asian corporations. Some have created special subsidiaries, with strong and liquid balance sheets, to issue these currencies and imbue them with greater credibility.

National Currencies

In many countries, national currencies will be used for a long time to come. They continue to play an important role within any country that has not joined a formal multinational currency integration system. Most exchanges continue to involve national currencies at least in partial payments, if only because they remain the official legal tender with which national taxes are being paid.

The main difference would be that national currencies would lose their monopoly as the medium of exchange. Payments could consist of a mix of national currencies, corporate scrips, or Internet currencies, even in a single transaction.

The only places where the national currencies have retained their monopoly are a few underdeveloped countries and backward dictatorships, where political control over the Internet has kept the cyber-economy completely shut out.

Regional Currencies

Under pressure to reduce long-distance transport, a significant source of harmful carbon emissions, many businesses are reorganizing their supply chains into regional networks. The C3 mechanism was one of the pioneers in this area. Supply chains have also emerged around specific industrial sectors, such as food production and processing or automobile components, and, of course, the regios in German-speaking Europe.

Even in the domain of conventional currencies, this trend is in evidence. Today, 14 U.S. states, namely, Colorado, Georgia, Idaho, Indiana, Missouri, Montana, New Hampshire, North Carolina, South Carolina, Tennessee, Utah, Vermont, Virginia, and Washington, have taken action to create their own state currency, usually backed by a precious metal such as gold or silver.[24] In the case of Utah, for example, the Utah Legislature has passed a bill allowing gold and silver coins to be used as legal tender in the state—and for the value of their precious metal, not just the face value of the coins. Utah's bill allows stores to accept gold and silver coins as legal tender. It also exempts gold and silver transactions from the state's capital gains tax, though that does not shield exchanges from federal taxes.[25]

Local Cooperative Currencies

In reaction to economic globalization and in parallel to it, organization of currencies at the local level has become very popular. The information revolution brought about a systematic reduction of production and service-related jobs. As jobs grew scarcer, communities created their own currencies to facilitate local exchanges among their members. Once critical mass was attained, cooperative currency clearing houses on the Internet made it possible for members of these communities to participate in the cyber-economy as well.

Functional Currencies

The field where the most creativity has emerged is special function currencies. There could be carbon-reducing currencies, energy-saving currencies, beautifying-neighborhood currencies, and currencies designed to stop overfishing in certain waters. There are systems like reputation currencies (such as seller ratings in the model pioneered by eBay) and learning currencies (the saber, talents, and alegres). The list of what is being and can be created is limited only by our imaginations and our abilities.

With all these currencies in circulation working in tandem with the conventional money, how would life be? What transformations would possibly take place? Let's take a glimpse at a possible future.

Chapter Twelve

OUR AVAILABLE FUTURE

The Cooperative Society

What if you slept, and what if in your sleep you dreamed, and what if in your dreams you went to heaven and there you plucked a strange and beautiful flower, and what if when you awoke you had the flower in your hand? Ah, what then?

SAMUEL TAYLOR COLERIDGE,
19th-century English poet and philosopher

Since the dawning of the Industrial Age and the instigation of the modern monetary system, no truly cooperative society has been able to operate, let alone thrive on a large scale.

The five scenarios that follow portray how a future society might look once it has transitioned from today's highly competitive structure to one based on greater cooperation and mutual support, within the span of one generation. The discrepancies between where we stand now and our possible future are enormous. The driver behind each of these transformations is a cooperative currency innovation. Such transformations are possible not because of the amount of money that is circulating but rather from the type of money that is in use.

These vignettes portray individuals and communities being enabled to shape their own lives, each arising from a history of uncertainty and insecurity, whether poor or rich. The first four relate to monetary technologies introduced in each segment of society—respectively, government, businesses, NGOs, and the individual—and the last story relates to the era of wisdom emerging from the postmodern industrial-knowledge age, bringing the monetary and societal systems into greater balance.

Foreseeing this available future can elicit a variety of strong reactions: delight and anticipation at the prospect or shock or despair because it seems so improbable, given what we have endured. New options for a brighter future can engender derisive and even dismissive cynicism—this simply can't happen as it has never happened before and, therefore, will never come to pass.

The good news, as evidenced in the previous pages, is that the knowhow and gumption to bring about this conversion already exist. It is not in-the-box solutions for the redistribution of wealth, bond mea sures, or enlightened self-interest from corporate entities that is catalyzing this evolution but, rather, ordinary people who are jumping outside the prescribed boundaries and simply rethinking and reengineering their money.[1]

MAE HONG SON PROVINCE, NORTHERN THAILAND, FEBRUARY 6, 2027

It was hard to tell Cha Cha's age, as she swept her raven-black hair back off her face with her earth-soiled hand, but it was clear that life had not been kind. She put her foot on the spade and leaned her lithe body up against the handle, taking a moment to rest from her toil in the community garden.

"I really wanted to find a way to restore confidence in government. For too long it has been the same. You know, cynical and resigned, very easy to be angry and frustrated. There's been enough bloodshed in my country," she remarked, as her face darkened. "We needed to start where we could. We needed to show good results quickly. It had to be easy—not much bother. Or else it wouldn't have worked."

She pointed to acres of verdant fields stretching beyond, as far as the eye can see. "We now have almost full employment. Everyone who wants to work can. The shops and markets are booming in trade. There's no one begging on the sidewalks. There's no mass exodus to the big cities anymore. There are no girls and boys walking the streets looking for customers and their next meal. Every child has access to education; everyone can get to see a doctor or a nurse practitioner. It may not be fancy, but everyone is taken care of. We changed from being one of the poorest regions in the county to one of the wealthiest in Asia within a decade," she said.

Now an Interior Ministry – appointed *na-yok umphur* (regional representative), Cha Cha worked her way up through the ranks swiftly, from an elected *pu-yai-baans*(delegate) for her village to the *kamnan* (mayor) for her district. She has known tough times herself. She, like a lot of women in these parts, is without a spouse. Husbands abandon their wives and children for a new partner and a fresh start, only to have the cycle repeat itself with yet another woman. She has had trouble making ends meet and providing for her children when her previous partners walked out.

As a result, there is nothing theoretical about her experience of poverty. And there was no book learning to find an answer. Her way out was culled from observing how the women took care of one another, sharing what they had and giving of themselves in terms of time, street smarts, and friendship.

"So how did we do it, you ask?" She posed rhetorically, pulling herself up to her full five feet, two inches.

"It took money! But not in the way you think," she said, shaking her finger. "Not baht, but civics. Yes, civics—money that does civic or public good. Starting with a couple of villages, we created local money so we had the cash to pay people to provide the goods and services that we so desperately needed. Anyone who was willing and able to work got paid in civics. With each success, it spread like wildfire.

"What is critical, looking back, and I suppose what made it really work, was when I got into regional government. We started paying off some old debts thanks to savings made possible with this new kind of money. Within two years, we had a balanced bud get, wiping out the deficit, and were able to fulfill our big-picture agenda. What's more, people were actually paying their contributions in advance for the following quarter. With each year, we expanded our programs, tackling new problems. We made, and continue to make, a very special effort to incorporate innovative ideas from the local communities.

"And, here we are, a decade later. Will I run for president in 2020? No comment," she said, with a twinkle in her eye.

OAKLAND, CALIFORNIA, SEPTEMBER 5, 2037, BOARDROOM OF THE BECHTEL CORPORATION

The following text is extracted from the minutes of a board meeting of the largest construction and civil engineering company in the world.

The Board considered the two main investment projects on today's agenda:

- A 25-year nature restoration project of the Southern Himalayan watershed
- A 100-year reforestation project of the sub-Sahara desert

The Board decided unanimously to implement the 100-year sub-Sahara project, given that the internal rate of return on this project is clearly superior to the 25-year project. The chairman added that the contribution of this project to overall global climate stability has been an additional incentive for him to vote for this project. The currency of all payments for goods and suppliers is the demurrage charged, similar to the Terra currency. The annual reports to the shareholders are similarly expressed in Terra.

LAKE VICTORIA, AFRICA, OCTOBER 7, 2023

Embu, a 23-year-old Kenyan Bantu-speaking woman and mother of one, takes the microphone and beams a broad, proud smile at the assembled group of representatives. They've traveled from far and wide across the expansive Nyanza Province, which borders on Lake Victoria, for this important quarterly joint NGO meeting. Delegates from across the culturally diverse region, including members of the Luo, Gusii, and Kuria tribes, sit in excited anticipation to hear the financial reports and updates on their area's comprehensive network of cooperatives and trade associations. Preliminary accounts and animated gossip, along with obvious evidence of vibrant commerce transacted daily, bode well for good news and a well-deserved celebration later that evening.

While waiting for the eager chatter to die down, some attendees quickly check their account balances on their mobile phones. Sammy sees that the consignment of goat skins and meat from his co-op to their neighbors across the border in Tanzania has been paid in full in *zutus,*local money that circulates in the ecoregion around Lake Victoria. This trading currency was designed to facilitate local commerce by keeping the zutu circulating within their larger community and has brought tangible wealth to the region.

Their local currencies are backed by time—one hour of work equals one unit—or by a commodity, such as timber. A special savings currency, called the *muti*and named after the Zulu word for "tree," is backed by shares in reforestation plantations. Sammy works there part-time. The future earnings from the trees harvested in 20 years will be helpful in looking after his parents' retirement, and, additionally, the new woodlands are reversing decades of soil erosion, enticing indigenous species back into the region.

His mobile e-purse carries several currencies: three national (euros, Kenyan, and Tanzanian shillings) and several local, including the zutu and the muti. There is an education currency called the *saber,* which has leveraged a government grant of 10 million 12 times over, each and every year. Based on his hours of mentoring younger students and helping them with their English and math homework, Sammy has earned saber credits, which have enabled him to pay the tuition for his long-distance learning degree in bookkeeping and business law.

Food, which was a major problem for decades, is now grown locally, either within the local forest or on organic farms, rather than imported. The vibrant forest supports a constructed ecosystem to provide bananas, coconuts, and other tropical fruits and nuts. Little labor is required since it is self-sustaining. The organic farms provide yields as high as conventional intensive farming methods while helping to build soil. The overall economics of the system, which includes grains, vegetables, and livestock, far exceed those of the massive farm that previously occupied and destroyed the land just outside the village. Labor is paid for using a time-backed local currency, where one hour of service equals one unit of currency. This money can be used to purchase a wide array of products and services in the local community and, by its design, tends to remain there.

Bebel, another meeting attendee, takes a moment and looks around the assembly hall with a certain satisfaction. The old building, which was constructed by the British in the early 1960s, has been totally retrofitted with passive energy features by Bebel and his team. Energy use in the community has been drastically slashed, while the residents still live and work in comfort. The new adjacent structure where to night's banquet will be held actually generates energy to feed into the local utility grid. Even though the temperature today is going to be high, and there is a large group assembled inside, these design modifications allow everyone to remain cool without the need for air conditioners. All appliances, when required, are highly efficient, often using as little as a tenth of the energy of comparable products built in 2010.

Embu clears her throat and raises her arm to call the house to order. The entrepreneurship and innovation that are clearly evident within the hall were ignited through an integrated series of trainings and programs. These encouraged each individual to have the self-assurance to trust their own observations of what was appropriate action, given their unique real-world awareness, experience, and knowledge. This newfound confidence—to be able to address issues on a grassroots level, along with an integrated plan of training, education, access to information, and the introduction of appropriate low-tech technologies and new monetary innovations—formed the lever that shifted their universe forever.

The air is electric with anticipation as the applause for Embu dies down.

"My dear colleagues and friends, I know you are all excited to get the financial reports and stories from our various co-op and team leaders on their collective breakthroughs and successes over the past few months. I know you've been talking among yourselves and have a sense of the good news we have to share," she begins.

"But there is something far more important I want to tell you. We have been contacted by some wai-Kukuyu in Nairobi. They live in terrible misery, with little food and no real opportunity, in the center of the capital in a heap of rubbish and filth.

"We have been asked to come and share our knowledge and capabilities with them. As we are country folk and not knowing the ways of the big towns, I was able to contact people in a faraway place called Curitiba, Brazil—on the other side of the world—who had rescued their own big town from terrible poverty, disease, and no hope 20 years ago, by using local money and local people's ideas—just like us.

"The news is I have asked and they have agreed to come to Kenya to help the Kukuyu." Her voice breaks with emotion.

There is a gasp of surprise and awe from the assembled group.

"So, my question to you, delegates and friends, can we, will we, use our time and abilities to help our brothers and sisters in Nairobi? Are we willing as Kenyans, no, better still, as fellow human beings, to make a difference and share the knowledge and resources that were so generously given to us? Are you with me?"

With that, all 300 attendees leap to their feet and roar a resounding "Yes!"

DUBLIN, IRELAND, AUGUST 5, 2020

The vintage sporting-green Morgan smoothly hugs the tight corner on Vico Road, as Stephen winds his way through the narrow coastal roads to Dalkey. The small village in the capital city's greater metropolitan area is just starting its day. The engine purrs as he pulls up in front of a trendy coffee shop. Nicholas, the car's owner, comes out, and Stephen, as he throws the keys to him, poses a question with a raised eyebrow.

"It's a great ride. Are you firm on the 15,000 quid?"

"Yeah, for 15,000 euros, she's yours."

Stephen exhales audibly as they take a table on the sidewalk café and order two expressi.

"Well, the car is in great shape. You've checked it out online?"

"Yeah, and I was hoping that we could do something on the price," Stephen adds hesitantly, as he reaches for his iPhone. Nick, in quick succession, pulls his out of his jacket pocket. Typical of their generation, they're very savvy, inured to marketing hype, and totally fluent in the latest technologies.

"Well, if your funds pass the sniff-test, I might be open to doing something. You're on Veri-funds, I presume?"

"Who isn't!" comes the almost indignant reply.

With a tap of his index finger, Stephen grants Nicholas access to view the pedigree of the various blocks of euros he'll be using for the transaction.

Nicholas pauses, waiting for the rating on the proffered funds to download. He glances quickly at his knock-off Cartier watch that he bought recently on his Erasmus year in Asia.

As they wait, the through-put of every euro being submitted for this negotiation since issuance is filtered through a preselected matrix of preferences. In Nicholas's case, they're for predominantly green and socially responsible companies, causes, customers, and citizens. Each end user can customize their preferences to support their personal principles and ideals. A rating of 10 would be a bull's-eye, a complete alignment of values between the seller and buyer.

The more a value set between the parties is discordant, the further the rating drops. A deal can be accommodated, nevertheless, if both parties agree to a discounting of the value of the currency. Again, the score is predetermined by each user's own rating tariff.

If the situation of a low rating occurs—a three or less—it indicates that the values are so out of sync that there's no amount of money that would close the deal, and both participants walk away. The exchange may not have happened, but both sides can take solace in the fact that they walked their talk and didn't put their money where their mouth was not.

"Um, we may have a problem here," claims Nicholas after a few moments.

"On first pass, it looks like a block of 4,000 euros was paid to shareholders by Petro-Co. They've just had an oil spill in the Caspian Sea. Their money is only worth 40 percent in my preterms, and that's only because they're doing a good cleanup job and not ripping the locals off."

"My aunt gave me that money for my birthday. She thought I would be able to spend it for full face value *because*of their efforts! Accidents do happen, you know."

"There may well be other takers out there, but I'm not inclined," says Nicholas as he starts to pocket his phone and takes a sip of his coffee.

"I would make up the difference, even if your rating is unbelievably tough and unreasonable!" Stephen sighs.

"No, even if you were to double the difference," declares Nicholas emphatically.

"There's no way we can come to terms, then? I really love the car."

"On principle, I can't. Not on this issue. Not today. Anyway, let me buy the coffee."

SÃO PAULO, BRAZIL, NOVEMBER 16, 2031

Jaime looks chuffed as he moves his knight into position. He sits back and sinks into the overstuffed armchair and takes another snip of his caipirinha. The fourth movement of Dvorák's *New World Symphony* plays in the background. A gentle breeze wafts through his friend's large and opulently appointed study, walled with floor-to-ceiling shelves of first-edition and leather-bound books. Mementos from foreign trips, personally autographed silver-framed photographs from the influential and famous, and gilt-edged degrees and statements of recognition are placed strategically to impress. The evening air is perfumed with the scent of lilac.

His opponent, Alejandro, ponders his next move. He exhales his cigar smoke slowly and declares, "My friend, I think you're going to beat me, again!"

"Well, a 10-year stretch in prison gives one a lot of time to perfect one's game!" replies Jaime.

Alejandro throws his head back and launches into a deep-barreled laugh. "It's a unique friendship, ours, the former car-jacker and the industrialist," he rejoins, regaining his composure and smiling broadly at his most improbable friend.

"My children and their kids all had to be specially chauffeured in armored cars to avoid the street rats," Alejandro continues. "Those days were hell. Miserable for everyone all round."

"And it went a lot deeper. You know, I watched my old man sit in his rocking chair waiting to die. He knew his family loved him, of course. But he felt useless in this age of technology. He felt washed-up as nobody really gave a toss about what he thought, what he had to offer. I suppose you would have called him a loser, like the vast majority of his generation."

Alejandro nods in agreement and adds, "My father had his orbit of considerable influence, as you can imagine. I never talked to him about this. But if I were to guess, I would say he was lonely, too, just like your Dad. For different reasons surely, but forlorn, nevertheless. Everybody was looking for something from him. Everyone! It was relentless and he ended up trusting no one."

"Our funerals will be different, very different from those of our parents," rejoins Jaime. "Just think of the crowd that will turn up, from all the walks of life that we've gotten to mingle with over these past decades. Folks that know us for what we gave and shared, the ones who have come to know us truly for who we are, not for what we might own and have."

"Love, actually!"

"Love and respect."

"And we don't have to wait for the eulogy at the wake to find out."

"Nope, isn't that the truth. My days now are filled with such contentment, wherever I go. I know I'm changing lives, be that in small ways."

The men look at each other. After a moment's silence and changing the mood, Jaime interjects, returning their attention to the game board. "So, do you want me to give you a hint?"

Chapter Thirteen

RETHINKING MONEY

From Scarcity to Sustainable Abundance

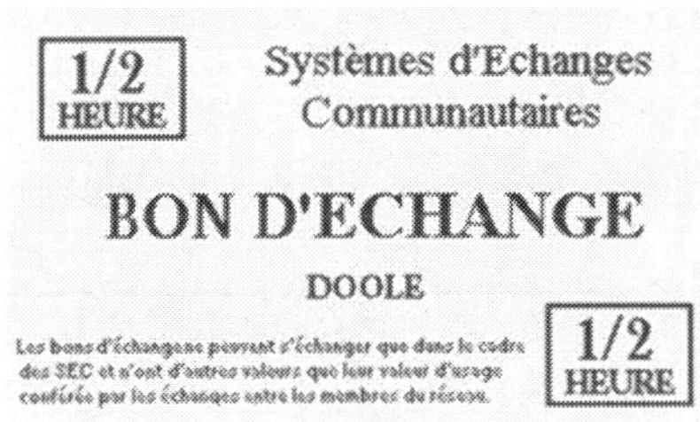

The debate on the future of money is not about inflation or deflation, fixed or flexible exchange rates, gold or paper standards, but about the kind of society in which money is to operate.[1]

GEORG SIMMEL, German philosopher and sociologist

Scarcity, particularly our warped view of monetary scarcity, which we inherited, can best be summed up in the following allegorical tale.

> A fisherman encounters a philosopher and happily informs her about his discovery: that all life in the sea is at least two inches long. Furthermore, the fishmonger has repeatedly made several market tests that prove his position unequivocally. Consequently, nobody wants fish smaller than two inches because they have never seen one. The philosopher smiles kindly and advises him gently,

> "There is a simple explanation for your findings: Your net has a two-inch mesh. If you were to use a net with finer-gauged netting, or employ another method, you would find that the ocean is a lot richer than you think. In fact, it's teeming with life. There are thousands of smaller species of fish in the sea, and oysters, clams, and snails that your nets will never catch. What's more, your research is skewed, since anyone you've ever surveyed could only buy seafood that's greater than two inches long, or wide, for that matter. Your fishing nets, dear man, predetermine your perception of reality."[2]

Donella Meadows, a systems thinker and advocate for sustainability, puts it another way: "Your paradigm is so intrinsic to your mental process that you are hardly aware of its existence until you try to communicate with someone with a different paradigm."[3]

The paradigm of the conventional, hypercompetitive money system is similar to the fisherman's net that limits what can be perceived and valued. Furthermore, because this purview has become so ingrained, to believe that there is another way, a cooperative way, is nigh impossible.

The dire consequences of this misperception are compounded by the many grave issues that now challenge humanity, such as the erosion of the middle class, economic growth without job creation, a deepening ecocrisis, the growing ranks of the uninsured, and an increasing illiterate and innumerate underclass.

For the most part, our educational systems remain rooted in the outdated and fractured Prussian model, which teaches people to take orders rather than think for themselves. Paired with the technological advances in communications, we are left swimming in an ever-engulfing sea of facts, unable to find meaning, never mind wisdom.

As entire economies are derailed, retirement plans for those in their golden years and the dreams of younger generations are dashed and left to burn on a funeral pyre of neglect. Growing sectors of the population remain disregarded and underserved. Furthermore, the failing economies make paupers of us all by eroding our well-being, our sense of security, and the honoring of our innate gifts and skills, and perhaps most profoundly, by threatening the very sustainability of our fragile blue-green planet.

There is plenty of blame to go around. While the rhetoric of culpability cites failed policies, the deeper causes are the flawed structure of the conventional competitive money system and the obstacles to examining it.

As we have seen, our current beliefs and practices about money, deliberated by high priests in the temples of central banks, were extrapolated from a series of economic assumptions based on the faulty and incomplete understanding of physics that prevailed at the end of the 19th century. They reflect the limited Newtonian view of a clockwork universe, static and immutable, rather than the more dynamic, complex, highly interdependent, and unpredictable universe of Bohr and the modern school of nonlinear dynamics.

Policy making, whether in business or in politics, based on forecasts distorted by the conventional money system is at best shortsighted, if not outright erroneous. Classic economic solutions tend to fall into one of two categories: to depend on the vicissitudes of the free market and rely on trickle-down economics or to implement strategies that attempt to redistribute wealth.

As long as conventional money retains its monopoly, there will always be insufficiency and untended needs. Indeed, this monopoly fuels both rampant fear of scarcity and its partner, greed. The traditional hyperrational explanations offered up for this ongoing universal suffering, disenfranchisement, and injustice fail to address the real issues.

Until the true problems are uncovered, real and sustainable solutions are unlikely. For example, it is nearly impossible for a corporation to plan for the long term because of the pressure to produce quarterly gains to satisfy their shareholders. According to research, 78 percent of executives would "sacrifice long-term value to meet earnings targets. Moreover, the recent rise in equity-based compensation and the sensitivity of CEO turnover to the stock price has likely increased managers' myopic tendencies."[4] Another survey polled 15 nations, most of them in the developing world, and found that the majority of people canvassed want their governments to take steps to fight climate change, even if that entails costs.[5]

Money is still the most powerful secular force.

But money is merely a human construct. And like any human-devised technology, it needs to be reviewed and revised regularly to increase functionality and work out the inevitable bugs. We need Money 2.0, a new monetary ecology in which an array of different currencies, both cooperative and competitive, flow through all levels of society and all sectors.

Then this technology upgrade—money—transmutes. As shown in the fisherman's net story, "scarcity is contextual and [this] technology [becomes] an abundance-liberating force."[6]

WORK VERSUS JOBS

The notion that we can get the global economy back on track by stuffing the technology genie back into the bottle and return to the halcyon days of well-paying employment is a myth. It's much more complex. Developments in science make it possible now for factories to operate in complete darkness, with robotics replacing the flesh- and-blood assembly-line workers, with alarming alacrity. Jobs in the United States have been exported en masse to China, where labor costs are much lower; yet even in China, plans are evolving to replace the human labor force with robots and androids.[7]

And it doesn't stop there.

What is being touted as the Third Industrial Revolution is now well underway. "The old way of making things involved taking lots of parts and screwing or welding them together. Now a product can be designed on a computer and 'printed' on a 3D printer, which creates a solid object by building up successive layers of material. The digital design can be tweaked with a few mouse clicks. The 3D printer can run unattended and can make many things which are too complex for a traditional factory to handle. In time, these amazing machines may be able to make almost anything, anywhere—from your garage to an African village."[8]

With the press of a button, the replacement for a broken vacuum cleaner part, for example, will be instantaneous and localized, if not at home, then at the neighborhood print shop. In such a scenario, industrial hubs with their networks of roads and railways that support the distribution of goods will become a thing of the past.

This movement to smaller and more localized production and distribution of goods will be widespread and universal. Energy, food cultivation, and water systems will be designed on a local scale but culminate in a matrix where everything scales from the smallest up to the largest while maintaining the fractal properties. Eventually, many more things will be designed to be distributed, scalable, and replicable. This ensures resilience and interdependence and consequently provides security and peace of mind.

Physicist Dr. Frank Baylin comments: "This is why, for instance, we see a multitude of smaller-scale, natural farms that follow nature's heartbeat, why truly renewable and sustainable energy systems will feature many smaller-scale, decentralized facilities in combination with just a few massive plants, and why cooperative currencies are so crucial for the survival of one-size-fits-all national, debt-based, fiat currencies. Furthermore, just as natural systems are inherently diverse, resilient, and able to rapidly self-repair when they are given half a chance, so can economic ecologies thrive when using an appropriate mix of conventional debt-based fiat and cooperative currencies that draw upon the existing but often unsourced talents and passions latent within any culture. If we do choose, however, to not go with the natural flow, we will suffer the obvious consequences of successive crises and ultimate failure."[9]

As these systems evolve, our concept of work will also be transformed.

The distinction between job and work is an important one to understand. The word *job*is relatively new, dating only from the Industrial Revolution. It was initially defined as a "pile of things to be done" or, even more precisely, "something done for hire, with a view for monetary profit."[10] In contrast, *work*is a very old word. Its first appearance in English dates from the Aelfric Homilies of the 11th century: "That work was begun under God's will." In English, the words *work* and *worship* have the same root. Some languages, such as Hebrew, still use the same word for "work" and "worship" today.

As new currencies are designed and circulated, many new means of making a living will emerge. Unlike today, when our passions most often are divorced from our jobs, work will encourage "following one's bliss." We will be remunerated for using our abilities and talents in the emergent multicurrency environment.

This is already happening, as ordinary people are doing extraordinary things within their communities.

By using additional monetary tools, new possibilities surface to meet the serious challenges of the 21st century. This is achieved not only by the mindful design of innovative cooperative monetary systems, including those already established, but also by those to come that will follow nature's grand design by creating a monetary ecosystem. This is a system where local, regional, and purpose-driven currencies balance out the role of the larger-scale national and supranational currencies and, by their scale and range, lead to a new paradigm of win-win, a system that benefits all.

Monetary scarcity can be a thing of the past. This core message has been communicated in various ways.[11]

It is powerful and compelling to realize that we now have in our hands the tools to fashion the world we envision for ourselves and future generations.

We seem to be just baby steps away from starting a journey of revelation and invention. Despite centuries of discoveries, astronomers and physicists say that only 5 percent of the universe is currently known,[12] let alone understood. Even closer to home, on our own planet, less than 5 percent of the oceans have been explored.[13] Furthermore, we certainly don't know what we don't know.

Humanity's ability to shift and adapt is grounded in education. Daniel H. Pink writes engagingly about the surfacing of predominantly right-brained thinkers, those who are mentally highly visual, intuitive, and nonlinear in their thinking, and how brains wired this way are the best hope for humanity's future. Pink says, "The future belongs to a different kind of person with a different kind of mind: designers, inventors, teachers, storytellers—creative and empathic right-brained thinkers whose abilities mark the fault line between who gets ahead and who doesn't."[14] New paradigms in education are beginning to take into consideration this increase in right-brain dominance, particularly in young children, providing a welcome alternative to the traditional Dickensian drill- and-kill methods.

"Frankly, it's not good enough to just simply think outside the box anymore. We need to throw the box away and think in an entirely different way. In order to do that, we need to teach our children *how*to learn by capitalizing on their individual strengths. And each is unique. That way a life of continual learning, adaptation and empowerment is possible. Each person can truly access his or her genius—a compass to follow one's individual bliss," comments Kimberly Kassner, author of *You're a Genius—And I Can Prove It!* Each person, when given the opportunity, becomes a unique and brilliant being.[15]

This shift away from paradigms that are seated in competition and unmitigated self-interest is taking place in other areas of endeavor as well.

"Traditional aid and economic development is analogous to the proverbial 'giving them fish or teaching them how to fish.' And too often, teaching them where the knowledge cannot be applied because the playing field is skewed against them and rules of the game are set by a few people from a scarcity mind-set. In the context of the globalized world today, the next crucial developmental shift is to not only give them fish and teach them how to fish, but to set new rules from a mindset of abundance based on a just and sustainable world giving them market access, financing, and the expertise to adapt the technologies of angling as the nature of fisheries will inevitably change; and nest these technical skills and systems understanding in people's agency—their transformational leadership capabilities," says Dr. Monica Sharma, former director of Leadership and Capacity Development for the United Nations.[16]

She explains that contemporary leaders of courage and compassion are operating from a profound space.

These leaders are pattern makers, not just problem solvers. They deal with what is not working by creating alternatives. They are able to identify, distinguish, design, and generate responses that integrate the different domains related to the entangled hierarchies of any given situation. They do more than solve complex societal problems at a surface level. They actively address the deeper dimensions of reality. They demonstrate that it is possible to design and implement programs differently: solving problems; synthesizing and making sense of the invisible patterns affecting reality, as well as endless incomprehensible bits of information; breaking new ground; and establishing alternatives—ethical and principled action sourcing their inner values and wisdom.

"This will ensure sustainability and ensure decisions based on their wisdom. This conscious full-spectrum approach truly supports the growth of economies and local communities, enabling everyone's deep participation in technological and system shifts, while being sourced in their wisdom and culture. This is how the new paradigm will be created for sustainable development to become a reality and genuinely thrive."

Sharma points out: "The persistence of poverty and the lack of opportunity to live and thrive for so many is a mea sure of our response to date. Our sense of scarcity, no matter how much we have; our definition of 'success,' where the proxy is basically money or 'wealth' without any sense of sufficiency; our rhetoric of partnership in the midst of systems set up for competition preclude creative responses. Our future depends on the choices we make. Will we continue doing the same things again and again, hoping to reverse the situation, or will we choose to generate a different reality?"

There is a deep yearning for a new context, a new story, a new mythology in which to interpret and play out the human experience.

Scholar, philosopher, and researcher in human capacities, Jean Houston, muses, "The new myth would be a myth of exchange. It's not simply the world monetary system with its multitrillion-dollar casino that runs around every day, which is the current mythos. The core of the new mythos is the world Mind—a world Spirit. This is where the ecology of the world spirit can be only partially financial. It has to be the spirit, the culture, the dance, the music, the generosity of people toward each other, and I think this is happening because of the rise of the women to full partnership with men in the whole domain of human affairs with a new emphasis on process rather than on product, on making things grow, cohere, relate. This is already the biggest shift, I think, in human sensibility."

She continues: "Take the fact that the Arab Spring, whatever happens with it, became the basis of the Occupy Movement, and what has happened there, the end of which we neither have seen nor can imagine. And it will end up in many movements, leading us into a deeper exploration and communication of the steps toward radical democracy and the gradual arising of a world civilization with high individuation of culture. This is a shift that is changing everything. As the great civilizations 4,000 years ago grew up along the great rivers—the Tigris, the Euphrates, the Ganges, the Nile, the Yellow River—so a whole new order of civilization is finding its outer mythic base in the Internet and social media and on the *innernet*in its inner mythic expression of psycho-spiritual growth and development."[17]

The new mythology is one of emancipation, the liberation to express in word and in deed each individual's gifts and abilities. This is fostered by a truly *co-operative* space of infinite possibilities, unlimited potential, and immeasurable creativity. Cooperative currencies are the ideal facilitator of this new mythology and its technologies, allowing regular folks to make an extraordinary difference in their own lives and in their communities.

To paraphrase the insightful words of the late Irish politician James Larkin, when tackling the issues facing a nation going through monumental changes, having just discarded the shackles of 700 years of colonialism: *It is not so much the bread on the table, but also the rose.* What Larkin was saying is still poignant and relevant today, almost a century later, that there is a deep yearning in all of us that goes beyond the practicalities of providing one's daily bread. There is a profound hunger for decency and beauty in such a seemingly graceless age.

And in the midst of all this, the good and the not so good, what continues to triumph is human ingenuity and the indomitable nature of the human spirit. History is full of incredible selfless acts of human kindness and bravery. On the other side of the coin, it no longer needs to be a game of apparent chance with victors and the vanquished. Rather, through intentionality, rigor, responsibility, and even forgiveness, it is possible to transmute the base metal of hypercompetitiveness, the bank-rupt denomination of the obsolete, into golden opportunities for all who so choose.

The dominant system of money has already been rethought, reengineered, and refashioned by ordinary people as they strive toward a more just civil society. Consequently, what is emerging is a civil society in which true wealth is defined not only in terms of financial assets but also as capital inherent in the spirit, creative genius, and unbounded potential of the ever-evolving human species.

Scarcity is indeed relative. Humanity may hit limits in material growth but there is unfathomable room for growth in work and creativity, and this for many future generations! By rethinking money, it is possible to enjoy even more than a period of prosperity but rather *a new era of genuine sustainable abundance.*

NOTES

Chapter Opener Currency Images

Chapter 1: Euro
Chapter 2: British Pound
Chapter 3: Japanese Yen
Chapter 4: Hands, New Zealand
Chapter 5: Brixton Pound, London
Chapter 6: Hanbat LETS, South Korea
Chapter 7: Madison HOURS, Madison, Wisconsin
Chapter 8: NOPPES, Amsterdam, The Netherlands
Chapter 9: Salt Spring Dollars, Canada
Chapter 10: Wörgl, Wörgl, Austria
Chapter 11: Talente Tauschkreis, Vorarlberg, Austria
Chapter 12: Boon Kud Chum, Thailand
Chapter 13: Doole Bon, Senegal, Africa

Introduction

[1] Alan Wilson Watts from his talk titled "From Time to Eternity." Transcript published in *The Culture of Counterculture*(Rutland, VT: C.E. Tuttle, 1999), 59.

[2] Gerard Caprio and Daniela Klingebiel, "Bank Insolvencies: Cross-Country Experience," Policy Research Working Paper, no.1620 (Washington, DC: World Bank, Policy and Research Department, 1996); J. Frankel and A. Rose, "Currency Crashes in Emerging Markets: An Empirical Treatment," *Journal of International Economics*4 (1996): 351–366; Graziela L. Kaminsky and

Carmen M. Reinhart, "The Twin Crisis: The Causes of Banking and Balance of Payment Problems," *American Economic Review*89, no.3 (1999): 473–500; and, for the data after 2006, Luc Laevan and Fabian Valencia, "Resolution of Banking Crises: The Good, the Bad, and the Ugly," IMF Working Paper 10/146 (Washington, DC: International Monetary Fund, 2010), 4. www.imf.org/external/pubs/ft/wp/2010/wp10146.pdf/.

[3] www.imf.org/external/pubs/ft/wp/2012/wp12202.pdf and www.telegraph.co.uk/finance/comment/9623863/IMFs-epic-plan-to-conjure-away-debt-and-dethrone-bankers.html.

[4] Edward Luce, "America's Dream Unravels," *Financial Times,*March 31, 2012.

Chapter 1

[1] Kimberly Palmer, "Do You Live in a High-Debt City?" Yahoo! Finance, September 8, 2010. http://finance.yahoo.com/.

[2] Gary Becker, "Will the Next Generation Be Better Off Than Their Parents, Generation?" Becker-Posner Blog. www.becker-posner-blog.com/2010/08/.

[3] "$22,350 a Year for a Family of Four or $10,890 for an Individual in the 48 Contiguous States and DC," *Federal Register*76, no.13 (2011): 3637–3638.

[4] Tami Luhby, "Government Assistance Expands," CNN Money, February 7, 2012. http://money.c

nn.com/2012/02/07/news/economy/government_assistance/index.htm.

[5] Jason Deparle, Robert Gebeloff, and Sabrina Tavernise, "Older, Suburban and Struggling, 'Near Poor' Startle the Census," *New York Times,*November 18, 2011.

[6] Richard Cranium, "Almost 80% of Americans Are Living Paycheck to Paycheck," Daily Kos, October 30, 2010. www.dailykos.com/story/2010/10/30/915125/-Almost-80-of-Americans-live-paycheck-to-paycheck-w-poll./-Almost-80-of-Americans-live-paycheck-to-paycheck-w-poll.

[7] Matt Krantz writes, "More than half of all workers have less than $25,000 in savings, according to a survey by the Employee Benefit Research Institute" in "Many Have Little or No Savings as Retirement Looms," *USA Today,* December 4, 2011.

[8] Haya El Nasser writes, "Today, you are one of 7 billion people on Earth. About half were added just in the past 40 years, and 3 billion more are expected by 2100" in "World Hits 7 Billion," *USA Today,* October 31, 2011.

[9] Translation by Dr. Alexander Tsoucatos.

[10] Paul J. Davies, "Downturn in China Spreads to Key Sectors," *Financial Times,* September 9, 2012.

[11] According to the U.S. government official poverty figures, 8.9 percent of those 65 and older were living in poverty in 2009. But when

out-of-pocket medical costs and other expenses are taken into account, the elderly poverty rate nearly doubles to 16.1 percent. See Philip Issa and Sheila R. Zedlewski, "Poverty among Older Americans, 2009," February 2011, Urban Institute, Program on Retirement Policy. www.urban.org/uploadedpdf/412296-Poverty-Among-Older-Americans.pdf.

[12] Dennis Cauchon, "Student Loans Outstanding Will Exceed $1 Trillion This Year," *USA Today,*October 25, 2011.

[13] www.nytimes.com/2011/11/03/education/average-student-loan-debt-grew-by-5-percent-in-2010.html: "Students who graduated from college in 2010 with student loans owed an average of $25 ,250, up 5 percent from the previous year.... The average debt—once again the highest on record—came as the class of 2010 faced an unemployment rate for new college graduates of 9.1 percent, the highest in recent years, according to the report by the Project on Student Debt, which pointed out that unemployment rates for those without college degrees were still higher."

[14] Jeevan Vasagar, "Graduates Warned of Record 70 Applicants for Every Job," *Guardian,* July 5, 2010.

[15] Paul Krugman, "Oligarchy, American Style," *New York Times,*November 3, 2011.

[16] Bernice H. Hill, *Money and the Spiritual Warrior*(Boulder, CO: Five Centuries Foundation, 2004), 56–59.

[17] Jacob Needleman, *Money and the Meaning of Life*(New York: Doubleday Currency, 1994), 239.

[18] "Boy in China Reportedly Sells Kidney to Purchase iPhone and iPad," Fox News, April 6, 2012. www.foxnews.com/world/2012/04/06/boy-in-china-reportedly-sells-kidney-to-purchase-iphone-and-ipad/#ixzz1tT3mSNV5.

[19] The female participants range from primarily school-aged girls to house wives. (交援) means "compensated dating" and is a practice that originated in Japan, where older men give money and/or luxury gifts. See www.chinahush.com/2011/11/24/young-compensated-dating-girls-in-shanghai/. Also, an anonymous girl postedon San Francisco's Craigslist site that she will offer herself to get tickets to Coachella. /24/young-compensated-dating-girls-in-shanghai/. Also, an anonymous girl posted on San Francisco's Craigslist site that she will offer herself to get tickets to Coachella. See http://elitedaily.com/elite/2012/girl-offer-sex-coachella-tickets/.

[20] "Policymakers, cognizant that 44 states project budget shortfalls in 2012, were exploring ways to let these states declare bankruptcy" in "States Most Likely to Go

Bankrupt," Daily Beast, January 26, 2011. www.thedailybeast.com/articles/2011/01/26/states-most-likely-to-go-bankrupt.html. Also, see "50 States in Debt," Daily Beast Business Section. www.thedailybeast.com/galleries/2010/06/14/50-states-in/01/26/states-most-likely-to-go-bankrupt.html.

[21] "Unlike cities, the states are barred from seeking protection in federal bankruptcy court. Any effort to change that status would have to clear high constitutional hurdles because the states are considered sovereign," in Mary Williams Walsh, "A Path Is Sought for States to Escape Their Debt Burdens," *New York Times,*January 20, 2011.

[22] Regan Morris, "Californian City of Stockton Files for Bankruptcy," BBC News, June 27, 2012. www.bbc.co.uk/news/world-us-canada-18605326.

[23] Ken Orski, "The Promise and Risks of Public-Private Partnerships," *Innovation NewsBriefs*21, no.6, April 5, 2010.

[24] François Morin, *Le Nouveau Mur de l'Argent*(Paris: Seuil, 2006), 228.

Chapter 2

[1] Aristotle, *Nichomachean Ethics*(350BC), 1133.

[2] Its official name was the *solidus.*It was first issued by Emperor Constantine (306–337AD) and circulated widely, even beyond the

Byzantine Empire in both Europe and Asia, until well into the Middle Ages.

[3] The true conspiracy saga of how this law was passed in the United States on the eve of Christmas 1913, just before World War I, is the topic of Edward Griffin, *The Creature from Jekyll Island: A Second Look at the Federal Reserve*(Westlake Village, CA: American Media, 1994).

[4] A governor of the Bank of En gland (a private company at that time) was being questioned by the British Parliament:

"Can you please inform us about how much gold there is at the Bank of En gland?"

"In ample sufficiency, Sir."

"Can you be more precise?"

"No, Sir."

[5] L. Randall Wray, *Understanding Modern Money: The Key to Full Employment and Price Stability*(Cheltenham, En gland: Edward Elgar, 1998), viii–ix.

[6] Steven D. Levitt and Stephen J. Dubner, *Freakonomics: A Rogue Economist Explores the Hidden Side of Everything*(New York: William Morrow, 2005), 15.

[7] Eric Beinhocker, *The Origins of Wealth: Evolution, Complexity and the Radical Remaking of Economics*(Boston: Harvard Business School Press, 2006). Beinhocker is a senior advisor to McKinsey and Company, and was

named by *Fortune Magazine*as "Business Leader of the Next Century." Chapters 2 and 3 of that book should be required reading for anybody who ever took or gave a course in economics.

[8] Eric Liu and Nick Hanauer, *The Gardens of Democracy: A New American Story of Citizenship, the Economy and the Role of Government*(Seattle, WA: Sasquatch Books, 2011).

[9] Gregory Bateson, *Steps to an Ecology of Mind*(New York: Ballantine, 1972).

[10] Clifford Cobb, Ted Halstead, and Jonathan Rowe, "If the GDP Is Up, Why Is America Down?" *Atlantic Monthly,*October 1995.

[11] Ibid.

[12] There have been two exceptions: Friedrich Hayek and Maurice Allais both received the Nobel in Economics, and both severely criticized the prevailing monetary paradigm. However, they expressed such criticism several years *after*having received the award.

[13] John Maynard Keynes, *The General Theory of Employment, Interest, and Money* (Amherst, NY: Prometheus Books, 1997). See Encyclopedia Britannica, September 10, 2012. www.britannica.com/EBchecked/topic/315921/John-Maynard-Keynes/315921suppinfo/Supplemental-Information.

Chapter 3

[1] Regulations specify that roughly 10 percent of a deposit needs to be kept as a reserve in case the customer withdraws the funds. Therefore, up to 90 percent is available to make new loans. Changing that percentage is one of the techniques whereby the Federal Reserve controls the quantities of credit money the banks will be able to create. The exact percentages also vary with the kind of deposit made: The longer the term of the deposit, the lower the percentage of "reserves" required. The 90 percent rule of this example, enabling a "multiplier" of about nine to one, is an illustrative average.

[2] Emeka Chiakwelu, "Nigeria Payment of Foreign Debt: The Largest Transfer of Wealth in Modern Time," Africa Political and Economic Strategic Center (Afripol). www.afripol.org.

[3] Anup Shah, "Poverty Facts and Stats," Global Issues, September 20, 2010.www.globalissues.org/article/26/poverty-facts-and-stats #src22.

[4] Geoffrey Ekenna, "Nigeria's Debt Back to $37b, Says Okonjo-Iweala," [Lagos] *Nigerian Compass*, August 27, 2011.

[5] The exact formula is $(1+i)^{(n-1)}$, where *i* is the interest rate and *n* the number of years of the deposit.

[6] R. Putnam, *Making Democracy Work: Civic Traditions in Modern Italy*(Prince ton, NJ: Princeton University Press, 1993).

[7] F. Fukuyama, *Trust: Social Virtues and the Creation of Prosperity*(New York: Free Press, 1996).

[8] M. Castell, *Das Informationszeitalter Bd.II*(Leverkusen, Germany: Leske & Budrich, 2002), 275ff.; and M. Castell, *Das Informationszeitalter Bd.III*(Leverkusen, Germany: Leske & Budrich, 2003), Chapter 3.

[9] G. Rodgers C. Gore, and J.B. Figueiredi (eds.), *Social Exclusion: Rhetoric, Reality, Responses*(Geneva: International Institute of Labour Studies, 1997); and E. Mingione, *Urban Poverty and the Underclass*(Oxford: Wiley-Blackwell, 1996).

[10] J. Coleman, *Foundations of Social Theory*(Cambridge, MA: Harvard University Press, 1990), especially Chapter 12; and R. Putnam, *Bowling Alone: The Collapse and Revival of the American Community*(New York: Simon & Schuster, 2000).

[11] John E. Yellen of the National Science Foundation in Washington, DC, has excavated !Kung archaeological sites with colleague Alison S. Brooks of George Washington University.

[12] John E. Yellen, "The Transformation of the Kalahari!Kung," *Scientific American* 262, no.4 (1990): 96–100. See also www.ralph-abraham .org/articles/MS%2383.Kung/kung2.html.

[13] The best works on the topic of gift economies are the classic by Marcel Mauss, "Essai sur le

Don: Forme et raison de l'échange dans les sociétés archaiques," *L'Année Sociologique* 1 (1923–1924): 30–186; and Lewis Hyde, *The Gift: Imagination and the Erotic Life of Property,* 3rd ed. (New York: Vintage Books, 1983). See full details in Bernard Lietaer, *The Future of Money* (London: Random House, 1999), Chapter 6.

[14] George Soros, *On Globalization*(Oxford: Public Affairs, 2002), 14.

[15] Joseph E. Stiglitz, "Of the 1%, by the 1%, for the 1%," *Vanity Fair,*May 2011.

[16] Correspondence with the authors via Margrit Kennedy.

[17] Report by the Congressional Bud get Office (CBO), ABC News, October 26, 2011. http://abcnews.go.com/Business/income-doubles-top-percent-1979/story?id=14817561.

[18] Arnold Toynbee, *A Study of History*(Oxford: Oxford University Press, 1960).

[19] Zbigniew Brzezinski, *The Choice: Global Domination or Global Leadership* (New York: Basic Books, 2004), 217.

[20] Richard Duncan, *The Dollar Crisis: Causes, Consequences, Cures* (Singapore: John Wiley & Sons, 2003).

[21] Putnam, *Making Democracy Work.*

[22] Fukuyama, *Trust.*

[23] Castell, *Das Informationszeitalter Bd.II.*and *Bd III.*

[24] Rodgers, et al., *Social Exclusion*and also E. Minigione, *Urban Poverty and the Underclass*(Oxford: Blackwell, 1996).

Chapter 4

[1] Glyn Davies, *A History of Money from Ancient Times to the Present Day* (Cardiff: University of Wales Press, 1994), 27.

[2] This definition has been explored by Rabbi Nilton Bonder in his book, *The Kabbalah of Money: Jewish Insights on Giving, Owning, and Receiving*(Boston: Shambhala Books, 1996).

[3] Estimate made by the authors based on conversations with practitioners globally.

[4] For more details, see Bernard Lietaer, Robert Ulanowicz, and Sally Goerner, "White Paper on All the Options for Managing Systemic Bank Crises," October 2008; Robert Ulanowicz, Sally Goerner, Bernard Lietaer, and Rocio Gomez, "Quantifying Sustainability: Efficiency, Resilience and the Return of Information Theory," *Journal of Ecological Complexity*, February–March 2010. See www.lietaer.com.

[5] Luc Laevan and Fabian Valencia, "Resolution of Banking Crises: The Good, the Bad, and the Ugly," IMF Working Paper 10/146 (Washington, DC: International Monetary Fund, 2010), 4. www.imf.org/external/pubs/ft/wp/2010/wp10146.pdf; Ge-rard Caprio and Daniela Klingebiel, "Bank Insolvencies: Cross-Country Experience," Policy Research Working Paper PRWP1620 (Washington,

DC: World Bank, 1996); rard Caprio and Daniela Klingebiel, "Bank Insolvencies: Cross-Country Experience," Policy Research Working Paper PRWP1620 (Washington, DC: World Bank, 1996); Graziela L. Kaminsky and Carmen M. Reinhart, "Twin Crises: The Causes of Banking and Balance-of-Payments Problems," *American Economic Review,*American Economic Association, 89, no.3 (June 1999): 473–500.

[6] Fritz Schwartz, *Das Experiment von Wörgl*(Bern, Switzerland: Genossens-chaft Verlag Freiwirtschaftlicher Schriften, 1951).

[7] See M. Amato, L. Fantacci, and L. Doria, *Complementary Currency Systems in a Historical Perspective*(Milan: Bocconi University, Department of Economic History,

[8] Marc Bloch, *Esquisse d'une histoire monétaire de l'Europe*(Paris: Armand Colin, 1954); Marcel Van der Beek, "Het Muntwezen in de Landen van Her-waartsover," in *Keizer Karels Geldbeurs: Geld en Financiën in de XVIe Eeuw*(Essays for a Cata log for Special Exhibitions held in Gent, April 1 to 24, 2000, and in Brussels, May 15 to June 30, 2000) (National Bank of Belgium, 2000), 147–169. 2003).

[9] Initially issued by Constantine (306–337 ad), its official name was the *solidus,* but it was generally known as the *bezant.*It was issued at the same weight (4.55 grams of gold) and purity (98 percent pure gold) for a record 700 years.

It circulated widely all over Europe and the Middle East, way beyond the borders of the Byzantine Empire.

[10] See Carlo M. Cipolla, *Il governo della moneta a Firenze e a Milano nei secoli XIV–XVI*(Bologna, Italy: Società editrice il Mulino, 1990).

[11] Fernand Braudel, *La dinamica del capitalismo*(Bologna, Italy: Società editrice il Mulino, 1981); Aldo de Maddalena, *La ricchezza dell'Europa*(Milan: Egea, 1992).

[12] G. Einaudi, "Teoria della moneta immaginaria nel tempo da Carlomagno alla Rivoluzione francese," *Rivista di Storia Economica*1, no.1 (Torino, 1936).

[13] Jean-Philippe Bouchaud and Marc Mézard, "Wealth Condensation in a Simple Model of Economy," 2000, www.thetransitioner.org/wiki/tiki-download _file.php?fileId=6. See also Jean-Philippe Bouchaud, "La (regrettable) complexité des systèmes économiques," *Pour la Science,* December 2003.

[14] David A. Bosnich, "The Principle of Subsidiarity." www.acton.org/publications/randl/rl_article_200.php: "Subsidiarity holds that nothing should be done by a larger and more complex organization, which can be done as well by a smaller and simpler /randl/rl_article_200.php: "Subsidiarity holds that nothing should be done by a larger and more complex organization,

which can be done as well by a smaller and simpler organization. In other words, any activity which can be performed by a more decentralized entity should be. This principle is a bulwark of limited government and personal freedom." The concept or principle is found in several constitutions around the world. For example, the Tenth Amendment to the U.S. Constitution asserts states' rights. Subsidiarity was established in European Union law by the Treaty of Maastricht, signed on February 7, 1992, and entered into force on November 1, 1993. The present formulation is contained in Article 5(2) of the Treaty on European Union (consolidated version following the Treaty of Lisbon, which entered into force on December 1, 2009).

[15] Its promoters included most leading American economists of the 1930s: Henry Simons and Paul Douglas from Chicago University, Irving Fisher from Yale, Frank Graham and Charles Whittlesley from Prince ton, and Earl Hamilton from Duke University—and also a young fledgling economist named Milton Friedman, who later came to be known for a very different set of monetary views.

[16] While the Chicago Plan or its most recent versions, such as the one presented in Joseph Huber and James Robertson, *Creating New Money: A Monetary Reform for the Information*

Age, New Economics Foundation, 2000, available as a free pdf download from www.jamesrobertson.com/subject-guide.htm#money. These authors propose to nationalize the money creation process; they have no intention of nationalizing the banking system itself. Banks would continue to compete with each other and to allocate financial resources as they do today. The only—but significant—difference is that their functioning would be based on 100 percent reserves, and they would therefore not be able to create debt money ex nihilo.

[17] www.imf.org/external/pubs/ft/wp/2012/wp12202.pdf and www.telegraph.co.uk/finance/comment/9623863/IMFs-epic-plan-to-conjure-away-debt-and-dethrone-bankers.html.

[18] F.A. Hayek, *Denationalisation of Money: The Argument Refined. The Theory and Practice of Concurrent Currencies*(Sussex, England: The Institute of Economic Affairs, first edition 1976, enlarged in 1978, 1990). See http://mises.org/books/denationalisation.pdf, p.28.

Chapter 5

[1] John Naisbitt, *Megatrends*(New York: Warner Books, 1982), 183.

[2] Paul Hawken, *Blessed Unrest: How the Largest Movement in the World Came into*

Being and Why No One Saw It Coming(New York: Viking, 2007), 4.

[3] Michael Linton, interview with Jacqui Dunne, December 9, 2011.

[4] Ibid.

[5] Edgar Cahn, interview with Jacqui Dunne, November 20, 2011.

[6] Ibid.

[7] Lisa Conlan, interview with Jacqui Dunne, January 9, 2012.

[8] Cahn, interview.

[9] Meltem Şendağ, interview with Jacqui Dunne, July 1, 2012.

[10] Cahn, interview.

[11] Ibid.

[12] Ibid.

[13] Stephanie Rearick, interview with Jacqui Dunne, May 22, 2012.

[14] Mira Luna, in conversation with Jacqui Dunne, June 29, 2012.

[15] Sharon Lee Schwartz, interview with Jacqui Dunne, January 3, 2012.

[16] "IRS Ruling," TimeBanks USA. http://besttimebank.org/Links/Time%20Dollar/IRS%20Ruling.htm.

[17] Margrit Kennedy, interview with Jacqui Dunne, June 1, 2012.

[18] Ibid.

[19] Margrit Kennedy and Bernard Lietaer: *Re-gional-waehrungen: Neue Wege zu nach-*

haltigem Wohlstand(Munich: Riemann Verlag, 2004).

[20] Civic Economics, "Andersonville Study of Retail Economics," BALLE Business Alliance for Local Living Economies, October 2004. www.livingeconomies.org.

[21] Kennedy, interview.

[22] Christian Gelleri, interview with Jacqui Dunne, January 17, 2012.

[23] Susan Witt, correspondence with Jacqui Dunne, November 1, 2011.

[24] Lawrence H. Officer and Samuel H. Williamson, "Purchasing Power of Money in the United States from 1774 to Present," Measuring Worth, 2011. www.measuringworth.com.

[25] Marjorie Deane and Robert Pringle, *The Central Banks*(New York: Viking, 1995), 352–354; United Nations Statistics Division, *International Labor Office Monthly Bulletin of Statistics, 1990 to 1996.* http://unstats.un.org/unsd/mbs/.

[26] Edgar Kampers, interview with Jacqui Dunne, March 19, 2012.

Chapter 6

[1] Speech, New York, October 25, 2010. See www.qfinance.com/finance-and-business-quotes/banking-business-quotes/banking.

[2] James Van Dyke, "'Bank Transfer Day,' What Really Just Happened?" Javelin Strategy and Research, January 26, 2012. www.javelinstrategy.com.

[3] "Move Your Money Movement This Saturday," CNN Money, November 4, 2011.

[4] Antoin E. Murphy, *Money in an Economy without Banks: The Case of Ireland* [(Manchester: Manchester School of Economics, March 1978).

[5] Michael Linton, interview with Jacqui Dunne, June 2, 2012.

[6] Murphy, *Money in an Economy without Banks.*

[7] Some people had access to British pounds; although usually accepted by merchants, these transactions were in a minority. See ibid.

[8] WIR Annual Report, 2010. www.wir.ch.

[9] James Stodder, "The Macro-Stability of Swiss WIR-Bank Spending: Balance and Leverage Effects," paper submitted to *Swiss Journal of Economics and Statistics,*2011.

[10] WIR Annual Report, 2010, 12. www.wir.ch.

[11] James Stodder, "Complementary Credit Networks and Macro-Economic Stability: Switzerland's Wirtschaftsring," *Jounal of Economic Behavior and Organization*72 (October 2009).

[12] James Stodder, "Reciprocal Exchange Networks: Implications for Macroeconomic Stability," paper presented at the International Electronic and Electrical Engineering (IEEE) Engineering Management Society (EMS), Albuquerque, NM, August 2000, 3.

[13] James Stodder and Bernard Lietaer, "The Macro-Stability of Swiss WIR-Bank Spending:

Balance, Velocity and Leverage," (forthcoming).

[14] Tobias Studer, "Le Système WIR dans l'optique d'un chercheur Américain," WirPlus. www.wir.ch.

[15] Amy Kirschner interview with Jacqui Dunne, December 2, 2011.

[16] João Joaquim de Melo Neto Segundo interviewed by Jacqui Dunne, December 28, 2011.

[17] "Cifras más reseñables, Corporación MONDRAGON" (Mondragon Corporation). www.mondragon-corporation.com/CAS/Magnitudes-Econ%C3%B3micas/Cifras-m%C3%A1s-rese%C3%B1ables.aspx.

[18] Henk Van Arkel, interview with Jacqui Dunne, December 16, 2011.

[19] Asier Ansorena, Asesor interviewed by Jacqui Dunne, January 13, 2012.

[20] Aurineide Alves Cordeiro interview based on written questions by Jacqui Dunne and translation by Aiser Ansorena.

[21] Celia de Anca and Cristina Trullols, "JAK Medlemsbank Free Interest Banking in a Changing Global Financial System," IE Business School, January 11, 2011. www.ie.edu/business-school/.

[22] Ibid.

[23] Mark Anielski, "An Assessment of Sweden's No-Interest Bank," The JAK Members Bank,

Sweden, 2003. Prepared by ANIELSKI Management Inc., Canada.

[24] Eddy Allen interview via personal correspondence with Jacqui Dunne, July 5, 2012.

[25] Fareed Zakaria, "The 'Angry Birds' Dress," CNN, December 13, 2012. globalpublicsquare .blogs.cnn.com.

[26] Mark Fischer interviewed by Jacqui Dunne, July 3, 2012.

[27] Lance Whitney, "Cell Phone Subscriptions to Hit 5 Billion Globally," CNET, February 16, 2010. http://reviews.cnet.com/8301-13970_7 -10454065-78.html#ixzz1k6sXaPmP.

[28] Ross Tieman, "Mobile Phone Operators Revolutionise Cash Transfers," *Financial Times,* June 3, 2008.

Chapter 7

[1] John Wasik, "Where Is the Real US Jobs Plan?" *Reuters Money,*September 2, 2011.

[2] Martin Ford, "The Lights in the Tunnel: Automation, Accelerating Technology and the Economy of the Future." www.thelightsinthetunnel.com.

[3] McKinsey Global Institute, "An Economy That Works: Job Creation and America's Future," June 2011. www.mckinsey.com/insights/mgi.

[4] Brian Arthur, *The Second Economy McKinsey Quartley,*September 10, 2012. www.mckinseyq uarterly.com/Thesecond_economy_285.

[5] Kevin Kliesen and Julia Maués, "Are Small Businesses the Biggest Producers of Jobs?"

Federal Reserve Bank of St. Louis. www.kiplinger.com/columns/onthejob/archive/10-jobs-that-didnt-exist-10-years-ago.html#ixzz1krNeoFAX.

[6] Henk Van Arkel, interview with Jacqui Dunne, December 16, 2011.

[7] Edgar Kampers, interview with Jacqui Dunne, June 3, 2012.

[8] Koen de Beer, interview with Jacqui Dunne, May 30, 2012.

[9] Arthur Brock, interview with Jacqui Dunne, July 7, 2012.

[10] Ned Smith, "Incubators Heat Up Chances of Small Business Success," *Business News Daily,*October 5, 2010.

[11] Sergio Lub, interview with Jacqui Dunne, July 7, 2012.

Chapter 8

[1] "Recycling is done at a plant (itself made from recycled materials) by previously unemployed people including the homeless and recovering alcoholics. Paper recycling alone saves the equivalent of 1,200 trees a day. Recovered materials are sold to local industries, and the proceeds used to fund social programs." The Brazilian city of Curitiba may be most livable city in the world. See http://hopebuilding.pbworks.com/w/page/19222330/Brazilian%20city%20of%20Curitiba20may%20be%20most%20livable%20city%20in%20the%20world.

[2] See www.sb05.com/plenary/Lerner.html.

[3] See www.globeaward.org/winner-city-2010.

[4] The 1993–1995 data is derived from Indústria, Comércio e Turismo Gestão Rafael Creca (December 1996). The respective growth rates are 8.6 percent per annum for Curitiba, 6 percent for the state of Paraná, and 5 percent for Brazil. The respective per capita growth rates between 1980 and 1995 are 277 percent for Curitiba, 190 percent for Paraná, and 192 percent for Brazil. Statistics from Informaciones Socioeconomicas, issued by the Prefeitura da Cidade Curitiba (1996) compared with the Brazilian databases of SACEN, IPARDES, and SICT/ICPI.

[5] Richard A. Epstein, "Beyond Austerity," *Defining Ideas: A Hoover Institute Journal,* May 1, 2012. www.hoover.org/publications/defining-ideas/article/116071.

[6] Matthew Boesler, "Introducing the 'Geuro': A Radical New Currency Idea to Solve All of Greece's Problems," *Business Insider,*May 20, 2012. www.businessinsider.com/introducing-the-geuro-a-new-parallel-currency-to-solve-all-of-greeces-problems-2012-5#ixzz1vbUNQjTC.

[7] Edgar Kampers, interview with Jacqui Dunne, June 3, 2012.

[8] Lisa Conlan, interview with Jacqui Dunne, December 28, 2011.

[9] Jeffrey Freed, interview with Jacqui Dunne, March 2, 2012.
[10] Igor Byttebier, interview with Jacqui Dunne, May 25, 2012.
[11] There was only one test so far.

Chapter 9

[1] Richard H. Timberlake, "Private Production of Scrip-Money in the Isolated Community," *Journal of Money, Credit and Banking*19, no.4 (1987): 437–447.
[2] David Pugh, interview with Jacqui Dunne, January 17, 2012.
[3] Ibid.
[4] Becky Booth, interview with Jacqui Dunne, December 6, 2011.
[5] Ceri Green, "Time2Grow Evaluation 2010–2011," TimeBanking Wales, 2011. www.timebankingwales.org.uk/userfiles/Time2Grow%20-%20%20Evaluation.pdf.
[6] Paul Glover, interview with Jacqui Dunne, June 20, 2012.
[7] Ibid.
[8] Ibid.
[9] Jacqui Dunne is a board member of A Human Right.
[10] Kosta Grammatis, interview with Jacqui Dunne, May 13, 2012.
[11] Bryan Walsh, "Trash Problems in Paradise," *Time*magazine, January 7, 2008. www.time.co

m/time/world/article/0,8599,1701095,00.html #ixzz1xtgStTME.

[12] Rui Izumi, associate professor at the School of Economics, Senshu University, in Tokyo, personal correspondence with Jacqui Dunne: "Major factors that have contributed to the growth of local currencies: First, and perhaps surprisingly, was a program national television in the late 1990s called *Michael Ende's Last Message.* This broadcast profiled complementary systems from the 1930s in Europe up [to] today's WIR, LETS, and other popular systems. It touched a collective nerve. At that time, Japan was in deflationary depression after the East-Asian financial crisis happened in 1997 and a bubble economic collapse in 1991, and these caused many Japanese people to wonder about speculation and money. Second, Toshiharu Kato, a bureaucrat at Department of Trade and Industry, created the term 'Eco-money.' Many people felt an affinity with the term rather than the phrase 'community or complementary currency,' and many books with the title containing the term 'Eco-money' were published."

[13] As quoted in Makoto Maruyama, "Local Currencies in New Zealand and Australia," in *Dynamics of Cultures and Systems in the Pacific Rim,*ed. Junji Koizumi (Osaka: Osaka University Press, 2003), 183.

[14] Izumi, personal correspondence.

[15] STRO and Stephen DeMeulenaere's proposal was a cofinalist in an Ashoka Change-maker's Competition in 2006.

[16] Gregory D. Kutz and John J. Ryan, "Hurricanes Katrina and Rita Disaster Relief: Improper and Potentially Fraudulent Individual Assistance Payments Estimated to Be between $600 Million and $1.4 Billion," United States Government Accountability Office (GAO), June 14, 2006.

[17] Stephen DeMeulenaere, interview with Jacqui Dunne, December 2, 2011.

[18] Edgar Cahn, founder of TimeBanking, interview with Jacqui Dunne, June 30, 2012.

Chapter 10

[1] William Butler Yeats, *The Collected Poems of W.B. Yeats*(London: Wordsworth, [1994), 81.

[2] Alex von Muralt, "The Wörgl Experiment with Depreciating Money," *Annals of Public and Cooperative Economics*10 (1934): 48–57. Also, see Fritz Schwartz, *Das Experiment von Wörgl* (Bern: Genossenschaft Verlag Freiwirtschaftlicher Schriften, 1951), 14.

[3] Wörgl's Heimat Museum; and Schwartz, *Das Experiment von Wörgl.*

[4] Irving Fisher, "Stamped Scrip and the Depression." Fourth Letter to the Editor, *The New Republic,*74 (April 12, 1933): 246.

[5] Before the Weimar Republic (1919–1933), there were marks. These were replaced by the Rentenmark in 1923 to counter inflation and by

the Reichsmark one year later on August 30, 1924, when the inflation slowed down. The Reichsmark was replaced with the Deutsche mark when it was introduced by a new currency law on June 20, 1948.

[6] Glyn Davies, *A History of Money: From Ancient Times to the Present Day* (Cardiff: University of Wales, 1994), 572–574.

[7] In 1929, the Wära Tauschgesellschaft was founded by two Gesell followers, Hans Timm and Reinhard Rödiger.

[8] Claude Million, PhD dissertation, "Nebenwährungen gegen Absatzstockung und Beschäftigungskrise—Die amerikanischen Versuche mit scrip während der Grossen Depression Humboldt" (Universität zu Berlin, April 1998).

[9] See letter from the Board of the Reichsbank (I 10513) to the Minister of Finance dated August 8, 1931 (Bundesbank Archiv R 31.01/15345, 145). See also Thomas Koudela: *Entwicklungsprojekt Ökonomie—Marktwirtschaft jenseits des Kapitalismus* (Kühbach-Unterbernbach, Germany: EWK-Verlag, 2004), 66–69.

[10] Margrit Kennedy, *Interest and Inflation Free Money*(Okemos, MI: Seva International, 1995), writes: "During the Weimar Republic (1924–1933), the central bank's president, Hjalmar Schacht, had the desire to create an 'honest' currency in Germany, which—in his understanding—meant a return to the gold

standard. Since he could not buy enough gold on the world market adequate to the amount of money in circulation, he began to reduce the latter. The shorter supply of money resulted in rising interest rates, thereby reducing the incentives and possibilities for investment, forcing firms into bankruptcy, and increasing unemployment, which led to the growth of radicalism and finally helped Hitler to gain more and more power."

[11] See John Weitz, *Hitler's Banker: Hjalmar Horace Greely Schacht*(London: Warner Books, 1999): In March 1930, Schacht stepped down from the position of Reichsbank chairman but returned to his job after Hitler's rise to power three years later.

[12] Ibid., 131.

[13] Official German unemployment statistics: "Arbeitarktdaten."

[14] Max Schwarz, *MdR—Biographisches Handbuch der Reichstage*(Hannover, Germany: Verlag für Literatur und Zeitgeschehen, 1965), 810–816.

[15] Fisher, *Stamp Scrip.*

[16] To the best of the authors' knowledge, no official explanation was given for this decision.

[17] H.W. Brands, *Traitor to His Class: The Privileged Life and Radical Presidency of Franklin Delano Roosevelt*(New York: Doubleday, 2008), quoted in *The Economist,*November 1, 2008, 83.

[18] Kim Severson, "Number of U.S. Hate Groups Is Rising, Report Says," *New York Times,* March 7, 2012.

[19] Sergio Lub, interview with Jacqui Dunne, July 7, 2012.

[20] Heloisa Primavera, interview with Jacqui Dunne, December 2, 2011, and July 9, 2012.

[21] Lub, interview.

[22] Edgar Kampers, interview with Jacqui Dunne, November 24, 2011.

Chapter 11

[1] John Stephen Lansing, lecture at http://longnow.org/seminars/02006/feb/13/perfect-order-a-thousand-years-in-bali.

[2] "Agent modeling is a class of computational models for simulating the actions and interactions of autonomous agents (both individual or collective entities such as organizations or groups) with a view to assessing their effects on the system as a whole." Wikipedia. http://en.wikipedia.org/w/index.php.

[3] Bernard Lietaer, "A World in Balance," *Reflections: The Journal of the Society Organizational Learning at MIT (SOL),*Summer 2003; and Bernard Lietaer and Stephen DeMeulenaere, "Sustaining Cultural Vitality in a Globalizing World: The Balinese Example," *International Journal for Social Economics,* September 2003.

[4] *Kepeng*is etymologically related to the word for "chip" or "fragment." This is likely a reference

to the traditional square hole in the middle of each uang kepeng coin. See S. Hassan and J. Echols, *Kamus Indonesia-Inggris*(Jakarta, Indonesia: PT Gramedia, 2004).

[5] Ida Bagus Sidemen, *Nilai Historis Uang Kepeng (Historical Value of Uang Kepeng)* (Denpasar, Indonesia: Larasan-Sejarah, 2002). The oldest uang kepeng found in Bali were minted by the Chinese Tang Dynasty (618–909AD). Other types of trading coins and brass gongs have been discovered in Bali, some of which originate from the Dong Son culture of Vietnam in the 4th century AD.

[6] Stephen DeMeulenaere, interview with Jacqui Dunne, January 2, 2012.

[7] Ibid.

[8] Hildred Geertz and Clifford Geertz, *Kinship in Bali*(Chicago: University of Chicago Press, 1978).

[9] DeMeulenaere, interview, December 2, 2011.

[10] See www.holacracy.com.

[11] Margrit Kennedy, interview with Jacqui Dunne, June 1, 2012.

[12] See www.regiogeld.de.

[13] Dee Hock, *One from Many: VISA and the Rise of Chaordic Organization*(San Francisco, CA: Berrett-Koehler, 2005).

[14] John Boik, interview with Jacqui Dunne, May 30, 2012.

[15] John Boik, "Creating Sustainable Societies: The Rebirth of Democracy and Local Economies," 2012. www.creatingsustainablesocieties.com.

[16] Henk Van Arkel, interview with Jacqui Dunne, December 14, 2011.

[17] Michael Linton, interview with Jacqui Dunne, December 9, 2011.

[18] Geert Jonker, "Efficient and Equitable Exchange in Air Traffic Management Plan Repair Using Spender-Signed Currency," University of Utrecht, the Netherlands (SIKS Dissertation Series #2008-25).

[19] Geert Jonker, interview with Jacqui Dunne, January 18, 2012.

[20] Ibid.

[21] Suetonius, *De Vita Caesarum—Divus Vespasianus.*Translation in English at www.fordham.edu/halsall/ancient/suetonius-vespasian.html.

[22] Dio Cassius (c. 40–110AD), *Historia,*Book 66, Chapter 14. Translation in English at www.braInfly.net/html/dio_cass.htm.

[23] Vespasian's name still is attached to public urinals in several languages: French (*vespasiennes)*, Italian (*vespasiani)*, and Romanian (*vespasiene).*

[24] See www.constitutionaltender.com.

[25] Stephen Dinan, "Utah Legislature Goes for Gold, Silver as Currency Options Seen as a

Hedge against Dollar Slide," *Washington Times,* March 10, 2011.

Chapter 12

[1] These cameo stories are presented as possibilities, as futures that could become available if we prove capable of rethinking our money. They are not intended as predictions for our future but rather as stories that capture a particular aspect of how different currencies could shape behavior patterns, thereby giving birth to another society.

Chapter 13

[1] Georg Simmel, *Philosophy of Money,* 2nd English ed. (London: Routledge, 1990).

[2] Story embellished from personal communications with Hans Peter Duerr, PhD in physics, former director of the Werner Heisenberg Institute of the Max Planck Institute in Munich, and author of *Für eine zivile Gesellschaft* (Munich: Deutscher Taschenbuch Verlag, 2000).

[3] Donella Meadows's Web site: www.donellameadows.org.

[4] Alex Edmans, "Blockholder Trading, Market Efficiency, and Managerial Myopia," *Journal of Finance* 64, no.6 (2009).

[5] World Bank, "Public Attitude toward Climate Change: Findings from a Multi-Country Poll," *World Development Report 2010: Development and Climate Change.* http://siteresources.world

bank.org/INTWDR2010/Resources/Background-report.pdf.

[6] Eric C. Anderson, quoted by Jeff Kluger, "Can James Cameron—or Anyone—Really Mine Asteroids?" *Time*magazine, April 25, 2012. www.time.com/time/health/article/0,8599,2112996,00.html#ixzz1yGzBgjr2.

[7] Lee Chyen Yee and Clare Jim, "Foxconn to Rely More on Robots; Could Use 1 Million in 3 years," Reuters News Agency, August 1, 2011. http://www.reuters.com/article/2011/08/01/us-foxconn-robots-idUSTRE77016B20110801.

[8] Editorial on manufacturing, "The Third Industrial Revolution, " *The Economist,*April 21, 2012.

[9] Frank Baylin, PhD, interview with Jacqui Dunne, March 10, 2012.

[10] "1550s, in phrase jobbe of worke 'piece of work' (contrasted with continuous labor), of uncertain origin, perhaps a variant of gobbe 'mass, lump' (c. 1400; see *gob)*via sense of 'a cart-load.' Sense of 'work done for pay' first recorded 1650s." See www.etymonline.com.

[11] For policy makers and academics, see Bernard Lietaer, Christian Arnsperger, Sally Goerner, and Stefan Brunnhuber, *Money and Sustainability: The Missing Link*(Axminster, England: Triarchy Press, 2012). For a practical how-to manual for using cooperative currencies at a city scale, see Gwendolyn Hallsmith and Bernard Lietaer, *Creating Wealth: Growing Lo-*

cal Economies with Local Currencies(Gabriola Island, BC: New Society, 2011). See also Margrit Kennedy, Bernard Lietaer, and John Rogers, *People Money: The Promise of Regional Currencies* (Axminster, England: Triarchy Press, 2012), for practical advice from and for implementers of regional systems.

[12] See www.redicecreations.com/article.php?id=10159.

[13] See oceanservice.noaa.gov/facts/exploration.html.

[14] Daniel H. Pink, *A Whole New Mind: Why Right-Brainers Will Rule the Future* (New York: Riverhead Books, 2005).

[15] Kimberly Kassner, interview with Jacqui Dunne, April 20, 2012.

[16] Dr. Monica Sharma, interview with Jacqui Dunne, March 17, 2012.

[17] Jean Houston, interview with Jacqui Dunne, December 18, 2011.

BIBLIOGRAPHY

Amato, M., Fantacci, L., and Doria, L. *Complementary Currency Systems in a Historical Perspective.* Milan: Bocconi University, Dept. of Economic History, 2003.

Anderson, Eric C., quoted by Jeff Kluger. "Can James Cameron—or Anyone—Really Mine Asteroids?" *Time* magazine, April 25, 2012. www.time.com/time/health/article/0,8599,2112996,00.html#ixzz1yGzBgjr2.

Anielski, Mark. "An Assessment of Sweden's No-Interest Bank." The JAK Members Bank, Sweden, 2003.

Aristotle. *Nicomachean Ethics,* 350BC.

Bateson, Gregory. *Steps to an Ecology of Mind.* New York: Ballantine, 1972.

Becker, Gary. "Will the Next Generation Be Better Off Than Their Parents' Generation?" Becker-Posner Blog. www.becker-posner-blog.com/2010/08.

Bloch, Marc. *Esquisse d'une histoire monétair de l'Europe.* Paris: Armand Colin, 1954.

Board of the Reichsbank (I10513) letter to the Minister of Finance dated August 9, 1931. Bundesbank Archiv R 31.01/15345.

Boesler, Matthew. "Introducing the 'Geuro': A Radical New Currency Idea to Solve All of Greece's Problems." *Business Insider,* May 20, 2012. www.businessinsider.com/introducing-the-geuro-a-new-parallel-currency-to-solve-all-of-greeces-problems-2012-5#ixzzlvbUNQjTC.

Boik, John. "Creating Sustainable Societies: The Rebirth of Democracy and Local Economies." 2012. www.creatingsustainablesocieties.com.

Bonder, Nilton. *The Kabbalah of Money: Jewish Insights on Giving, Owning, and Receiving.* Boston: Shambhala Books, 1996.

Bosnich, David A. "The Principle of Subsidiarity." www.acton.org/publications/randl/rl_article_200.php.

Bouchaud, Jean-Philippe, and Mézard, Marc. "Wealth Condensation in a Simple Model of Economy." 2000. www.thetransitioner.org/wiki/tiki-download_file.php?fileId=6.

_____. "La (regrettable) complexité des systèmes économiques." *Pour la Science,* December 2003.

Brands, H.W. *Traitor to His Class: The Privileged Life and Radical Presidency of Franklin Delano Roosevelt.* New York: Doubleday, 2008. Quoted in *The Economist,* November 1, 2008.

Braudel, Fernand. *La dinamica del capitalismo.* Bologna, Italy: Società editrice il Mulino, 1981.

Brzezinski, Zbigniew. *The Choice: Global Domination or Global Leadership.* New York: Basic Books, 2004.

Cassius, Dio (c. 40–110 ad). *Historia,* Book 66, Ch.14. Translation in English at www.brainfly.net/html/dio_cass.htm.

Castell, M. *Das Informationszeitalter BD.II.* Leverkusen, Germany: Leske & Budrich, 2002.

_____. *Informationszeitalter BD.III.* Leverkusen, Germany: Leske & Budrich, 2003.

Cauchon, Dennis. "Student Loans Outstanding Will Exceed $1 Trillion This Year." *USA Today,* October 25, 2011.

Chiakwelu, Emeka. "Nigeria Payment of Foreign Debt: The Largest Transfer of Wealth in Modern Time." Africa Political and Economic Strategic Center (Afripol). www.afripol.org.

Cipolla, Carlo M. *Il governo della moneta a Firenze e a Milano nei secoli XIV–XVI.* Bologna, Italy: Società editriceil Mulino, 1990.

Civic Economics. "Andersonville Study of Retail Economics." BALLE Business Alliance for Local Living Economies, October 2004. www.livingeconomies.org .

Cobb, Clifford, Halstead, Ted, and Rowe, Jonathan. "If the GDP Is Up, Why Is America Down?" *Atlantic Monthly,*October 1995.

Coleman, J. *Foundations of Social Theory.*Cambridge, MA: Harvard University Press, 1990.

Cranium, Richard. "Almost 80% of Americans Are Living Paycheck to Paycheck." *Daily Kos,* October 30, 2010. www.dailykos.com/story/2010/10/30/915125/-Almost-80-of-Americans-live-paycheck-to-paycheck-w-poll.

Davies, Glyn. *A History of Money from Ancient Times to the Present Day.*Cardiff: University of Wales Press, 1994.

de Anca, Celia, and Trullols, Christina. "JAK Medlemsbank Free Interest Banking in a Changing

Global Financial System." IE Business School. January 11, 2011. www.ie.edu/business-school/.

Deane, Marjorie, and Pringle, Robert. *The Central Banks.* New York: Viking, 1995.

Deparle, Jason, Gebeloff, Robert, and Tavernise, Sabrina. "Older, Suburban and Struggling, 'New Poor' Startle the Census." *New York Times,* November 18, 2011.

Dinan, Stephen. "Utah Legislature Goes for Gold, Silver as Currency Options Seen as a Hedge against Dollar Slide." *Washington Times,* March 10, 2011.

Economist. "The Third Industrial Revolution," April 21, 2012.

Edmans, Alex. "Blockholder Trading, Market Efficiency and Managerial Myopia." *Journal of Finance,* 2009.

Einaudi, G. "Teoria della moneta immaginaria nel tempo da Carlomagno alla Rivoluzione francese." *Rivista di Storia Economica* 1, no.1 (1936).

Ekenna, Geoffrey. "Nigeria's Debt Back to $37b, Says Okonjo-Iweala." *Nigerian Compass,* August 27, 2011.

El Nasser, Haya. "World Hits 7 Billion." *USA Today,* October 31, 2011.

Epstein, Richard A. "Beyond Austerity." *Defining Ideas: A Hoover Institute Journal,* May 1, 2012. www.hoover.org/publications/defining-ideas/article/116071.

Federal Register 76, no.13 (2011).

Fisher, Irving. *Stamp Scrip.* New York: Adelphi, 1933.

Ford, Martin. "The Lights in the Tunnel: Automation, Accelerating Technology and the Economy of the

Future." October 2009. www.thelightsinthetunnelco m.

Fukuyama, F. *Trust: Social Virtues and the Creation of Prosperity.*New York: Free Press, 1996.

"Gallery of States in Debt." Daily Beast Business Section, June 14, 2010. www.thedailybeast.com/gal leries/2010/06/14/50-states-in-debt-html.

Geertz, Hildred, and Geertz, Clifford. *Kinship in Bali.*Chicago: University of Chicago Press, 1978.

Green, Ceri. "Time2Grow Evaluation 2010–2011." TimeBanking Wales, 2011. www.timebankingwales.o rg.uk/userfiles/Time2Grow%20-%20%20Evaluation.p df.

Griffin, Edward. *The Creature from Jekyll Island: A Second Look at the Federal Reserve.* Westlake Village, CA: American Media, 1994.

Hassan, S., and Echols, J. *Kamus Indonesia-Inggris.* Jakarta, Indonesia: PT Gramedia, 2004.

Hawken, Paul. *Blessed Unrest: How the Largest Movement in the World Came into Being and Why No One Saw It Coming.*New York: Viking, 2007.

Henderson, Hazel. *Building a Win-Win World.*San Francisco, CA: Berrett-Koehler, 1996.

Henderson, Hazel, with Simran Sethi. *Ethical Markets Growing the Green Economy.* White River Junction, VT: Chelsea Green, 2006.

Hill, Bernice. *Money and the Spiritual Warrior.*Boulder, CO: Five Centuries Foundation, 2004.

Hyde, Lewis. *The Gift: Imagination and the Erotic Life of Property,*3rd ed. New York: Vintage Books, 1983.

"International Labor Office Monthly Bulletin of Statistics 1990–1996." United Nations Statistics Division. http://unstats.un.org/unsd/mbs/.

"IRS Ruling." TimeBanks USA. www.timedollar.org.

Issa, Philip, and Zedlewski, Sheila R. "Poverty among Older Americans, 2009." Urban Institute Program on Retirement Policy, January 27, 2011. www.urban.org/uploadedpdf/412296-Poverty-Among-Older-Americans.pdf.

Jonker, Geert. "Efficient and Equitable Exchange in Air Traffic Management Plan Repair Using Spender-Signed Currency." SIKS Dissertation series #2008-25. Netherlands: University of Utrecht, 2008.

Keynes, John Maynard. *The General Theory of Employment, Interest, and Money.* Amherst, NY: Prometheus Books, 1997.

Kliesen, Kevin, and Maués, Julia. "Are Small Businesses the Biggest Producers of Jobs?" Federal Reserve Bank of St. Louis. www.stlouisfed.org/publications/re/.

Koudela, Thomas. "Entwicklungsprojekt Ökonomie—Marktwirtschaft jenseits des Kapitalismus." Kühbach-Unterbernbach, Germany: EWK-Verlag, 2004.

Krantz, Matt. "Many Have Little or No Savings as Retirement Looms." *USA Today,* December 4, 2011.

Krugman, Paul. "Oligarchy, American Style." *New York Times,*November 3, 2011.

Kutz, Gregory D., and Ryan, John J. "Hurricanes Katrina and Rita Disaster Relief: Improper and Potentially Fraudulent Individual Assistance Payments Estimated to Be between $600 Million and $1.4 Billion." United States Government Accountability Office (GAO), June 14, 2006.

Laevan, Luc, and Valencia, Fabian. "Resolution of Banking Crises: The Good, the Bad, and the Ugly." International Monetary Fund working paper 1/146. Washington, DC: International Monetary Fund, 2010. www.imf.org/external/pubs/ft/wp/2010/wp10146.pdf.

Lansing, John Stephen. Lecture at www.longnow.org/seminars/02006/feb/13/perfect-order-a-thousand-years-in-bali.

Levitt, Steven D., and Dubner, Stephen J. *Freakonomics: A Rogue Economist Explores the Hidden Side of Everything.* New York: William Morrow, 2005.

Lewin, Tamar. "College Graduates' Debt Burden Grew, Yet Again, in 2010." *New York Times,* November 2, 2011. www.nytimes.com/2011/11/03/education/average-student-loan-debt-grew-by-5-percent-in-2010.html.

Lietaer, Bernard. "A World in Balance." *Reflections: The Journal of the Society for Organizational Learning at MIT (SOL),* Summer 2003.

Lietaer, Bernard, and DeMeulenaere, Stephen. "Sustaining Cultural Vitality in a Globalizing World:

The Balinese Example." *International Journal for Social Economics,*September 2003.

Lietaer, B., Ulanowicz, R., and Goerner, S. "White Paper on All the Options for Managing a Systemic Bank Crisis." October 2008. www.lietaer.com/images/White_Paper_on_Systemic_Banking_Crises_final.pdf.

Liu, Eric, and Hanauer, Nick. *The Gardens of Democracy: A New American Story of Citizenship, the Economy and the Role of Government.*Seattle, WA: Sasquatch Books, 2011.

Luhby, Tami. "Government Assistance Expands." CNN Money, February 7, 2012. http://money.cnn.com/2012/02/07/news/economy/government_assistance/index.htm.

Maruyama, Makoto. "Local Currencies in New Zealand and Australia." In *Dynamics of Cultures and Systems in the Pacific Rim,*ed. Junji Koizumi. Osaka, Japan: Osaka University Press, 2003.

Mauss, Marcel. "Essai sur le Don: Forme et raison de l'échange dans les sociétés archaiques." *L'Année Sociologique*1 (1923–1924).

McKinsey Global Institute. "An Economy That Works: Job Creation and America's Future." June 2011. www.mckinsey.com/insights/mgi.

Million, Claude. PhD dissertation, "Nebenwahrungen gegen Absatzstockung and Beschäftigungskrise—Die amerikanischen Versuche mit scrip wahrend der Grossen Depression Humboldt." University of Berlin, April 1998.

Minigione, E. *Urban Poverty and the Underclass.*Oxford: Blackwell, 1996.

Morris, Regan. "Californian City Faces Bankruptcy." *BBC News,*June 27, 2010. www.bbc.co.uk/news/world-us-canada-18605326.

"Move Your Money Movement This Saturday." *CNN Money,*November 4, 2011.

Murphy, Antoin E. "Money in an Economy without Banks: The Case of Ireland." Manchester School of Economics, March 1978.

Naisbitt, John. *Megatrends.*New York: Warner Books, 1982.

Needleman, Jacob. *Money and the Meaning of Life.*New York: Doubleday Currency, 1994.

New York Post."Boy in China Reportedly Sells Kidney to Purchase iPhone and iPad," April 6, 2012. Reported on Foxnews.com. www.foxnews.com/world/2012/04/06/boy-in-china-reportedly-sells-kidney-to-purchase-iphone-and-ipad/#ixzz1T3mSNV5.

Officer, Lawrence, and Williamson, Samuel H. "Purchasing Power of Money in the United States from 1774 to Present." Measuring Worth, 2011. www.measuringworth.com.

Orski, Ken. "The Promise and Risks of Public-Private Partnerships," *Innovation NewsBriefs* 21, no.6 (2010).

Pink, Daniel H. *A Whole New Mind: Why Right-Brainers Will Rule the Future.*New York: Riverhead Books, 2005.

Pippin, Robert, and del Caro, Adrian. *Nietz sche: Thus Spoke Zarathustra.*Cambridge: Cambridge University Press, 2006.

Putnam, R. *Making Democracy Work: Civic Traditions in Modern Italy.*Prince ton, NJ: Prince ton University Press, 1993.

_____. *Bowling Alone: The Collapse and Revival of the American Community.*New York: Simon & Schuster, 2000.

Rand, Ayn. *Atlas Shrugged.*New York: Dutton Adult Centennial Edition, 2005.

Report by the Congressional Bud get Office (CBO). ABC News, October 26, 2 011. www.abcnews.go.com/Business/income-doubles-top-percent-1979/story?id=14817561.

Rodgers, G., Gore, C., and Figueiredi, J.B., eds. *Social Exclusion: Rhetoric, Reality, Responses.*Geneva: International Institute of Labor Studies, 1997.

Schwartz, Fritz. *Das Experiment von Wörgl.*Bern, Germany: Genossenschaft Verlag Freiwirtschaftlicher Schriften, 1951.

Schwarz, Marx. *MdR—Biographisches Handbuch der Reichstage.*Hannover, Germany: Verlag für Literatur und Zeitgeschehen, 1965.

Severson, Kim. "Number of U.S. Hate Groups Is Rising, Report Says." *New York Times,* March 7, 2012.

Shah, Anup. "Poverty Facts and Stats." *Global Issues,*September 20, 2010. www.globalissues.org/article/26/poverty-facts-and-stats#src22.

Sidemen, Ida Bagus. *Nilai Historis Uang Kepeng (Historial Value of Uang Kepeng).* Bali, Indonesia: Larasan-Sejarah, 2002.

Simmel, Georg. *Philosophy of Money,*2nd English ed. London: Routledge, 1990.

Smith, Ned. "Incubators Heat Up Chances of Small Business Success." *Business News Daily,* October 5, 2010.

Soros, George. *On Globalization.*Oxford: Public Affairs, 2002.

"States Most Likely to Go Bankrupt." Daily Beast, January 26, 2011.

www.thedailybeast.com/articles/2011/01/26/states-most-likely-to-go-bank.rupt.html.

Stiglitz, Joseph E. "Of the 1%, by the 1%, for the 1%." *Vanity Fair,*May 2011.

Stodder, James. "Complementary Credit Networks and Macro-Economic Stability: Switzerland's Wirtschaftsring." *Journal of Economic Behavior and Organization*72 (2009).

Studer, James. "Reciprocal Exchange Networks: Implications for Macroeconomic Stability." Paper presented at the International Electronic and Electrical Engineering (IEEE) Engineering Management Society (EMS). Albuquerque, NM, August 2000.

Studer, Tobias. "Le Système WIR dans l'optique d'un chercheur Américan." WirPlus. www.wir.ch.

Suetonius. *De Vita Caesarum—Divus Vespasianus.*Translation in English at www.fordham.edu/halsall/ancient/suetonius-vespasian.html.

Thompson, Michael. *Organising and Disorganising: A Dynamic and Non-Linear Theory of Institutional Emergence and Its Implications.*Devon, En gland: Triarchy Press, 2008.

Tieman, Ross. "Mobile Phone Operators Revolutionize Cash Transfers." *Financial Times,* June 3, 2008.

Timberlake, Richard H. "Private Production of Scrip-Money in the Isolated Community." *Journal of Money, Credit and Banking*19, no.4 (1987).

Toynbee, Arnold. *A Study of History.*Oxford: Oxford University Press.

Ulanowicz, R., Goerner, S., Lietaer, B., and Gomez, R. "Quantifying Sustainability: Efficiency, Resilience and the Return of Information Theory." *Ecological Complexity,*March 2009. www.sciencedirect.com/s cience.

Van der Beek, Marcel. "Essays for a Cata log for Special Exhibitions held in Ghent," April 1 to 24, 2000, and in Brussels May 15 to June 20, 2000.

Van Dyke, James. " 'Bank Transfer Day,' What Really Just Happened?" Javelin Strategy and Research, January 26, 2012. www.javelinstrategy .com.

Vasagar, Jeevan. "Graduates Warned of Record 70 Applicants for Every Job." *Guardian,* July 5, 2010.

Von Muralt, Alex. "The Wörgl Experiment with Depreciating Money." *Annals of Public and Cooperative Economics*10 (1934).

Walsh, Bryan. "Trash Problems in Paradise." *Time*magazine, January 7, 2008. www.time.com/time/world/article/0,8599,1701095,00.html#ixzz1xtgStTME.

Walsh, Mary Williams. "A Path Is Sought for States to Escape Their Debt Burdens." *New York Times,*January 20, 2011.

Wasik, John. "Where Is the Real US Jobs Plan?" *Reuters Money,*September 2, 2011.

Weitz, John. *Hitler's Banker: Hjalmar Horace Greely Schacht.*London: Warner Books, 1999.

Whitney, Lance. "Cell Phone Subscriptions to Hit 5 Billion Globally." CNET, February 16, 2010. http://reviews.cnet.com/8301-13970_7-10454065-78.html#ixzz1K6sXaPmP.

Wikipedia contributors. "Agent Modeling." Wikipedia, the Free Encycloped ia. http://en.wikipedia.org/wiki/Agent-based_model.

WIR Annual Report 2010. www.wir.ch.

World Bank. "Public Attitude towards Climate Change: Findings from a Multi-Country Poll." World Development Report 1020: Development and Climate Change. http://siteresources.worldbank.org/INTWDR2010/Resources/Background-report.pdf.

Wray, L. Randall. *Understanding Modern Money: The Key to Full Employment and Price Stability.* Cheltenham, England: Edward Elgar Publishing, 1998.

Yeats, William Butler. *The Collected Poems of W.B. Yeats.*London: Wordsworth Editions, 1994.

Yee, Lee Chyen, and Jim, Clare. "Foxconn to Rely More on Robots; Could Use 1 Million in 3 Years. Reuters News Agency, August 1, 2011. http://www.reuters.com/article/2011/08/01/us-foxconn-robots-idUSTRE77016B20110801.

Yellen, John E. "The Transformation of the Kalahari !Kung." *Scientific American*262, no.4 (1990).

ACKNOWLEDGEMENTS

A special word of thanks to Ed and Deb Shapiro, Frank Baylin, Kimberly Kassner, Nigel Seale, Aureya Magdalen, Jean Houston, Paul Ray, Jan Coleman, and Sally Dunne-Lee. To Michelle Bishop for her diligent assistance with some of the research. Also, to our agents David Nelson and Neil Gudovitz at Waterside Productions for their consummate support and guidance.

To Steve Piersanti, president of Berrett-Koehler, for holding a clear vision for the book with us, while guiding us through the rigors and practicalities of getting it down on paper.

This book is the result of, quite literally, thousands of conversations over time and scores of interviews across the globe during the course of writing this book. Unfortunately, while many discussions didn't make it into the book, they were seminal in shaping our work. There are too many people to thank here by name for their time, contributions, and generosity of spirit. Know that you are all held in our hearts with deep and abiding gratitude.

ABOUT THE AUTHORS

Photo credit: Rick Cummings.

BERNARD LIETAERis one of the most knowledgeable people in the world about money and financial systems.

Bernard has been a star since 1969, when he received an MBA from MIT and *Time*magazine selected him as one of the top-10 graduates of U.S. business schools. His post-graduate thesis, entitled *Financial Management of Foreign Exchange,*was published by MIT Press in 1970 and received wide attention in the financial world. In his thesis, he discussed applying nonlinear programming to global currency management for multinational corporations. This was considered the first book to explore the applications of systems theory to international finance. It described how to optimize currency management for corporations working in a large number of countries and currencies, and included the techniques to deal with floating exchanges, at the time a rare occurrence limited to some exotic currencies in Latin America. A major U.S. bank negotiated exclusive rights to Bernard's approach prompting him to start a new career and move to South America. He developed, for the largest mining company in Peru, a new system for worldwide allocation of mining resources, which ended up being used to optimize two-thirds of all foreign exchange earnings of Peru. Subsequently, he wrote the only book (published in 1979) to foretell the Latin American debt crisis that exploded as he predicted in the early 1980s.

Later, Bernard was widely credited with being one of the principal architects of the euro, the single European currency. This came about after he accepted a job offer as the head of the Organization and Computer Department at the Central Bank in Belgium. Because Belgium received the chairmanship of the European Currency Unit (the ECU), his first project at the Bank was the design and implementation of the convergence system, which evolved into the euro in January, 1999. During this period, Bernard was appointed president of the electronic payment system in Belgium, considered the most inclusive and cost-effective payment system in the world. In 1987, Bernard left the Central Bank and cofounded one of the first large-scale off-shore currency trading funds. During his three-year tenure as its general manager and currency trader, from 1987 to mid-1991, the largest of these funds (Gaia Hedge II) was rated by the Micropal survey as the top performer among 75 currency hedge funds and among all 1,800 offshore funds worldwide. In 1990, *Business Week* named Bernard "the world's top trader."

In the mid-1990s, Bernard changed his focus. He has spent the past two decades as one of the world's leading designers and implementers of cooperative currencies. He has consulted with communities, governments, banks, and businesses around the globe. He has written several books on the topic of money, including the classic, *The Future of Money,* along with hundreds of articles and interviews. One of Bernard's current projects in terms of new currencies is the Trade Reference Currency, which is a privately-issued, cooperative, global reference currency that is backed by a noninflationary, standardized basket of the dozen most important commodities and services in the global market. It is poised to drastically change barter and counter-trade along with creating stability and predictability in the financial and business sectors by providing a robust standard of value for international trade. Most importantly, it will resolve the current conflict between short-term financial interest and long-term sustainability thereby providing, for the first time since the gold-standard days, an international standard of value that is inflation-resistant. This mechanism would work in parallel with national currencies. Currently, Bernard is a Research Fellow at the Center for Sustainable Resources of the University of California at Berkeley. He is also Visiting Professor at the Finance University of Moscow.

He is a member of the Club of Rome; a Fellow at the World Academy of Arts and Sciences, the World Business Academy, and the European Academy of Sciences and Arts; and a founding member of the Global Futures Forum. He currently resides in his native Belgium. He is fluent in English, French, Spanish, German, and Dutch, and reads Latin and Greek.

JACQUI DUNNEis an award-winning journalist from Ireland, founder and CEO of Danu Resources, and a leader in helping entrepreneurs develop technologies that restore the earth's equilibrium globally.

Danu Resources is a for-profit organization organization brings together and aligns donors and projects that focus on environmental and energy initiatives to move the world to greater sustainability while empowering people with dignity and the essentials of life. Danu's unique value is its ability to work from a future reference point that draws out the greatness, and builds upon the strengths, of both the donor and the company or initiative, thus creating a flourishing paradigm shift for people and the planet. Where feasible, ventures operate using a multiple-currency ecosystem.

She serves on the board of, or is an advisor to, several U.S. and international companies. These firms are engaged in innovative solutions in the domains of green energy (the Swedish corporation Mimer Energy and Blue Energy in Canada), decentralized local food production (Perpetua in the United States), and a natural resolution for nuclear and other waste streams, Amo Terra. She is a principal strategist with the launching of the business-to-business currency, the Terra, that is designed to create more stability and predictability in the financial and business sectors by providing a mechanism for contractual, payment, and planning purposes worldwide.

In terms of philanthropy, Jacqui sits on the board of A Human Right, which is dedicated to providing free basic Internet and phone access to developing countries and underserved regions internationally, using spare satellite capacity.

An award-winning journalist, she started her career in her native Ireland. While still in college, Jacqui reported on a freelance basis on Spain's transition to democracy in the late 1970s for both the *Irish Times*and RTE (Irish Radio). Later, she joined the *Sunday Inde pen dent*as a staff reporter and features writer and covered a variety of stories from the political unrest in Northern Ireland to famine in Ethiopia. For several years, she wrote a monthly column for the *Irish Tattler* and codesigned special events for the magazine to encourage women's entrepreneurship.

In New York, she wrote for *Interview Magazine, Elle,*and the *Daily News,*then headed west to San Francisco, where she wrote for *Grassroots/Dresdner RCM Bank,*compiling investigative reports on companies and industry sector analysis. She produced radio interviews with thought leaders and was an occasional on-air host for *New Dimensions Radio,*syndicated to NPR and community radio stations nationally and overseas.

In order to gain experience in how business really works, Jacqui conducted market research for multinational biotech and pharmaceutical companies. She was vice president of a former boutique technology public and investor relations company, ContentOne, which handled media and investor relations for firms ranging from start-ups to publicly traded companies.

Lately, she has worked as a content editor for *Money and Sustainability—The Missing Link, A Report from the Club of Rome,* which reveals the hidden dynamics among the conventional money system, climate change, and ecological sustainability. This report was addressed to Finance Watch, an in de pen dent European public interest association tasked by the European Union with reporting on the causes of the current banking and financial debacle.

*Rethinking Money*is her first book. She currently resides in Colorado.

Berrett–Koehler
Publishers

Berrett-Koehler is an independent publisher dedicated to an ambitious mission: Creating a World That Works for All.

We believe that to truly create a better world, action is needed at all levels—individual, organizational, and societal. At the individual level, our publications help people align their lives with their values and with their aspirations for a better world. At the organizational level, our publications promote progressive leadership and management practices, socially responsible approaches to business, and humane and effective organizations. At the societal level, our publications advance social and economic justice, shared prosperity, sustainability, and new solutions to national and global issues.

A major theme of our publications is "Opening Up New Space." Berrett-Koehler titles challenge conventional thinking, introduce new ideas, and foster positive change. Their common quest is changing the underlying beliefs, mindsets, institutions, and structures that keep generating the same cycles of problems, no matter who our leaders are or what improvement programs we adopt.

We strive to practice what we preach—to operate our publishing company in line with the ideas in our books. At the core of our approach is stewardship, which we define as a deep sense of responsibility to administer the company for the benefit of all of our "stakeholder" groups: authors, customers, employees, investors, service providers, and the communities and environment around us.

We are grateful to the thousands of readers, authors, and other friends of the company who consider themselves to be part of the "BK Community." We hope that you, too, will join us in our mission.

A BK Currents Book

This book is part of our BK Currents series. BK Currents books advance social and economic justice by exploring the critical intersections between business and society. Offering a unique combination of thoughtful analysis and progressive alternatives, BK Currents books promote positive change at the national and global levels. To find out more, visit www.bkconnection.com

Berrett–Koehler Publishers

A community dedicated to creating a world that works for all

Visit Our Website: www.bkconnection.com

Read book excerpts, see author videos and Internet movies, read our authors' blogs, join discussion groups, download book apps, find out about the BK Affiliate Network, browse subject-area libraries of books, get special discounts, and more!

Subscribe to Our Free E-Newsletter, the *BK Communiqué*

Be the first to hear about new publications, special discount offers, exclusive articles, news about bestsellers, and more! Get on the list for our free e-newsletter by going to www.bkconnection.com.

Get Quantity Discounts

Berrett-Koehler books are available at quantity discounts for orders of ten or more copies. Please call us toll-free at (800) 929-2929 or email us at bkp .orders@aidcvt.com.

Join the BK Community

BKcommunity.com is a virtual meeting place where people from around the world can engage with kindred spirits to create a world that works for all. BKcommunity.com members may create their own profiles, blog, start and participate in forums and discussion groups, post photos and videos, answer surveys, announce and register for upcoming events, and chat with others online in real time. Please join the conversation!

A

B

D

E

F

H

I

N

Q

R

S

T

U

V

W

Y

Z

43135294R00226

Made in the USA
Lexington, KY
18 July 2015